WORKING CLASS USA
The Power and the Movement

WORKING CLASS USA

The Power and the Movement

by
GUS HALL

INTERNATIONAL PUBLISHERS, New York

Drawings by Laszlo Kubinyi

Library of Congress Cataloging in Publication Data
Hall, Gus.
    Working Class USA: The Power and the Movement.

    Includes index.
    1. Labor and laboring class—United States—History.
2. Social conflict—United States—History. 3. Communist
Party of the United States of America—History. I. Title.
HD8066.H29   1987   305.5"62"0973   87-3232
ISBN 0-7178-0660-X
ISBN 0-7178-0659-6 (pbk.)

Contents

WORKER'S FLASHBACKS

Acknowledgements

This book is a collective product. It was conceived and compiled by George Meyers, Joe Brandt, Scott Marshall and Tom Hopkins.

In addition, there are many others who contributed their talents, through hard work and long hours. Without them, this book would not have been possible.

Gus Hall
A Worker's Life

by Phillip Bonosky

Gus Hall
A Worker's Life

By Phillip Bonosky

BACK IN 1931, A GROUP OF WELL-KNOWN WRITERS, HEADED BY Theodore Dreiser, and under the auspices of the newly-formed National Committee for the Defense of Political Prisoners, went to investigate what was the truth about the killings of coal miners in the part of Kentucky that would later be known as "bloody Harlan."

Responding to the report which this committee made, Sherwood Anderson, author of *Winesburg, Ohio* and other books that would make him famous, appeared at a New York City mass meeting protesting the Harlan County terror. His speech was titled, "I Want to Be Counted" and, among other things, he had this to say:

> I remember what a man said to me a short time ago. I was on a train and talking to this man. . . . He was a large manufacturer. "You are a writer, Anderson." he said. "You write stories and novels, books, etc.?"
>
> "Yes."

"Well," he said, "I could not do that (but) . . . what it would take you a whole book to say I could say in two words . . . 'You're fired.' "

And a bit later, Anderson again:

A friend of mine down South asked me recently: "What is the difference between a Socialist and a Communist?" I couldn't tell him the technical difference. I didn't know. I am myself a story teller, not a political economist. "I don't know," I said. "I guess the Communists mean it."

It was a good guess. The difference between most radical, Left, New Left, Socialist and quasi-Socialist parties that speak for, or in any case say they are speaking for, the working class — and the Communist Party, is just that: the Communists mean what they say.

And no matter how dense the fog of confusion that is wrapped around the relationship of boss and worker, one fact clearly emerges when you get down to the bone: the boss has the power to hire and fire, to pick up his factory and skip the country, or shut down whole factories altogether leaving thousands of workers totally stranded.

It is this destructive power that apologists for corporate America dare call "progress." It is this enormous waste of human lives that is pictured as the inevitable cost of social development.

It's all a lie. The grim reality exposes the real failure of American capitalism and most acutely in its virulent form of "Reaganomics." But an ideological gloss is spread over the reality. Gus Hall puts it this way:

We must never lose sight of the fact that in no country and at no time in history has a dying class spent so much on its ideological efforts as does the capitalist class in these United States. In money alone it runs into billions each year. This is most likely the single largest effort being exerted on any one thing in our land.

Few there are today who cannot see that labor is under

massive attack. For the first time in over 50 years organized (and unorganized) workers are literally fighting for their lives today. This is the new aspect of what is still the old war: the war for survival. After decades of apparent tolerance, of union negotiating successes, of what seemed like social acceptance at last, the utopian dream that the lion and the lamb could lie down together in peace has been violently shattered.

Today labor stands in peril of losing even the most elementary gains which had cost the working class so much in blood and tears, and which the nation had every right to believe had been permanently incorporated in the laws of the land. The one thing that had not changed however was the power that lay in those two words that Sherwood Anderson heard pronounced by that large manufacturer: "You're fired."

"You're fired!" is exactly what President Reagan told the 12,000 air traffic control workers who had dared to go on strike in 1981. Reagan, a confessed labor spy and FBI informant when he was head of the Screen Actors Guild, in brutally firing the air traffic control workers and destroying their union, sent out a signal to corporate America that the last remnant of the old Roosevelt days were over, and open season on the working class had now been declared.

Corporate America was not long in picking up the signal. The attack on labor that followed almost instantly on Reagan's words reached an intensity unequalled in all past history. With the government coming out openly as a strikebreaker, corporations with labor-baiting, spy-infested departments primed for action, were not far behind. A veritable orgy of labor-bashing began and has not subsided up until this very moment. Labor knows it has to fight back, and is groping for the best weapons it can find.

But it is up against a formidable and sly enemy. Unlike the past, the modern attack on labor has taken on diverse forms, though the aim remains the same: to disarm the American working class and reduce it to impotence. Capitalism still has the whip-hand and it is using it. While still resorting to brute force — to police, state troopers, to the "persuasion" of clubs

and guns — to break some strikes, corporate America now resorts even more readily to a whole spectrum of other, more
subtle and tricky devices. It has launched a crusade to win over
the middle class and to alienate young workers from the older
veterans of the working class. It has raised the very question of
unionism itself.

Numerous corporations have also taken their shops overseas, where they exploit cheap labor, then export the cheaper
products back into the USA to undermine the wage scales and
living standards of the American worker.

So successful has the concerted drive by Big Business (with
Ronald Reagan's sanction) against the wages and working conditions of the American working class proven to be that it was
possible for Wall Street to boast that "hourly compensation
rose only four-tenths of one percent (in 1986), the smallest
quarterly increase since the third quarter of 1960" which represented as a whole the fact that "unit labor costs fell at a 2.3
percent rate. . . . " (*New York Times*, May 5, 1987.)

Taken as a whole, the American working class is falling behind — larger and larger sections see their living standards
sinking closer and closer to the bare minimum needed for subsistence.

But corporate America has not ended its drive against the
working class by undermining its wage scales and living standards. It wants to reduce labor to impotence — to throw it back
to its barest beginnings — that is, over 150 years ago when the
first strike of 600 carpenters in Boston was successfully broken
by that familiar combination of court and police.

The crime that the carpenters were then found guilty of, by
a court made up of representatives of the "master class," was
the crime of "conspiracy" to win a ten-hour day. Even then, the
basic issues were clear to the workers, as the Preamble to the
Mechanics Union of Trade Associations' Constitution in 1827
clearly shows:

> When the disposition and efforts of one part of mankind to oppress
> another have become too manifest to be mistaken and too pernicious
> to their consequences to be endured, it has often been found nec-

essary for those who feel aggrieved to associate for the purpose of affording to each other mutual protection from oppression.

It went on to say:

Do not all the streams of wealth which flow in every direction and are emptied into and absorbed by the coffers of the unproductive, exclusively take their rise in the bones, marrow, and muscles of the industrial classes? In return for which, exclusive of bare subsistence (which likewise is a produce of their own industry) they receive — not anything.

And they were answered by a judge, when they went on strike, who found that "to associate for the purpose of . . . mutual protection" really amounted to a "conspiracy" to fix the cost of the product they produced, and that this represented a "restraint of trade," and was illegal. The employers of the carpenters were astonished that their own God-fearing workers had actually thought up the idea of going out on strike, and declared:

We cannot believe this project (setting up a union of carpenters) to have originated with any of the faithful and industrious sons of New England but are compelled to consider an evil of foreign growth, and one which, we hope and trust, will never take root in the favored soil of Massachusetts (1825).

In 1825, Karl Marx was only 27 and was almost totally unknown in America. Eugene Debs was to be born 30 years later (1855), V.I. Lenin in 1870. Nor could the subversion of the carpenters in 1825-27 be blamed on Gus Hall, who wasn't born until 1910.

ARVO GUS HALBERG (HE WOULD SHORTEN HIS NAME later), was born in a worker's family in Iron, Minnesota. His mother's lullabies were workers' songs. Gus was the fifth in a family that would eventually number ten children. His parents had been Finnish immigrants who were already conscious socialists before they came to America. Almost the moment his foot touched Minnesota soil, Gus's father, Matt Halberg, plunged into the struggle to organize the Mesaba iron ore workers, and this, and other such struggles to organize the unorganized, earned for him a place on the employers' permanent blacklist.

Being on a blacklist made life very hard for the Halberg family. "We lived in semi-starvation," Hall says simply of those days. Matt was a carpenter, and made a catch-as-catch-can living doing carpentry work on a free-lance basis. He built everything, including the house — a log cabin — in which Gus was born, but his specialty was building staircases. People in that area still point to a staircase Gus's father had built years before.

Nevertheless, Hall's childhood was by no means a gloomy one. Deprived though the children of the Halberg family were of what's called "creature comforts," and as often as they had to stint on this and that, there was always plenty of food for the mind. The Halberg household was a kind of way-station for workingclass militants passing through who stopped over for a meal and a place to spend the night — but who brought with them the latest news hot from class struggle fronts. Ideas flourished, arguments back and forth rocked the calm of the neighborhood. Matt Halberg was a friend of Big Bill Haywood. And both he and his wife were founding members of the Communist Party in 1919 (along with John Reed, about whom the movie *Reds* was made.)

Gus Hall had to quit school at the age of 15 in order to help feed the growing family. Nevertheless, though his formal schooling ended at the 8th grade — when it was "legal" to get working papers — his real education had only begun.

Later, in his writings, Gus would make a big point of attacking the idea that "uneducated" workers, because they lacked a school education, couldn't think. "U.S. capitalism has always promoted the concept that thinking should be limited to the chosen few," he's written. And he pointed out that this slander of workers is not new. In fact, as far back as the middle 1880s, Frederick Engels, co-worker of Karl Marx, and great Marxist in his own right (whom Gus is fond of quoting), was already saying that "the uneducated workers, who can easily be made to grasp the most difficult economic analyses, excel our superci-lious 'cultured' folk, for whom such ticklish problems remain insoluble for their whole life long." Gus also quotes Marx's ob-servation at about the same time that "before the proletariat fights out its victories on the barricades and in the line of battle, it gives notice of its impending rule with a series of intellectual victories."

Such "intellectual victories" from workingclass intellectuals were very much on the order of the day when the very exis-tence of the working class itself was being called into question by bourgeois intellectuals of every stripe. Houdini, the great illusionist, might have been able to make an elephant disap-pear in front of your eyes, but even Houdini wasn't so mad as to believe he could make an entire class of hundreds of millions of workers disappear the same way!

At 15, Gus was a full-fledged worker — as big physically as he would ever get to be. He started to work in the Northern lumber camps. He was a "four-mule skinner;" he floated logs down the river to the saw mill; he spent many lonely weeks deep in the woods with no other company but squirrels and chipmunks and other lumberjacks.

But even then, though life was hard, it wasn't intellectually empty. Gus would write much later: "The old-time lumberjack tended to think about the world in more philosophical terms than practical or immediate. . . . I was surprised at their great interest in culture. As a matter of fact, it seems that the great majority of the world's poets and songwriters were in these lumber camps. I read more poetry that was never published than all the poetry I've read since. . . . "

Gus's knack of knowing how to live alone without being intellectually lonely would stand him in good stead later when he had to pass weeks in solitary confinement at Leavenworth. There, too, books and thoughts were his companions.

Revolutionary talk wasn't unusual in a household whose two leading members had been founding members of the Com-munist Party. At 17, Gus himself officially joined the Commu-nist Party. Nobody pushed him. "I'm often asked how and why I became a Communist," he writes. "My answer has always been that in a sense I was born a Communist. Father came from a long line of rebels and radicals."

And further:

> My parents and family were co-workers in the class struggle. They inspired me. They set the example. They were the critics. It was easy for me to become a revolutionary. In becoming a radical and a rebel I simply followed a family custom of some generations. Even going to prison for political reasons was following a family tradition of long standing. I am the proud recipient of the only material family heirloom. It is a wooden sugar bowl carved in prison by a great-great-grandfather. He was the one who wasn't hung. . . .

But being born in a Communist family does not in itself explain why Gus not only remained a committed Communist but threw himself actively into the struggle to realize its principles. Devotion does not by itself explain it. Fanatics and cultists are also devoted to their causes. To remain devoted to Marxism-Leninism one has to be convinced that it is right; that its policies and principles meet the objective demands of life itself. As Lenin said about Marxism: "The teaching of Marx is all-powerful because it is true." Theories have to prove themselves in practice; they have to be true. In any case, those who are otherwise powerless must have the truth on their side.

And as Gus was educated not only by books but by practice, he learned from the talk around the dinner table, from his parents' comments on the political scene, and there was always a book by Marx or Engels or Lenin, by Eugene Debs, or any of the other radical writers of the day, within easy reach. Books gave him perspective. But he learned most of all in what Mother Jones was fond of calling her "College of Hard Knocks," life itself.

And yet, Gus is far from being an activist only who may know what he's doing but isn't always clear why he is doing it, nor where his activity is carrying him. Again, reacting against those who would like to picture workers as non-thinkers, Gus emphasizes over and over the need to understand the full reasons for action, and to fit every action into the perspective opened by theory. Born a Communist, nevertheless, every day of his life experience had to justify Gus's choice. Gus learned to read books as part of life, and life, though full of surprises, of turns and twists, of zigzags, would come to read like a book that had been written by the working class of the world.

Thus, when Gus started to work in the lumber camps, he didn't have to go through any soul-searching over whether or not he should join the union. Joining the union was, with his background, a natural thing to do. Was it also the right thing to do? Did experience justify theory — theory learned at home around the dinner table as a child? Yes, a thousand times over. Not only was it natural to join whatever union existed, it was just as natural to go right ahead and organize one if it didn't exist. Did the 70-year-old man regret those actions of the 17-year-old boy? Not once in all the intervening years! And, as his jobs changed, his union affiliation changed along with them — from the International Woodworkers of America, later the International Association of Bridge, Structural and Ornamental Iron Workers Union — this last union, in actual fact, he helped to set up. Gus's instinct was always the worker's instinct — a union man's.

T HE AMERICAN 1920s, WHEN GUS WAS GROWING UP, HAS gone down in American history with a variety of tags — like the "roaring twenties," the "jazz age," the era of the flapper and bootlegger, when writers like Ernest Hemingway and F. Scott Fitzgerald fled America's shores for the Left bank of Paris and there became the "lost generation."

But if America's middle-class intellectuals fled America to escape what they felt was its stultifying cultural atmosphere, this wasn't possible for workingclass America which had to stay at home in the mill towns and company towns, literally slaving from morning until night in the desperate attempt to scrape together what amounted to subsistence wages to keep their families alive. America, except for a minority of craft workers, was open-shop America. It was unorganized America. It was an America whose working class was generally seen at the time, as the great writer Theodore Dreiser puts it:

> Actually, as a worker, he is laughed at and, in times of unrest and contest, spit upon as a malcontent, a weakling, a radical, an undesirable citizen, one who had not the understanding and hence not the right to complain of the ills by which he finds himself beset. Herded, insofar as the majority of him is concerned, in work warrants called towns, watched over as the slaves of the South were watched over in the days before the Civil War, by the spies and agents of the immense cooperative associations of wealth, in the factories and mines and mills for which he now works, warred upon by veritable armies of mercenaries employed by these giants . . . in order to overawe him and subdue him; he finds himself discharged, starved, and then blacklisted and shot down when he strikes; he finds himself, as I have said before, frustrated, ignored, and denied by his church, his press, his paid officials and his supine and traitorous government. (*Harlan Miners Speak*, 1932.)

Workingclass America was (and still is) a blank in the history of American literature, as is school-taught history itself, and Black workers didn't rate more than a glance. But despite the fact that they didn't exist for the artistic intellectuals, living off father's money, and discovering courage as a spectacle of "grace under pressure" watching toreadors spearing bulls in Spain, nevertheless working America did exist and learned about courage first-hand on the picket line and discovered heroes in the ordinary men and women who faced the muzzles of the sheriff's guns.

America had become monopoly America by the turn of the century. So brutal was monopoly America in its suppression of all workingclass struggle for elementary human rights that by 1912, Morgan-owned U.S. Steel would boast that none of its mills were any longer in danger of being unionized. At the same time it could point to a gross income of $745 million which, in 1912, was more than the entire income of the USA itself for that year — which was $692 million. If it wanted to, the Morgan banks could have bought out the whole United States! They contented themselves with buying up Senators,

Congressmen and whole state legislatures, instead.

To gross this huge bagful of profits, American monopoly had to squeeze the American working class to the bone. But not without resistance. Fierce class battles were being fought in every industrial area in the country. The 1919 steel strike, with some 22 workers killed, though it was defeated, had shaken corporate America in its roots. The 1920 Palmer Raids on "the reds" had torn civil liberties of American workers and "dissidents" to shreds. The arrest of Tom Mooney and Sacco and Vanzetti on frame-up charges — with the execution of Sacco and Vanzetti — marked the lengths to which reaction was ready to go to terrorize the working class. Always the terror had a practical aim. Even while the steel strikers were being ridden down by the Coal-and-Iron police in Western Pennsylvania, members of President Harding's cabinet were stealing the oil and land resources of the country hand over fist, in what became known as the Teapot Dome scandal, a forerunner of Watergate and Iran-gate of today.

Lynchings in the South and "race riots," often instigated by the police in the North, were a continuous reality in that "jazz age" of the 1920s. Sweat shops in both the South and particularly in New York City cut short the lives of thousands of children and women from overwork and disease, and many were slaughtered in the fire-trap buildings they were forced to work in.

Wages, despite the general "prosperity" never more than just sufficed for a subsistence existence of the majority of the unorganized industrial workers whose struggles to get organized were relentlessly drowned in blood.

Ten months before the Stock Market Crash of 1929, President Calvin Coolidge, surveying the land, found it good:

In the domestic field there is tranquility and contentment, harmonious relations between management and wage earner, freedom from industrial strife, and the highest record of years of prosperity. . . . The great wealth created by our enterprise and industry, and saved by our economy, has had the widest distribution among the people, and has gone out in a steady stream to serve the charity and business of the world. . . . The country can regard the future with optimism.

Even then, if he had just looked out of his window, or taken a casual auto trip through parts of the country, it would have been impossible for him not to have seen the tens of thousands of men and women out of work. With a workforce much smaller than it is today, nevertheless, in that period of "the highest record of prosperity" some four million people were out of work! And instead of "contentment" reigning every- where, in actual fact millions of other workers, though "em- ployed," were paid so little that their life was no more than a slow starvation. The average wage of the American worker in 1927 was $1,300 a year. According to the Bureau of Labor Statis- tics, a typical family of five (three children) needed to earn at least $2,064.95 to live with any measure of decency in New York City. In San Francisco the minimum wage needed for a family of five was $2,556.62. Even by employers' calculations — who calculate the "necessary" minimum wage much lower — the average worker's income still fell below the minimum by $405 a year. Profits, however, zoomed. In 1927 the value of pro- ducts manufactured increased by $800 million above the value of products in 1925.

The astonishing thing is how successfully the real plight of the working class was concealed from both the public at large and even from sections of the working class itself. Only now and then studies by philanthropic organizations provided a glimpse of the fact that far from the "great wealth" having the "widest distribution among the people," the people were actu- ally getting less and less back of what they produced.

Reported the Rand School of Social Sciences:

Due to the constant speeding up in American industry the increas- ing number of accidents, the unwholesomeness of many of the materials handled, and other factors, the expectation of life of adult American workers is continuously growing shorter. (Rand School of Social Science, 1929.)

In fact, a worker who was over 37 could expect to live 1.39 years less than before. The truth was that American capitalism was killing its workers at a fantastic rate. Some 35,000 were killed outright in the mines and mills and factories (1927) with 3,500,000 injured. Working men tended to die in their fifties. At 45, most men were considered unemployable and were fired.

If machines and accidents didn't kill them at their work sites, they died at home from diseases induced by foul working conditions. Among iron and steel workers, for instance, death from pneumonia was 15.9 percent higher than among the general public. Iron and steel workers, textile workers and coal miners were particularly susceptible to pulmonary illnesses caused by breathing in polluted air at work.

In 1928, something like 1,060,858 children were working full time (six days a week). Most of them were under 14 years of age. They, too, compared with school children their own age, showed the unmistakable signs of seriously-undermined health. Child labor would be abolished (at least in factories if not in the fields) only in the mid-1930s — and only as a result of trade union agitation against it.

Most of the industrial working class was unorganized and literally at the mercy of their capitalist employers who had no mercy on them. A certain percentage of craft workers were organized and their lives were relatively decent. But the vast majority of America's workers were naked before wolves.

At the same time much work was also done at home, both by children and their parents, who were paid by the piece. Such wages were even lower, especially for women, whose average pay in factories and shops fell far below what the male worker made — and his wages too were quite low. (In New York, full-time women's average wages dropped from $19.08 a week in September 1927, to $18.73 in 1928. Men's average wages for the same time, and for practically the same work, came closer to $34.08.)

Just slightly before the Wall Street Crash of 1929, Herbert Hoover, now president, looking the same scene over that Calvin Coolidge had looked at, pronounced:

> We have not yet reached the goal, but given a chance to go forward with the (Republican) politics of the last eight years, we shall soon, with the help of God, be within sight of the day when poverty will be banished from the nation.

Then came October 29, "black Tuesday," when the Stock Market collapsed. Almost overnight, the GNP fell from a high (in 1929) of $81 billion to a low of $41 billion (1932). Some 13 million workers lost their jobs. Nine million savings accounts were wiped out. Some 275,000 families lost their homes and were thrown out on the street. Some 250,000 teenagers (the present writer among them) "took to the road," homeless and jobless and school-less. Over 300,000 Black people left the starving South to come to the starving North. Schools were closed or the school day was cut short all over the country and thousands of teachers lost their jobs. That year, 1932, more people left America than entered it. Marriages were postponed, births were down, suicides were up and death by diseases brought on by malnutrition began to soar.

An enormous national catastrophe and yet "nothing" had happened! No earthquake had shaken the country, no great tornado had torn the towns apart; there was not even a flood. No armies had marched through the land laying waste to the fields and factories. Thousands of mills and factories closed their doors, but at no tyrant's command. Day by day suddenly all of America was to see something that Calvin Coolidge had been unable to see — long lines of starving people waiting for a bowl of free soup!

When people asked why, they were told that too much had been produced. The country was glutted with unsaleable goods, they were told: too much to sell, but the people had too little with which to buy.

Yet, even that formula seemed strange — for people needed food, clothing, homes; they were starving, going about in ragged clothing; they were being thrown out of their homes and building shacks in abandoned fields out of scrap in "Hoovervilles," and the factories and mills all stood idle. And while people wanted meat, pigs were destroyed. And while babies cried for milk, dairy farmers poured their milk into the gutters, refusing to sell it below cost.

The people turned to the wise men for answers. And here is what the wise men said. One day after the Crash, Herbert Hoover intoned: "The traditional business of the country, that is, production and distribution of commodities, is on a sound and prosperous basis."

Later that same year, November 4, the great Henry Ford, who had claimed that he was going to refute Karl Marx with "the $5 day," would confide that "things are better today than they were yesterday." And, not to be outdone, on December 10, Charles M. Schwab, chairman of the board of Bethlehem Steel, told a waiting world: "Never before has American business been as firmly entrenched for prosperity as it is today."

And J.P. Morgan, the most powerful banker in the world, whose money had saved Mussolini's Italy, and whose tinkering with the financial markets was credited with setting off the panic, would tell the nation in 1936, that "if you destroy the leisure class, you destroy civilization. By the leisure class, I mean the families who employ one servant — twenty-five to thirty million families."

This "great financier" believed that the Depression could be cured by hiring more servants!

At the same time, Andrew W. Mellon, also an admirer of Benito Mussolini, and hailed in the prints as the "greatest Secretary of the Treasury since Alexander Hamilton" (who proved the truth of that by awarding himself a tax rebate of almost $3 million and much more to his fellow bankers), told a clutch of Wall Street manipulators: "Conditions today are neither as critical nor so unprecedented as to justify a lack of faith in our capacity for dealing with them in our accustomed way."

Looking the scene over, and considering the ideas that had been advanced to explain the economic debacle, Will Rogers, the wit and newspaper columnist, had this to say: "It's almost worth the Depression to find out how little our big men know."

Thus, in 1929, America was obviously in the hands of

fools, rogues, nuts (J.P. Morgan consulted a notorious fortune teller, Evangeline Adams, on his financial moves), thieves, liars and just plain incompetents. Their stupidity, avarice and arrogance caused enormous suffering to millions of people and almost wrecked the country. Nothing was so clear as the fact that the "captains of industry," "helmsmen at the tiller of the ship of state" knew absolutely nothing about either the laws that governed industry nor the laws that governed the state.

Shocked, bewildered, disorganized, it was at this point that millions of Americans began to look elsewhere for answers to their burning questions. The mood was anything but complacent. "Will there be a revolution? This was the question that weighed heavily on many Americans' minds and hearts in 1931 and 1932," starts a chapter heading in a compilation of reports of the times. (*The Great Depression,* David A. Shannon, editor, Prentice-Hall, 1960.) And to find the answer to this question, many turned to the — up until then, almost ignored — Communist Party. Answers to this and other questions led to an unparalleled growth of the small Communist Party which attained a card membership of close to 100,000 by the beginning of World War II, with an influence going far beyond its membership.

At the same time, people began to look across the seas to the Soviet Union which, until then, had also existed marginally in their attention. So desperate was the situation for millions of Americans who were totally unemployed, literally beginning to starve, that they were ready to turn to any source that offered them hope and — most important — a job.

And, in the October 8, 1931 issue of *Business Week* it would be no surprise to anyone to read:

New Yorkers dominated the flow of Americans who have decided, at least for the time being, to cast their lot with the Russians. . . . More than 100,000 applications have been received at the Amtorg's New York office for the 6,000 [job offers in the USSR]. . . .

Three principal reasons are advanced for wanting the positions [in the USSR]: 1) unemployment; 2) disgust with conditions here; 3) interest in the Soviet experiment. . . .

"**I** LANDED IN MAHONING VALLEY IN THE MIDDLE OF AN-
other disaster, the economic crisis of the 1930s," Gus
Hall remembers. He was already a veteran of "disasters" for the working class. During the '20s, he had been in the
very thick of the class battles which had — despite what Coolidge said — raged in the industrial valleys of the nation. He
had led Hunger Marches. He had been involved in strikes.
Now, as a member of SWOC (Steel Workers Organizing Committee), and directly under its president, Phil Murray's authority, he was prepared to devote all his energy and talent to helping to organize the unorganized steelworkers.

John L. Lewis, leader of the United Mineworkers of America, had split from the AFL and had set out to organize the millions of unorganized industrial workers in the country. But he
lacked experienced workers to do it. Labor organizers didn't
grow on trees. There was one place however where they did
exist, and Lewis had no compunctions about tapping that
source: the Communist Party.

And there is where he found them. Communists had been
agitating for years in anticipation of precisely this moment,
when the workers would be organized into unions on an industrial basis — that is, everybody in the plant, from machinists to sweepers — they volunteered, almost *en masse*, to do
the job.

Among them was Gus.

Then, as a member of the SWOC staff, Gus found himself
in Mahoning Valley, Ohio. Here is what it was like:

Life then was raw and brutal. Hungry families were evicted from
their homes. There were soup lines. Death from so-called "natural
causes" of people weakened by hunger, increased dramatically.
There were no unemployment checks, relief checks, or old-age pensions. And there were no welfare systems people could turn to for
emergency relief.

But, in spite of the hunger and misery, there was hope because
there was a fightback. . . .

There were strikes. And not a week passed in Youngstown

without some kind of mass demonstrations, petitions, hunger marches. And for some of us the county jail became a second home. It was a common sight to see the marshals coming to evict families from their homes; the neighbors getting together taking the furniture off the street and putting it back into the house. . . .

Yes, there were strikes. But what was remarkable about these strikes was the fact that, though there were literally 13 million workers unemployed, and hungry, relatively few tried to scab!

This was probably the first time in labor history when unemployed workers as a whole refused to allow themselves to be used to take away the jobs of strikers. Why?

The answer to this, and to other changes in the behavior of workers, employed and unemployed at this period, is simple enough, though hardly acknowledged in the official histories of the times. And it can be stated flatly. The difference between the fact that in earlier days, unemployed workers always could be recruited as scabs to break a strike, and now — when they could not — was the existence of the Communist Party.

In and out of season, the Communists had preached (on soapboxes and off them) that all workers had the same interests in common. Though unemployed, a worker was still a worker — he was brother to the man who was lucky enough to be working. What had happened in the 1919 steel strike was not to be repeated in the 1930s. Then, Black plantation workers recruited by company agents were locked into freight cars and found themselves at the end of their journey right smack in the middle of the struck plants. Some tried to break out.

But hostility and resentment developed. History now sees this episode as a classic case of how corporations use and foster racism. Mutual distrust existed between Black and white workers in the steel mills for years and it was the general opinion among top AFL labor bureaucrats that for this, and other reasons, steelworkers could not be organized.

Communists were well aware of the history of hostility between Black and white workers. But more than that: they knew the real reason for it. William Z. Foster, now (in the 1930s) a

Communist leader, and then (1919) the chief organizer of the steel strike, understood the basic class reason for it better than anybody at the time.

Communists early understood that the key to victory in all class struggles was cooperation between Black and white workers. Early in the Depression years, it was in the Unemployed Councils, later the Workers Alliance, where thousands of Black and white workers met for the first time on an equal basis and learned, through direct experience, that the interests of both Black and white workers were indeed the same.

One of the unique contributions which the Communists made to the drive to organize the CIO was to bring this knowledge and experience, gained from these earlier struggles, to help solve the difficult problem of reaching Black workers who, in those days, were suspicious of all whites and tended to remain aloof from the union.

Ben Carreathers, a Communist leader, himself a Black veteran of the unemployed struggles, was particularly well equipped to persuade Black steelworkers in the Pittsburgh area that it was in their real interest to join the CIO. He personally signed up hundreds of workers and astonished Phil Murray who had felt that Aliquippa, a sheriff-controlled company town, was out of reach.

Communists had driven home to the unemployed from the very beginning that, basic to everything, they were all workers, and as workers they had a right to a job. The spirit in the unemployed movement was always militant. At no time did the unemployed come to their "masters," hat in hand, begging for a handout. They demanded. This militancy, encouraged by the Communists, reflected an ideological, class view. It climaxed on March 6, 1930 when tens of thousands of unemployed workers took to the streets, at the call of the Communist Party, and demonstrated for jobs.

Such unemployed workers were always reminded that they were not the enemies but the class brothers of men and women who happened still to be unemployed. In fact, during strikes, a contingent of the unemployed, often Black and white, always showed up on the picket line in solidarity. This class unity was the main reason why it proved to be impossible to break the various strikes that, in earlier days, the workers might not have dared to call for fear of scabs.

In addition, the fact that the Communists launched a campaign, that ultimately spread all over the world, to save the Scottsboro youth, later Angelo Herndon, from the electric chair, also left a deep impression on the Black masses.

These struggles had not only had practical results. They had a profound psychological effect on the masses as well. They saved the millions of unemployed and oppressed from a sense of despair — a sense of their impotence, of their futility, of their insignificance.

These struggles maintained the psychological and mental health of the masses. They gave the workers a sense of their own potential power, and of their inherent worth. When Communists told the workers that it was they who produced all the wealth — and the capitalists who took it all — this was not mere demagogy. This was the truth.

And indeed because it was true was why it had such a profound effect. Black and white unity, on a basis of complete equality, was very new and considered extremist then. And yet, it was not a new idea to the Communists. In fact, it was first enunciated by that first Communist of the world, Karl Marx himself, who more than a hundred years earlier, had put the idea in very concrete terms: "Labour cannot emancipate itself in the white skin where in the black it is branded."

Few in the middle 1800s were capable of such profound insight. For these immortal words alone, Karl Marx would have deserved to go down in history as the greatest liberator of all time. More than a hundred years later one worker was saying:

The key to mass struggles is workingclass unity. And the main ingredient of steelworkers' unity has always been the unity of Black and white workers. The question has now emerged as an integral part of the present crisis in steel because steelworkers cannot win without unity. And there can be no solid unity without a struggle against racism — racism that the steel corporations have fostered and practiced for over a hundred years.

The bottom line in the struggle against racism in the steel industry is the struggle for economic parity for Black, Puerto Rican and Chicano workers with their white class brothers and sisters.

This is Gus Hall speaking — a true son of Karl Marx. Through him speak Marxists of all countries, who have never faltered on this basic tenet in their ideology.

THERE WERE FURTHER CONTRIBUTIONS WHICH THE COMMUnists made in their struggle to bring workers to full consciousness of who and what they were. Not only did the Communists champion the rights of the unemployed, of Black people, of the mill and mine and factory workers. They also raised, in those desperate days, a healing perspective of struggle for millions of alienated and, in effect, socially discarded youth. In raising the goal of socialism, the Communists gave the youth something to strive for which was not only possible but which was within grasp — socialism was no longer a utopian dream but a living reality. These youth were ideologically brought *to* the working class, not estranged from it.

When Spanish democracy was being murdered in the late 1930s by a conspiracy of the imperialist powers, some 3,000 American youth, most of them Communists, volunteered to go to the help of democratic Spain, seeing in that action their international duty to their class brothers. This action has marked the highest moral achievement American youth, most of them from the working class (Black and white and women too), had ever reached. Their actions, their beliefs, their sacrifices also proved that moral corruption of the youth had to be imposed by social forces. Youth are not naturally corrupt. Another contribution to changing the American way of life directly attributable to the Communists was the way in which they changed the style of struggle. In the '30s, if you saw a picket line you assumed those were Communists on it. Very often the assumption was correct. If you saw Black and white demonstrations, you assumed Communists had a hand in them. You were often right. If you saw women on demonstrations — leaving their kitchens behind — you could be almost certain that these women were Communist-inspired. Demonstrations, protests, mass marches and movements — all this was the hallmark of Communist influence and organization. If you saw men and women (Gus among them) hauling furniture back into a house from which the sheriff and his men had carried it, you weren't far wrong if you guessed Communists were there.

Communists proved to the ordinary worker that property wasn't sacred. They told the farmer that the land belonged rightly to those who put their life into it, and helped save farms from being sold at auctions. The Communists showed the connections between Big Business (capitalism) and politics, between Big Business and war, between Big Business and racism, between Big Business and unemployment.

They argued that writers and painters and artists of all stripes had the right to practice their art and demanded subsidies from the government (to which they had paid taxes) to practice their art even though unemployed. And the result was the famous WPA arts projects (musicians, theater, writers, etc.). The hit song of a Broadway musical (put on by the garment workers' union) started with:

> Sing me a song of social significance
> All other songs are taboo.

In fact, so thoroughgoing, so widespread, so convincing were the ideas that welled out of the Communist activists, and so thoroughly absorbed by the people, that some version of Marxism (from the grossly distorted to the most enlightened) was factually accepted as the normal thinking of the times. So much so that Joseph Wood Krutch, a well-known writer for the *Nation* then (forgotten now) complained at the time that most people he knew were unconscious Marxists.

Indeed, the real education of the people took a Marxist direction. Schools devoted to teaching the workers the elements of Marxism sprouted all over the country, and such schools did point the direction to where the genuine education of the masses must go. But the "unconscious" education of the people, many of whom never met a live Communist, also took the same direction, and it is a symptom of the times that even President Roosevelt himself felt obliged to describe his political philosophy as a "little left of center" to get the ear of the people.

Perhaps the greatest contribution which the Marxists of the '30s made to the working class was to teach it how to think and what to think about. It was a great milestone in the ongoing struggle for full liberation when even portions of the working class came to recognize themselves as being a class, and learned how to think in their own interests.

American Marxists oriented that section of the working class which it influenced directly (about three million workers) to recognize the class features of fascism, not only abroad (it was easy to see that Mussolini and Hitler were no democrats) but in the home-grown American variety, especially as it presented itself in Huey Long's formula: "If Fascism came to America, it would be on a program of Americanism." It is to the eternal credit of the American Marxists that they were able to educate untold millions of Americans in the class origins of anti-Semitism and in the class origins of white chauvinism and male supremacy. These concepts, so new then, and such an unmistakable mark of the Communist (as the FBI well understood), are today widespread, even if in a distorted form.

When Gus says, "The Communist Party brought me up," literally tens of thousands of workers could also echo, in some degree, the same basic idea. The 1930s were a learning and a teaching time. The Communist Party played a decisive role in the education of the American working class and to preserve and continue that heritage is a fundamental part of the class struggle today.

G US HALL WAS IN THE VERY MIDDLE OF IT. IN FACT, HIS FBI dossier is probably the thickest the Department can show. He was often in jail. But being jailed, as he himself has observed, was an occupational hazard for a revolutionary. In any case, all of his jailings were in connection with the struggle to organize the unorganized. He remembers best his jailing during the 1937 Little Steel Strike when an attempt to frame him on a dynamite charge led to his arrest.

Gus had been put in charge of organizing the steelworkers in Mahoning Valley, in Niles and Warren, Ohio. When the word to pull the workers out came, he pulled them out. That strike was no small thing. Before it was ended, there would be casualties, particularly of ten people at Republic Steel in Chicago, owned by Tom Girdler.

Tom Girdler was a notorious open-shop hard-liner. His boast that he would sooner "pick apples" than sign a contract with the then-SWOC (Steel Workers Organizing Committee) is often referred to as an example of ultimate corporate arrogance.

But, in his autobiography, *Bootstraps*, he reveals just how ignorant and bigoted he was. He not only saw the strikes as the work of Communists, but he identified Communists with darkness, with men of swarthy complexions, "probably Italian." Earlier, at a congressional investigation, he had admitted candidly enough that "I never knew a steel plant that didn't have guns and ammunition to protect its property." (*Time* magazine, June 14, 1935.)

He was only telling the truth when he confessed that all plants were equipped with gunmen and were backed up with stores of ammunition. The 1937 LaFollette Senate Investigating Committee would later reveal what a vast undercover system of spies, paid by the corporations, existed within the labor movement, especially its most militant section. Big Business has always functioned hand-in-glove with the criminal underworld, and never more closely than in the militant '30s — except during the period of Reaganism, which out-corrupts all others.

It was reliably estimated that 230 spy agencies serviced the majority of America's corporations, many of which today sponsor genteel cultural events on TV. These agencies put anywhere from 40,000 to 135,000 agents into the field. There were 41,000 union locals in the country then, and new ones coming into existence every day with the CIO, and it was estimated that every one of them had its own spy, paid for by the corporation and making regular reports to the corporation on what was said and done at the local union meetings.

These spies — who were the co-workers of a certain actor named Ronald Reagan, soon to be active in the Screen Actors Guild — were not just passive agents of the corporation within the union who just took notes. They often assumed active roles in deciding union tactics. Some even became officers of their locals. As such, they were in a position not only to name the militants in the union (thus having them fired) but to promote actions which proved to be dangerous or self-defeating.

For these services, the corporations paid a total of $80 million a year — a huge sum indeed for those times. In addition they shelled out millions more for guns and ammunition which they stocked on their premises. It was a common sight in the steel valleys to see the mills "protected" by barbed wire (often electrified) fences with machine-gun "nests" perched at strategic corners with a clear view of the mill yards and the streets outside. A virtual private army with the right to kill any worker who "passed" on company property was at the command of corporate America, many of whom were represented by gorillas like Tom Girdler. In addition to their own private armies, the corporations could call on the local police and the State Troopers at will.

Philip Murray (who headed the Steel Workers Organizing Committee) sent Gus to Chicago and while he was there a warrant was issued for Gus's arrest. Gus's first notice that he was being sought by the police came in a story he read in the Chicago papers. "I sent a telegram to the newspapers and the sheriff, who said I was a fugitive, and that I was being hunted in six states. I told them I would be back. Do you know what they did? Both the papers and the sheriff kept the telegram secret. When I hurried back they arrested me and slapped one of the highest bails ever slapped on anyone there — $50,000."

It was on the anarchist-stereotype of a "revolutionary" as a compulsive bomber that the charge against Gus as a "dynamiter" was based. The frame-up was sworn to by the in-house spy (provided by one of the national spy outfits) who had actually planted the sticks of dynamite himself. National

Guardsmen then had "happily" discovered them and immediately Gus was accused of plotting to blow up the plant, apparently on the idea that if the workers had no plant to work in, that too would solve the strike. "All the time," Gus says, "I was in Chicago."

But to be in Chicago when they want you to plant dynamite in Ohio is no problem for the police. They don't need you to be actually present. They perform that chore for you themselves. "Witnesses" were bought and paid for according to the going rate and said their piece. "But," says Gus, "before the trial was over, the man (chief witness) was sent to prison for the criminally insane."

That was then, of course. Today, in the age of Ronald Reagan, they send them to the White House. Even so the case dragged on, with the judge showing his impatience at the clumsiness of the frame-up more and more openly. Finally, losing his patience altogether, the judge made it clear he'd accept a compromise and one was struck. Gus was "convicted" of a misdemeanor and fined $500 for knocking down a post. "I shouldn't even have agreed to that," he says, looking back.

Phil Murray, who headed the successful drive to organize steel, paid Gus a great compliment on his ability to persuade the workers to accept the union and then to go out on strike at its call. "We have the best organization in Warren," he noted publicly. And, in fact, the Warren-Niles-Youngstown strike was the best-organized, most efficiently run, with the best self-discipline.

But what struck Gus most memorably was how the workers behaved when they went on strike. They had never been on strike before. In fact, they had never been in a union before. Nor, on the other hand, did they have any real illusions about the humanity of their bosses.

The Little Steel Strike of 1937 was a bitter, bloody strike. The Girdler forces had thrown down the gauntlet to the CIO and made it clear that they would resist unionization with all the power at their command. Bloody clashes between strikers and police and scabs broke out at several places, but climaxed in June in the Memorial Day Massacre at the Republic Steel

Company in South Chicago where ten people (not all strikers) were mowed down by the police. There were three Communist Party members among them. A contemporary news account reports it this way:

> Then suddenly, without apparent warning, there is a terrific roar of pistol shots, and men in the front ranks of the marchers go down like grass before a scythe . . . a dozen falling simultaneously in a heap. . . .
>
> Instantly the police charge on the marchers with riot sticks flying. At the same time tear gas grenades are seen sailing into the mass of demonstrators, and clouds of gas rise over them. Most of the crowd is now in flight. The only discernible case of resistance is that of a marcher with a placard on a stick, which he uses in an attempt to fend off a charging policeman . . . he goes down in a shower of blows. . . .
>
> Although the ground is strewn with dead and wounded, and the mass of marchers are in precipitate flight down the dirt road and across the field, a number of individuals . . . have remained behind, caught in the midst of the charging police. . . . Groups of policemen close in on these isolated individuals and go to work on them with their clubs. . . . One (policeman) strikes him horizontally across the face, using his club as he would wield a baseball bat. Another crashes it down on top of his head and still another's whipping him across the back.
>
> These men try to protect their heads with their arms, but it is only a matter of a second or two until they go down. In one such scene . . . a policeman gives the fallen man a final smash on the head before moving on to the next job. (*Post-Dispatch* Bureau, June 16, 1937.)

Nothing so bloody took place at Warren, Ohio. Nevertheless Gus was to describe the scene:

> It was hardly dark and when I reached the pickets (before the steel plant) I didn't believe what I saw. The dark side looked like a scene from the First World War — a battlefield. The Republic Steel plant in Warren was big enough for the landing of planes. So Republic hired small planes filled with food and scabs from around the country. And that's how they brought in the strikebreakers.

But, he added, many of the steelworkers "were deer hunt-ers. So they got out their guns and . . . shot at the scab planes enough so that two of them crashed on landing. . . . This was the end of Republic's scab flights."

Gus, too, was a hunter as all woodsmen were and deer hunting is very popular among miners and steelworkers, and simply their reputation as good shots was enough to intimidate goons from the company side. Years later when Gus made himself unavailable and the FBI set out to look for him and were told by Gus's brother that Gus was out hunting in the "deep timber" and if they wanted him they were welcome to go and find him, the FBI agents' reply was: "Do you think we're crazy? Go after Gus knowing he has a gun in those deep woods?!"

But the truth is that Gus had learned early that one man with a rifle can't do much to advance the cause of the workers. As the old song goes, the emancipation of the workers is the work of the workers themselves. He was to be sent on other assignments by Phil Murray, especially to trouble spots where he was most needed. He helped organize workers in the can factories in Brooklyn, workers in Washburn Wire in the Bronx. . . .

And then he did something that surprised everybody. With Big Steel signing a contract with the CIO, followed by Little Steel in due course, a secure job as a union bureaucrat was as-sured him. But it was at this precise moment that Gus, though the highest-paid organizer on the SWOC staff, sent in his resig-nation.

That in itself was a shock. What followed was even more shocking. For Gus left the possibility of a well-paying job in the union hierarchy to become a section organizer of the Commu-nist Party of Youngstown, Ohio — for $20 a week when it was there.

Why did he do it? He would not have denied that trade union work was necessary and useful. But he felt the need to go further than the limitations imposed by trade unions alone. He wanted to help raise the consciousness of workers above the level they had reached with their awareness of the need to build and join a union. He wanted to introduce workers to a consciousness of socialism — to convince them that their rights would never be assured under capitalism, and that not even their hard-won trade union gains, not even their unions, were safe under capitalist rule. What Tom Girdler could not do with guns, the courts would do for him with a scratch of a judge's pen! Workers had to go directly into workingclass politics.

Meanwhile, he wanted to keep the union, whose origins had been so militant, as an organization responsive to the needs of the rank-and-file worker, free of the rot of bureaucracy, of corruption, of sweetheart deals with the corporations. "I felt I was making my best contribution to the steelworkers by helping to build up a core of Communists." For, Gus went on to say: "They'd guarantee that the union would remain a fighting organization. Don't forget, the steel union was largely built under Communist leadership," a fact of history not often recollected too willingly in official quarters.

But why such faith in Communists? Weren't Communists people? Weren't they prey to the same temptations and susceptible to the same pressures as were other workers? What guarantee was there that Communists wouldn't sell out to the other side for temporary partisan advantages?

Although Gus was never reluctant to tout the virtues of Communists he didn't really have to. The history of Communists in the labor movement spoke for itself. Despite the rivers of slander poured over Communists in the past decades, nobody has ever charged Communists with dishonesty, with stealing from the union treasuries, of making careers and fattening their bankbooks at the expense of the union membership, of striking back-door deals with the corporations they were supposed to be opposing. They have made mistakes and have been the first to admit it. But one "mistake" they never made. They never sold out the workers, nor became part of the huge general corruption which characterizes American life today.

And nobody exemplifies these qualities — this utter devotion to the cause of the worker — more than Gus himself. Win or lose, up or down, in good times or in bad times. Gus's compass has always pointed a steady north — north on history's compass being where the working class is. He has fought to keep the perspective clear. He has exposed all theories, no matter how smartly decked out in the glad rags of opportunism, that tended to undermine the basic, determining role of the working class.

Still, he has changed with the times. But "change" had to be organic, to grow logically out of the past, rooted in the needs of the working class, proven to be necessary by the test of struggle. The class struggle never ceases, he points out. It changes its face, its methods, its tactics constantly, and it is absolutely imperative for a workingclass party to keep pace with its maneuvers, or it will be caught off base and will pay dearly for it.

But perhaps the main distinction between Communists — Gus Hall in particular — and others in the workingclass movement is the one that Sherwood Anderson spotted years ago: "They mean it."

THOUGH GUS MANAGED TO EVADE THE TRAP SET FOR HIM BY the company spies in 1937, he would not be so lucky in the years to come. In the 1940s he, along with other members of the Communist Party, would be jailed on the charge of election fraud — which, boiled down, consisted of nothing more than having someone who signed a petition to put the Communist Party on the ballot swear in court that he had been misled by the Communists in putting his signature down. By that time, with another spasm of anti-Communism riding the media-induced waves of hysteria, any jury would have found Communists guilty of any crime the government chose to charge them with.

Gus was indicted, along with other leaders of the Communist Party, and in due course found guilty by an FBI-combed jury, and sent to jail.

Two years later, but only after the Communist Party launched a campaign for the right of Communists to serve in the war, Gus was drafted into the Navy, took his boot training at the Great Lakes, and was sent to the Pacific and wound up on Guam. Gus was one of 14,000 Communists drafted and who served (many with great honor) in World War II.

There, on Guam, he would see many things that made him aware even more profoundly than before of the contradictions inherent in America's participation in the war against fascism. The American people entered the war to stop fascism, but corporate America supported the war, not to defeat fascism, but to clear the Germans out of the commercial markets of the world (and along with them the Japanese). Gus was to see even on Guam how the interests of corporate America clashed directly with the interests of the people.

Ships were unloaded (at Guam) by the hundreds with goods from the U.S. They were unloaded onto huge caravans of trucks that carried and dumped these goods from a high platform to huge fires below . . . fires fueled by dumping endless barrels of high octane gasoline used by airplanes. What were the material goods that were being fed into the fires of Guam? Shiploads . . . of new shoes, finest bedsheets, office equipment, motorcycles, rope, clothing of every description — socks, pants, shirts, raincoats — portable electric plants, each costing tens of thousands of dollars . . . burned in the fires that lit up the nights of Guam. These goods came straight from the factories. They were all goods that the people in the U.S. and on Guam could have used. There were many items that were in short supply in the U.S.

The young sailors especially from smaller towns and the farms, who participated in the destruction kept asking: 'How come?'

How come indeed! The sight of destruction of new and useful products, so badly needed in Guam, and back home where the home folks were trying to make ends meet on ration stamps, puzzled and then sickened those young boys lately from the American heartland. Did they come to learn that the manufacturers of those goods that the army never used had a secret contract with the government which directed the army to destroy all such goods in order to keep the price at home at a profitable high? To sell them on the "free market" would have knocked prices down. There was a key lesson there in the huge wastefulness of capitalism and the privileged position which the monopolists hold in that system if those young soldiers had the eyes to see it!

Gus was always the Communist. Wake him up out of the middle of the night and he will come up a Communist! Communism was bred in his bone. This is not to say, however, that his view of life, especially of workingclass life, is mainly negative. His hatred of capitalism is for the evil it does — especially to the working class and all the oppressed, to the nation itself. Within his hatred of capitalism, however, is a vision of how magnificent this country could be if the tremendous creative forces of the people, so much of which now is wasted serving the interests of capitalists, were truly liberated.

This is no utopian ideal. The world, already one-third socialist, is ripe for socialism everywhere, and mainly it is American imperialism that stands between the ideal and the reality. A country in which 6,000 teenagers kill themselves while some 400,000 make the attempt, yearly, is not a country that can stand up before the eyes of the world and boast about itself or point the finger of "abuse of human rights" at anybody! And what is one to say about the moral health of a nation where an estimated six million people spend $110 billion yearly on cocaine while tens of thousands are homeless?

O N JULY 22, 1948, GUS HALL WAS ARRESTED ONCE AGAIN. This time it was along with 11 other leaders of the Communist Party, U.S.A. The charge, under the Smith Act, claimed that the Communist leaders were guilty of "conspiring to teach and advocate the necessity for the overthrow of the U.S. government by force and violence."

In 1948, the Communist Party had already been in existence for almost 30 years. In all that time, it had actively promoted its ideas however it could: through its newspaper the *Daily Worker*, in magazines, books, by speaking in lecture halls, at union meetings or out on the street. The one thing it did not want to do: keep its aims secret from the people. It ran candidates for office year after year.

And in all that time no proof was ever produced that these charges had any basis in fact. Supreme Court Justice Hugo Black, in his dissenting opinion, put the case quite clearly, and time has more than vindicated him:

> These petitioners were not charged with an attempt to overthrow the government. They were not charged with non-verbal acts of any kind designed to overthrow the government. They were not even charged with saying anything or writing anything designed to over-throw the government.
>
> The charge was that they agreed to assemble and to talk and to publish certain ideas at a later date: the indictment is that they con-spired to organize the Communist Party and to use speech or news-papers and other publications in the future to teach and advocate the forcible overthrow of the government.
>
> No matter how it is worded, this is a virulent form of prior censorship of speech and press. . . .

And so it was. It was even more: it was an echo taken from the arsenal of the very enemy just defeated, at an enormous cost in blood: the Nazis. They, too, had outlawed the Commu-nist Party of Germany and had executed 700,000 Party mem-bers during the war. . . .

T O GO INTO THE ORIGIN AND REASONS FOR THE COLD WAR IS not the function of this piece. Suffice it to say that with the war's end, a massive effort was launched by the most reactionary, most imperialist-minded forces in America to reverse the anti-fascist consequences of the anti-fascist war. Hitler was dead, but fascism, now wrapped in stars and stripes, was not to be buried with him. A visit to the cemetery of Bitburg by Ronald Reagan over 30 years later to commem-orate the SS Hitlerite dead loomed as the inevitable climax to the policy now enunciated by American reaction. With the death of European fascism and Japanese militarism the world had moved "too far to the Left" to satisfy the newborn ambi-tions for world hegemony that now took over in that part of the American ruling class which had never been reconciled to the anti-fascist aims of the war and now went to work to rob the people of their victory.

The American working class had fully supported the war and the CIO had taken part in 1945 in setting up a World Federation of Trade Unions in Paris, which aimed to unite the workers of the capitalist countries with the workers of the socialist countries in one single organization to preserve the victory won by the allied forces and to promote the ends of democracy everywhere. It also actively helped set up the UN. This participation of the advanced wing of the American working class (the AFL refused to participate), in setting up a world federation of workers marked the high-water point to which the American working class had reached. It remains an historic moment, despite later defections.

On March 6, 1946, Winston Churchill, speaking at Fulton, Missouri, with President Truman (who had not long before broken the railroad strike) at his side, delivered what has gone down now in history as the "Iron Curtain" speech, which is credited with being the most significant single act announcing a fundamental change in the policy that had been the key to winning the war against the fascist Axis. The Soviet Union, yesterday's honored ally, was now declared to be the enemy.

Everything changed after that. Not only were the 12 leading Communists arrested under a law specifically tailored for Cold War ends. But witchhunts were now launched in every area of social life. With the exploding of the atomic bomb over two Japanese cities in 1945, America announced by that act that only she possessed what was now decisive power in the world. America's tone toward the rest of the world changed almost overnight from the reasonable "good neighbor" accounts of the Roosevelt era to the openly chauvinist, jingoist, domineering type of the world bully. The "ugly American" was born.

Anti-Communism has been, and remains, the single most important weapon against the peace of the world in the arsenal of imperialism. Hardly had the Nazis been defeated on the field of battle than their ideas — anti-democratic, anti-Semitic, racist, reactionary — were retranslated into Yankee American and took on a new life.

The Communist Party was the immediate target of the neo-reactionaries. To justify the attack on the Communists, a hysterical "spy" atmosphere was deliberately created. Spies were invented and "found" everywhere. Hunts for Reds were launched on a massive scale. Some "930,000 . . . investigations (were) conducted by the Bureau (FBI) from 1955 to 1978. In a single year, 1972, the Bureau opened some 65,000 domestic files with an internal or national classification." (Sen. Frank Church hearings, Volume II.)

To launch the ideological rollback from an expectation of further democracy, a hope for peace and international detente, Senator Vandenburg of Michigan, one of the chief architects of the Cold War, is quoted as saying: "We've got to scare the hell out of the American people. . . . "

In this atmosphere (with the Korean War now enflaming it even more) it was foredoomed that the leaders of the Communist Party would be convicted. The intimidated jury would have convicted them of anything the government asked for — stealing moonbeams or bringing on winter. This jury had been drawn from the middle class; it had been combed and re-combed by the FBI for "subversive" ideas which they themselves might inadvertently have contacted the way children do cold germs, and was organically incapable of "independently" coming to a judgement — such a "judgement" in any case was built into the indictment.

The 11 leaders of the Communist Party (William Z. Foster was separated from the trial because of illness) were sentenced to five years in prison. Four of them, including Gus Hall, failed to show up to start their prison terms. Gus was later located in Mexico City in October 1951, kidnapped by the FBI who had no right to be in Mexico, and illegally transported across the Mexican border. Three more years were slapped on top of his five-year sentence.

Judge Harold Medina, whose considerable fortune came out of the way he handled the estate of widows who were his clients, presided over the "Trial of the Twelve." His contemptuous dismissal of the defense and the brutal way in which he sent defense lawyers to jail when they protested his arrogance not only intimidated witnesses but the jurors as well, whose "guilty" verdict was assured long before the trial ended.

At the same time, Medina pictured himself as a martyr and told the press later that all the time he had suffered during the trial because he kept hearing a voice telling him to "Jump!" He made certain that he didn't pass open windows!

P RISONS — AMERICAN FEDERAL PRISONS — AREN'T COUNTRY clubs (at least for revolutionaries, though they well may be for Watergate criminals and Wall Street thieves). Life there was cramped, empty, monotonous and mind-numbing. For Gus it presented him with the problem of how to keep mentally alert despite the bleakness of almost every kind of mental stimulus. Books could be taken from the prison library, but the library was limited. Some books could be ordered from outside. It was possible to read a newspaper. But letters to and from were severely censored and visits were limited to the family (a thousand miles away) and to attorneys. Food was bad. And though the other prisoners treated Gus with respect, there was little prospect of such communication to be found there.

One day Gus saw an old, wizened man come out of the cell next to his. He was hardly able to exchange greetings. The old man turned out to be the notorious Machine-Gun Kelly who had been one of Hoover's top "wanted" men during the 1930s as a bank robber. Years in prison had reduced him to this mumbling old man. "He had no perspective," Gus said of him.

Gus, of course, did have perspective. He knew the fight would go on. This was not imperialism's century. It was really and truly the "century of the common man." Later at a celebration of his 60th birthday he would note then what he already believed:

I am old enough to have lived and struggled in a period of history when imperialism was the dominant factor. It ruled and exploited, it killed and maimed and starved hundreds of millions throughout the world. . . .

I am old enough to have lived and struggled at a time when the

U.S. workers were unorganized —at a time when the boss was the total authority on all matters. But now the working class in the basic industries is organized, and I am young enough to be confident that I will live to see the day when these unions are led by the militant, progressive Left and Communist workers of our land. . . .

Changes had indeed occurred in those 60 turbulent years. The year 1970 also marked 53 years since the revolution in Russia, which is the date that the modern working class marks the beginning of its practical liberation. The revolutionary power let loose over the entire world during those momentous few weeks in November, 1917, in what was then St. Petersburg, has not abated for more than a moment ever since. That revolutionary explosion spread shock waves throughout the world — welcomed by the working class, feared and hated by the capitalists in every country, not least in the U.S. which, in 1919, sent an expeditionary force of 5,000 into Russia in an attempt to (in Churchill's words) "strangle the baby in its crib."

In prison Gus read a lot. He also decided to use his sudden leisure time to fill in the gaps in his formal education, and he buckled down to study physics and chemistry. His tutor was a scientist who, as it happened, had worked for Albert Einstein. He had wound up in prison (for five years) because he had briefly been a member of the Young Communist League in his youth and later, in filling out an application for a government job, he'd forgotten that fact and had written "no" where he should have written "yes." This one wrong word cost him five years of his life and the end of his career.

But, what was an ill wind for him was a good one for Gus. For Gus now had the personal tutorial services of a highly-developed scientist with whose help Gus went deep into the world of science.

It must be said, however, that prison being what it is, and Gus's connections with the outside world severely limited to only a few letters a month, and then only to his immediate family and lawyers, the scope for applying his newly-won knowledge in science was not very broad. In fact, his audience rather narrowed down to one small pre-teenaged boy, his son Arvo.

Still, with him Gus could let loose. His letters to his young son took up all the vital matters in that boy's life — baseball, football, movies, books, school, how to behave to mother and sister, and every so often Gus initiated his son into the mysteries of science. For example, on the matter of fat rain.

He informed Arvo that "a thunderstorm rains up as well as down," a statement which certainly must have plucked up that boy's ears. For Gus went on: "When a cloud is forming there is a strong wind blowing up as it first raises up and only when the clouds and raindrops get too heavy for the wind, do we get the rain down here on earth. So the raindrops that we get are only the fatsos that can't fly any more. And if any one tells you it's raining you have a right to ask which way — up or down?"

The letters are full of observations (strictly circumscribed) on what was taking place in the world. Nothing seemed too trivial or too unimportant to notice. On another occasion Gus wrote Arvo (Oct. 20, 1953):

> I don't recall if I ever told you how once I started to train a chipmunk while deer hunting. As you will find out some day, the best deer hunter is the one with the most patience. You find a nice spot and then just sit and freeze there and wait until some impatient hunter moves around and chases the deer to you.
>
> One day as I was sitting and taking in the beauty that only a forest can have, a chipmunk stuck its head from a hole, only a few feet from me. When I did not move, it began to make small spitting-hissing noises at me. At first, I decided to mimic the chipmunk. But, after a while, I took the lead in making the same kind of noises and the old chip would follow me. When I stopped, he stopped. After a long period of this, instead of making one noise, I started to make two short hisses and, to my great surprise, the old chipmunk made the same two noises I did.
>
> We had quite a time. I don't know which of us enjoyed it more. Afterward, I had a feeling the chipmunk was not playing with me at all but was telling me in no uncertain terms to get off his pile of nuts, covered in the dirt I was sitting on. The old chip outlasted me. I was still making the two noises I had taught it.

But it did not have confidence in me, because when I came back to the same place a day or so later he had dug up his storage of nuts and moved them to a new place.

Surely a man who can talk to chipmunks and learn from them can talk to anybody and learn from anything? Later, he would tell Arvo how, when he, Gus, was a little boy, he was mistaken by his favorite horse for a hank of hay — rather his boy's hair was. "The horse . . . thought my hair was more hay and he took one yank and through the window I went."

He would recall (again to Arvo, Dec. 5, 1953):

I promised to tell you about the smartest wild bear I ever saw. . . . When I was about Barbara's age, for three or four winters I worked in the deep woods of Minnesota as a lumberjack. I cut and sawed logs. One of the most honored jobs in the eyes of the old lumberjacks is to drive a four-horse team to haul logs. I was possibly the youngest "four-horse skinner" in the woods.

But, as you know, bears sleep and hibernate all winter. But, one year, I stayed in the camp into the Spring to take part in driving the logs down a lake and river.

So, after the snow melted and it got warm, a big bear used to come behind the camp in the evening and dig some food in the dump. We noticed the bear would go after old milk and syrup cans. The bear had learned to hit the cans with its big claws and make holes in them. So, we put full, unopened cans in the dump. And, believe it or not, this educated bear would hit those cans with its feet and make holes with its claws and drink the milk and syrup. The old bear didn't need to buy a can opener, because he had five of them on each foot. I suppose after this the old bear showed how it is done to his or her children and, by now, I imagine the woods of northern Minnesota are full of can-opening bears.

Mebbe so. Whether that's progress or not in the world of bears is a question. But those who can read between the lines of these comments about chipmunks and fat rain, and how to teach bears to open cans will see where the link between such observations about animals in the wild and the class struggle among humans connects up. The man who can learn from watching chipmunks, horses, fish, bears, rain and keep his sense of humor going under all circumstances, can also learn from a lifetime of watching how the working class lives —being part of it all the time — its struggles to win and why it wins and why it loses.

His thinking on that subject is not something that came casually to mind on an otherwise empty afternoon when he had nothing else to do. A lifetime, literally starting in the cradle, of thought, tested by action, is behind every word that follows in this book. None of the assertions made here are made irresponsibly. In prison, Gus turned all these ideas over and over in his mind, and like everyone who has had to fight for his ideas, and pay the price of holding them, he had to answer the vital question: am I right, or am I wrong? Are those putting me behind bars right? Or are they wrong? Unlike cultists, visionaries or fanatics, Gus had to subject his ideas to an objective test: they had to measure up in the real world; they had to be true.

He has put it clearly enough:

A true Marxist is one who not only knows the experience of the past, knows theory, understands the Marxist dialectical-historical method, but applies it to the specific situation as a good scientist should.

The first prerequisite for such application is to know the specific — to be close to it; to understand it not superficially but in its many-sidedness — its past, present and future, to know what caused it and what effects it will have; to know in what direction it is moving, how it is related to other surrounding specific phenomena.

And he adds:

As in the case of all fields of science, the study of Marxism is not a matter of studying or memorizing set phrases or formulas. The study and the development of this science, as well as the growth of one's own understanding, is itself a living continuous process. It is the study of the laws of motion or social development.

But that was precisely the point. That Marxism was a science was being questioned everywhere. The government had outlawed Marxism entirely; had branded those who held Marxist ideas as criminals. And even in those quarters that did concede that Marxism was a science, it was not also conceded that leaders of the existing Communist Parties were themselves masters of this science. The split in the ranks of world communism was most dramatically visible in the split between China and the USSR. For many in the world this "split" was conclusive evidence that Marxism itself was fatally flawed as a tool for grasping the motive forces changing the world.

In particular, the basic concept of Marxism that the working class was the key force in changing the world was attacked most fiercely of all. This hit at the very heart of Marxism. In its place, dozens of "new" theories were advanced that varied all the way from the Maoist concept of revolutionary change rising from the peasants, from the "Third World," to the notion that students, or else that the socially alienated criminals, *lumpens*, etc., had now become the real revolutionary force replacing the working class. In the USA, the further theory was advanced that the only revolutionary force was represented by the liberation struggle of Black people. In addition, voices were raised contrasting "Marxism" to "Leninism."

But whoever rose up to attack Marxism-Leninism as it was being actually practiced, the essence of their criticism always tended to undermine the basic Marxist concept of the decisive role of the working class in the class struggle.

Gus Hall was not yet the general secretary of the Communist Party of the USA. But he was already profoundly involved in the struggle that whirled around its principles. While he was still in prison, an attempt to turn the policy of the Communist Party around, to gut its revolutionary essence, and most pointedly to water down or eliminate altogether the key role of the working class, was made by elements within the Party headed by John Gates who was then a member of the Central Committee of the Communist Party and editor of the *Daily Worker*.

Gus had to watch all these developments that struck at the very heart of his own ideas, his own life in fact, stuck behind prison walls and unable to take part directly in the polemics which were threatening to tear the Party apart.

When Gus was finally freed from prison and could speak publicly again, he had this to say: "Like many others, I also spent some time in prison thinking over the past and evaluating the past and the present. But like most of the comrades who went to prison, I must say that I did not have any difficulty in not coming to the conclusion that Gates reached [that the Communist Party should liquidate itself — P.B.]. I think one of the significant things that Gates said was that he started his thinking in prison. In this thinking — and there is a lot of time to do it — I always took precautions not to allow something else to enter into it. I kept this pretty well to myself. The something else was cowardice."

There is cowardice and there is cowardice. There is physical cowardice — fear of being physically hurt — which is most familiar and most easily forgivable.

But there is also moral cowardice, which is not forgivable. A leader committed to principle is morally bound to defend principle against all odds. He has the trust of others, and that trust must be held sacred.

In the struggle now opening up so fiercely, moral courage was at a premium. Some individuals who were not afraid to face bullets collapsed before the blandishments of capitalism. Deserting principle, deserting the conviction that the working class was the force to change society in a revolutionary direction — and all that such a basic concept gave birth to — was, on the moral level, the same as a soldier turning tail in the face of the enemy and running for cover. Standing on principle was not an act of blind faith (as some enemies charged) but a decision based on practical experience over a prolonged period of time.

Precisely was this true in the United States: that of all the forces working in the direction of progress and change, the working class was key. Nor was Gus impressed by the argument that the working class itself had changed such that, in effect, it no longer existed, or if it could be said to exist, it had been totally adopted by the capitalists who had completely tamed it.

In 1959, at its 17th Convention, the Communist Party

elected Gus Hall as its general secretary. Later, Henry Winston would be elected as national chairman of the Party.

Almost immediately Gus made it clear that as the leader of the Communist Party he had no intention of watering down its revolutionary essence. He emphasized that the Communist Party was and would remain the party of the working class and of all the oppressed. The goal of the Party was to bring about a fundamental restructuring of society, of extending democracy far beyond bourgeois limits until it became, in the 19th century writer William Dean Howell's words (shared by his friend Mark Twain), an "economic democracy," i.e. socialism. The road toward this goal lay along the struggle of the people led by the working class and its vanguard party.

To reassert this goal and the means to achieve it in 1959 was in itself an act of courage as well as foresight. For the world was aflame with anti-Communist, anti-Soviet agitation and actions. Ideologically, the enemies of Marxism-Leninism claimed victory and were reading their funeral orations over what it identified as the corpse of the "Old Left" — a sly characterization of the Communist Party as being out-of-date, as tied hopelessly and dogmatically to past, outworn concepts.

Actually the target of all these "new" ideas, no matter how they were dressed up in "revolutionary" clothing, was always the living militant Communist Party. Behind all their concepts which they advanced as new and which transcended "old Marxism-Leninism" was one idea; and this is how Gus would spear it!

One of the basic theoretical concepts that has of late come under question and suspicion and is in fact openly challenged, is the Marxist concept that the working class is the only consistent progressive and revolutionary class in our society — that all social progress must of necessity increasingly lean and develop on this class as the basis for advancement.

This Marxist concept holds that the working class is the only class whose long-range interests are not tied to the *status quo* of capitalism but whose class interests necessitate the advance of all society through the elimination of capitalism and the construction of a socialist community — a system having the ultimate purpose of ensuring a life of abundance and of creativity for all the earth's inhabitants.

And, at his 60th birthday celebration, he summed it up:

The 60-year span of my life is witness to the total futility of denying history's direction. My first childhood memories are political. I am old enough to remember the effects of the first heartbeat of the beginning of the world revolutionary transition from capitalism to socialism. . . . The socialist heart now beats in over one-third of the world. That is definitely the direction of history.

That indeed — "that is the direction of history" — has been confirmed even more solidly since then. In the following ten years, most of the parties that claimed to represent the Left crashed on the hard rock of life itself. Maoism died a natural death. The notion that the alienated of society had replaced the working class as a revolutionary force simply faded away in smoke. Black freedom fighters in America recognized that only in alliance with the working class could the interests of the Black minority oppressed hope for full emancipation and true liberation. The various "national communisms," including Eurocommunism, had their brief day in the sun and then collapsed.

Capitalism had not changed its spots. It had no solution for the basic problems either in America or the world at large. In fact, American capitalism was caught in a triple-tiered crisis out of which there is no exit, and continues to stagger from one economic breakdown to the next. The danger of war, always present since American imperialism became aware of its world power, had increased enormously with the advent of the Reagan gang into Washington. In fact, Reagan has managed to place into the center of world attention the very survival of the human race itself.

One of Gus Hall's greatest services to the working class and to all people of goodwill everywhere was his early analysis of the fatal connection between so-called Reaganism and the political gambles and adventures that issued from it. Gus never tired of driving home to the working class, first of all, and to other progressives in general, the enormous danger in which the world now stands directly as a result of the Reagan foreign policy, the heart of which Reagan himself summed up as uncompromising opposition to the Soviet Union as the "source of all evil."

Reagan had the arrogance to confront the American people with the proposition: wouldn't you prefer to risk going down in flames to save the Stock Market, than to live in the same planet with the "evil one?" And rejecting the formula as totally false, Gus has pointed out that the real alternative facing Americans and all people is: life and peace and co-existence, or total annihilation.

The campaign to arouse the people to the need to struggle for a sane foreign policy culminated in actions like the April 25th massive demonstrations in Washington and San Francisco in the year of this writing (1987) where tens of thousands of Americans —spurred on by trade unionists in larger numbers than ever — made it clear that grassroots America wanted peace and wanted it now. Reagan's foreign policy stood nakedly exposed to the world as criminal with the exposure of Iran-contra wheelings and dealings in an attempt to fund the anti-Nicaraguan cutthroats.

In the April 25th demonstration, the thousand-strong contingent of the Communist Party, at whose head Gus Hall marched, was cheered by the onlookers who — despite years of anti-Communist propaganda — found that they were, perhaps even to their surprise, pleased to see the Communists out in strength. It was reassuring to them that what they were seeing was living proof that not only were the Communists alive and well but that their being there — with banners flying — proved that they represented forces in the working class that were irreducible and indestructible.

And it was a bit of history — and greater history to come — marching in the person of Gus Hall, who had survived years in Leavenworth, various plots to assassinate him, oceans of slander, and though born and raised "in the belly of the beast" had demonstrated, through his person, that the heart of the

American working class was sound, that the party Gus represented was organic to the country and to the class, and that the policies of class struggle he had spent his life fighting for were more and more manifest in the course of events.

Gus's election as general secretary of the Communist Party in 1959 opened up an intense period of intellectual and organizational activity that has not tapered off for more than a moment ever since. Not only was Gus confronted with the urgent job of rebuilding and unifying the Communist Party around the central question of its workingclass principles and revolutionary direction. He had to convince what was then a largely confused section of both the Left activists and the working class in general that this was the correct line to follow.

The same doubts and confusions about the basic nature of Marxism also characterized sections of the international Communist movement and Gus was deeply involved in international debates on these issues. He came out solidly against all forms of revisionism, of watering down the workingclass essence of Marxism, of every attempt to accommodate the American Left to the service of American imperialism in no matter what disguise it presented itself. Thus, he was an early opponent of Maoism, of Zionism, of Eurocommunism, of the "New Left," and of old Trotskyism in its new forms. At all times he was an enemy of the war-makers, of mindless anti-Sovietism, of every attempt to sell the working class short.

Today, he is recognized internationally as a genuine leader not only of the American Left but as an inspiration to militant revolutionaries and Communists everywhere — from South Africa to Sverdlovsk.

Capitalism had exposed itself. Reagan had proven to the world that capitalism, in its dying phase, goes to war against democracy, and in order to save themselves all democratic-minded people must join together.

This, too, was the thought of W.E.B. Du Bois, the great Black leader, scholar and historian, whose thinking had been so influential in shaping the thought of progressives everywhere. His own rich life led him to apply for membership in the Communist Party, USA (October, 1961) saying that, "Capitalism cannot reform itself; it is doomed to self-destruction. . . . "

Speaking before an audience at a symposium "Marxism and the Bicentennial" (April 24, 1976), Gus Hall wound up his review of "Two Hundred Years of the Class Struggle" with this confident prediction:

I feel it safe to say that when the next centennial rolls around there will be a new relic in our socialist U.S. museums. The people will view the relics of capitalism in amazement and disbelief, as they ponder: "What insanity! A small minority of thieves, worthless, idle leeches got rich by exploiting the great majority of the people! . . . What insanity that nations had enough killing power to destroy each other ten times over. . . . What an odd period it must have been! Human beings inhabiting the same celestial body were divided into nations, races, classes. . . .

"And it was all based on an economic system called capitalism, motivated by something called exploitation and profit. It is hard to believe this was part of our history!"

WORKING
CLASS
USA
The Power and the Movement

About This Book

THROUGHOUT THE AGES RULING CLASSES HAVE DOWNPLAYED, covered up and suppressed the notion that there is any such thing as a class struggle. And yet human history is one story after another of the people — working people — fighting for and winning their freedom from exploiters and oppressors. That is the class struggle.

Nowhere in the world is it more important to keep this fact in mind than in our country with a ruling class unmatched by any in its efforts to deny that the class struggle exists — especially in our "classless" USA.

The class struggle in the United States is practically an untold story. It is not taught in the schools, never mentioned by Republicans or Democrats, there are no shows about it on TV nor stories in the major newspapers. But it goes on as a daily part of our lives. It affects everything.

To try and understand what's happening today without seeing the class struggle is like trying to drive without seeing the road. Before long you'll end up in a ditch!

Even within the workingclass movement there have been those who have denied that the class struggle is with us for as long as we have had capitalism. Especially during and following the period of McCarthyism — the counteroffensive of Big Business — there was a deafening chorus of those saying the class struggle was gone forever. But how long and how loud someone says it doesn't make it so. Capitalism's tightening squeeze on the U.S. working class (under Reaganism it has become a stranglehold) and the growing militancy, unity and leftward movement of the trade union movement is ample proof that the class struggle has not gone away — just the opposite.

This book is not a history of the class struggle in the United States, but there is a lot of history in it. Understanding the class struggle today requires knowing something about how it developed into what it is. And an essential part of that is knowing the link between the class struggle and the Communist Party. That is the untold story within the untold story!

Since its birth the Communist Party, USA has fought for policies of class struggle trade unionism, for unity of the working class, for raising class consciousness — the awareness in the working class of its own great power. These factors serve as a barometer of how advanced the class struggle is at any given time: the more militant the policies of class struggle trade unionism, the higher the level of unity within the class, the greater the class consciousness — then the greater the advance in the class struggle.

The selections in this book were written at different times, under different conditions and for different audiences. This many-flavored character gives the book an extra dimension. But it is also true that there are certain threads, or steel cables, running through the diversity.

The greatest victories to date for the U.S. working class were during the rise of industrial trade unionism in the 1930s and '40s. Conditions were ripe for great advance. Workers were ready to fight after years of suffering the massive unemployment of the Great Depression, and after the movements of the unemployed, initiated by the Communist Party, had pointed the way to struggle.

Building the Union in Steel: Thirty Years of Struggle discusses in some detail the rise of the union in steel, how it came about as part of the militant policies of class struggle trade unionism, policies that Communists had been fighting for since the 1919 steel strike. It shows how the struggle for workingclass unity, Black-white unity in the first place, was key to victory, and that the Communist Party's contribution was essential. And it tells about how Communists were a part of every phase of organizing in steel. This example holds true for the other mass production industries.

Needless to say the "captains of industry," who had for so long considered themselves invincible, were none too pleased about being forced to make concessions to "their" working class. And forced they were. Many industrialists who swore they would never negotiate with a union were forced to sign contracts.

But the class struggle changes with objective conditions, and conditions had changed enough after the Second World War to allow Big Business to go on the counteroffensive. *Big Business's Counteroffensive and the Anti-Communist Hysteria* discusses this period. Written in the 1960s, it is published here for the first time.

U.S. imperialism was more powerful than any in all of history. It was able to throw its weight around overseas and at home. It could afford to buy a little bit of "labor peace" while launching a vicious attack against the advanced units of class struggle in the U.S. — the Communist Party and the Left as a whole. Certain mistakes in the tactics of the Party in dealing with a very difficult situation made their job easier.

It is no accident that during that period the policies of militant class struggle trade unionism were by and large replaced by policies of class collaboration, that the class unity forged in struggle was fractured, and that Communists and other Left forces were attacked and in many cases hounded out of the trade unions.

The question of how Communists should work in the trade unions after the McCarthy onslaught was a very important one that carries lessons for today. The basic lesson in *Communist Approach to Building the Unions* is that to fight for our policies the Party and the Left can never be "armchair critics" but must be actively involved in the search for solutions. These solutions — then as now — are not always easy to come by.

As always, the class struggle continued to change as objective conditions did. By the late 1950s and into the '60s, at the very time that Big Business hoped that it had achieved an enforced "labor peace" forever, times were changing. U.S. imperialism was suffering defeats; the socialist community was gaining strength and the movements for national liberation were scoring victories around the world. At home the contradiction was growing between the rank and file of labor, left at the mercy of the bosses, and a top labor leadership completely in the lap of Big Business — particularly AFL-CIO president George Meany and cohort Jay Lovestone.

Labor in the Post-McCarthy Period discusses this period and the need for building rank-and-file movements in the labor movement and the imperative of all-sided workingclass unity. Helping the rank and file of the trade union movement make this turn was an essential responsibility of the Communist Party.

The Rank-and-File Movement and the Emerging Left goes further into these factors as they developed with the rise of the militant rank-and-file movements and radical caucuses of the late 1960s and early '70s.

Another question of burning importance for the working class in that period was its relationship to corporate war aims in Vietnam. *Hard Hats and Hard Facts: The Vietnam War* is from a pamphlet issued and distributed in response to a staged march of construction workers in New York, in support of Nixon's war policies. Though the battle areas have changed from Vietnam to Central America, Southern Africa and other areas, the interests of the U.S. working class in fighting U.S. imperialism's aggressions are the same.

Once again, as the objective situation changed, the class struggle changed with it. U.S. capitalism developed a new disease, the structural crisis, that characteristically it passed along to workers at home. Corporation heads stated openly that they were in the business of making money, not steel, autos, machine tools, rubber, etc., and they could make more money by closing down plants in the U.S. and moving them overseas — to exploit cheap labor in countries where U.S. military aid to

Right-wing and fascist governments had guaranteed a "union-free environment."

Not only was U.S. Big Business making superprofits overseas, it had a new club to hold over the heads of workers at home — the threat of plant closings. A labor movement wracked by class collaborationism, by disunity, and without a big enough Communist Party and Left was not in the position to fight back effectively.

Beat the Steel Crisis! Save Every Job! (1977) is a speech made in Youngstown, Ohio, when it was newly shaken by the closing of the steel mills there. It discusses what elements are needed for mounting a fightback against the structural crisis in the U.S. This speech, incidentally, marks the first time that the concept of nationalizing our basic industries was raised as a timely solution to the structural crisis.

How to fight back, always important, became critical for the labor movement, particularly how to develop further the leftward trend in the rank and file in order to pressure for greater workingclass militancy and unity. This is discussed in *Why a Left-Center Coalition.*

Today, as a result of all these developments, a new wind is blowing through the working class and the trade union movement: a qualitatively new level of militancy, of unity, of class consciousness and growth of the Left. It really comes as no surprise. It is an outgrowth of the sharpening class struggle, of the changes in objective conditions which have forced the working class to fight back.

The Old and the New, New Framework for the Class Struggle, and *One Hundred Years of Heroic Class Struggle* all examine the new situation in the working class and trade union movement. The past points the way to the future: in order to face the new challenges, to deal with tremendous problems faced by the working class, there needs to be even more militancy and class struggle policies, even greater levels of working-class unity, and a much bigger and more influential Communist Party, USA.

Today, the ruling class sits on the horns of a sharpening

dilemma, faced with a capitalist society on the decline — internationally and domestically — in virtually every area, and a working class that is fighting mad, increasingly so. Whether the U.S. ruling class will decide to back off and give concessions, or attempt to pursue the discredited "Reagan revolution," depends to a great extent on the unity, the militancy, determination and creative ideas on the part of the workingclass and trade union movement, and the leadership the Communist Party is able to provide.

Part II goes further into the elements the working class needs for its further advance. The most basic of all basics for the working class is a scientific understanding of its central position in capitalist society as the revolutionary class and the greatest force for progress. The article, *The Working Class,* goes into this question at some length. It was written in 1966 as the introduction to a book on the working class and, because of the day-to-day pressures of struggle, it has remained unpublished until now.

The Living Science looks at Marxism-Leninism, the science of the working class, as a dynamic science that must continuously be updated with the class struggle itself. There are no blueprints. This has never been more true than today when we workingclass scientists need to apply our science creatively to our new conditions and problems. *Workingclass Intellectuals* discusses why this process must not be left solely to those outside the working class.

An understanding of the political party of the working class, the Communist Party, is an indispensable part of any study of the class struggle. *The Communist Party, USA* discusses how the Party was no accident of history, nor a "foreign import," but a logical outgrowth of the objective conditions created by U.S. capitalism. History founded the Communist Party as much as did its founding members.

What the working class needs today is more class struggle trade unionism, greater levels of unity, more political independence, greater class consciousness — in other words what the working class needs today is a bigger and stronger Communist Party, USA. *Fighting Big Business Ideas,* and *Adding the*

"Plus" though written almost 40 years apart, discuss the role and responsibilities of Communists in the workingclass movement.

Communists have always pursued a policy of industrial concentration, with special emphasis on the basic section of the industrial working class. Basic industrial workers occupy a special position in the engine room of capitalism, and the system has developed in them a high degree of collectivity and cooperation. For this reason, industrial workers are the most revolutionary section of the working class.

But here too, changes in objective conditions bring changes in the class struggle. The structural crisis has decimated many of the basic industries in the United States, so that some industries that were once the backbone of our economy may never return to the U.S. under capitalism. This fact requires changes in the Party's policy of industrial concentration. To take into account the most recent developments, *Industrial Concentration and the Changing Class Struggle* was written for this book.

"United we stand and divided we fall" — these words sum up hundreds of years of hard experience of the working class. The U.S. working class is particularly diverse: multinational, multiracial, men and women, young and old; class unity is a central question. Within that the need for Black-white unity has been and remains foremost. And with the rapid entry of great numbers of women into the U.S. workforce in recent decades, the question of unity with and equality for women has taken on greater importance.

Black-White Unity and the Working Class and *Women and the Working Class* both date from before the creation of the Coalition of Black Trade Unionists (CBTU) and the Coalition of Labor Union Women (CLUW) — very important forms of organization for the further development of workingclass unity.

Today's transnational capitalism raises the question of the role of the U.S. working class in the world to ever greater importance. Part III deals with a number of sides to this question.

World Workingclass Unity (1969) discusses the class struggle in the world arena: the contest between capitalism and socialism. Since that time the fact that socialism is winning the contest has become even clearer. The class struggle in the developed capitalist countries is an integral component of the historic revolutionary transition taking place.

New Problems of Capitalism: Fighting the Transnationals presents some recent thinking on how to deal with the very difficult problem of imports and exports. As leaders in our trade union movement are increasingly aware, much more international trade union cooperation is needed to fight today's transnational megacorporations. *Class Struggle is the Frame of Reference* develops further thinking on this, emphasizing that the class struggle is the motive force for change in the world arena as much as in the USA.

Socialism — what is it, can it happen here? — is a question on the minds of more and more workers and people generally in the U.S. today. *Lenin and the U.S. Working Class* discusses the impact of socialism's first appearance, the October Revolution, for the U.S. working class.

Where Workers Have Power, was written in response to an anti-Soviet, anti-workingclass slander by then-president of the United Auto Workers Douglas Fraser. It holds capitalism in the U.S. and socialism in the USSR up to the light for comparison from the perspective of the working class. Guess which comes out on top — and time has more than supported the conclusions!

The book ends with some *Worker's Flashbacks,* stories about workers and workers' struggles — all true. Many of these stories have their humorous side and nevertheless provide insight into the indomitable character and fighting spirit of our working class, USA.

There is no subject of more importance or consequence than the class struggle. There is no power greater than the working class. And there is no more noble struggle than for the working class to rid humanity forever of the dog-eat-dog of exploitative class society. It is my hope that this book will give aid and understanding to my fellow workers and fighters in this greatest of all struggles.

Gus Hall
New York City

July, 1987

Development of
the Class Struggle
in the United States

takes a fight to win

The Rise of
Industrial Trade Unionism

Building the Union in Steel:
Thirty Years of Struggle

[From: "Thirty Years of Struggle for a Steelworkers' Union and a Workingclass Ideology," Political Affairs, September, 1949 — slightly abridged; written in prison while serving a sentence for protesting Judge Harold Medina's gag rules.]

PRISONS AND JAILS ARE SO MUCH A PART OF THE HISTORY OF THE class struggle in the United States that my surroundings here at the Federal Detention Prison are truly appropriate for the writing of this article on the struggles of the steelworkers.

This year marks the 30th anniversary of two major landmarks in American labor history. It is 30 years since the founding of the Communist Party, USA, and 30 years since the first successful organizing campaign of the steelworkers and the Great Steel Strike of 1919.

It is not an accident that these two anniversaries coincide. For it was the same working class that had attained a new maturity thirty years ago, which gave birth to the Communist Party and to the epic struggles of the steelworkers. Many of the same individuals took part in both of these historic events.

Our beloved William Z. Foster[1] was the initiator, leader, and organizer of the campaign to organize the steelworkers and of the history-making strike that followed. Shortly after the strike and the founding meetings of our Party, Comrade Foster, in 1921, led a group of militantly progressive trade union leaders and members into this newly founded Marxist-Leninist Party of the working class: Jack Johnstone, Charles Krumbein, Scotty Williams, and many others. It was the blending of the experiences of the U.S. working class — embodied in these outstanding trade union leaders — with the science of Marxism-Leninism that laid a firm foundation for the Communist Party of the United States of America.

The organization of a political party was not something new for the American people. But the Communist Party was and is not just another party. The Communist Party is the Party of the working class, and its theory and practice are rooted in the revolutionary science of Marxism-Leninism.

The founding of our Party therefore added a new quality to the class struggle in America and marked the beginning of the end for the era of drifting, spontaneous movements and utopian schemes. Now the working class had a revolutionary Party that was armed with a scientific understanding of capitalist development and with the accumulated, generalized experience in struggle of the workers of the United States and of the whole world. Now the working class had a rudder, a guide on the difficult road to liberation — to socialism.

The newly founded Party had to study and master the Marxist-Leninist science and become skilled in applying it to the problems of the class struggle in our country. And it had to undertake the bitter, uncompromising struggle against the reformist, social democratic ideology of class collaboration, of opportunism, which had paralyzed the working class for decades.

For the steelworkers, as for the whole working class, the founding of our Party marked a qualitatively new stage in the struggle for industrial, militantly progressive unionism.

LARGE-SCALED MASS PRODUCTION — MONOPOLY-CON-trolled industry — began to dot the landscape of America during the last half of the 19th century. There took place the two-fold process of rapidly expanding production and the narrowing down of industrial ownership and control. This continuing process has placed domination of the economic and political life of the country into the hands of a few major finance-capitalist groups.

The emergence of the trusts, as Lenin brilliantly showed in his classic study, *Imperialism: The Highest Stage of Capitalism,* is marked by reaction all along the line, by greatly intensified exploitation and oppression, by growing and deepening class struggles. In the United States the offensive of capitalist reaction included a bitter, violent assault on the small and weak trade union movement, which had evolved on the basis of small-scale production.

The working class was not prepared for this attack politically, ideologically or organizationally. The small unions of skilled workers, organized by crafts and dominated by the Gompers ideology of pure-and-simple unionism, were no match for the emerging industrial giants.

The magnates of the steel industry were in the leadership of the union-smashing drive.

As Foster states in his book, *The Great Steel Strike,*[2] written after the Great Steel Strike of 1919, conditions in the steel industry approximated outright peonage. The workers slaved in the mills for twelve and more hours a day, many of them for seven days a week. Wages were at the starvation level. Working conditions were murderous. Accidents, constantly growing speedup, brow-beating by foremen and a virtual reign of boss terror fed the anger of the thousands of immigrant workers who had fled Europe in the hope of achieving a better life in this country. The communities were dominated by the open hirelings and lackeys of the steel trusts.

Unionism quickly took hold among the steelworkers, "and by the later 1880s, grace to the activities of many unions, notably among which were the old Sons of Vulcan, the Knights of

Labor and the Amalgamated Association of Iron, Steel and Tin Workers, considerable organization existed among the men employed in the iron and steel mills throughout the country."

The Amalgamated Association (AA), the largest of these unions, achieved a high point of 24,000 members in 1891. Organized mainly in the Carnegie mills in and near Homestead, Pa., the AA consisted almost entirely of highly skilled men, ignoring the masses of unskilled workers. Nevertheless, the union had won a contract with Carnegie and in 1889, after a short strike, successfully resisted Carnegie's attempt to slash wages.

The historic 1892 strike of the workers in the Carnegie Steel plant in Homestead, which lasted five months and was joined by workers in many large mills in the Pittsburgh district, was the reply of the workers to Carnegie's continued union-busting and wage-cutting drive. Five hundred Pinkerton gunmen, hired by Carnegie and his newly-acquired slave driver, Henry C. Frick, used river barges to unleash their murderous assault on the strikers. The story of this famous struggle is still related today by steelworkers to their grandchildren.

The AA was virtually driven out of the mills after the 1901 strike against the newly formed U.S. Steel Corporation. Thoroughly "tamed" by this time, especially under its new president, M.F. Tighe, the AA made its last-ditch stand in 1909 when the steel barons served notice — by instituting a wage cut — that nothing short of the open shop would be acceptable to them. The bitter 14-month strike which resulted was doomed from the outset. Thereafter, the AA was purely a paper organization whose main "contribution" was in acting as a vehicle for transmitting the ideology of the capitalist class into the ranks of the steelworkers.

Slowly but surely the paralyzing, defeatist idea that "it is impossible to organize the workers in the basic, mass production industries" penetrated into the ranks of the trade unions and the working class. Long before Hitler, American Big Business used the line of "invincibility." This capitalist propaganda, spread by the class collaborationist labor leaders, was the first obstacle in the path of all attempts at large-scale union organization. Before anything could be done about organizing the steelworkers, the "theory" of Big Business invincibility had to be destroyed in the ranks of the AFL.

At the 1918 AFL convention, rank-and-file pressure resulted in the unanimous adoption of a resolution to organize the steelworkers, submitted by William Z. Foster, then secretary-treasurer of the committee organizing the meatpacking workers in Chicago. The stage was set for an attempt at the "impossible," although many of the AFL leaders privately predicted failure for the campaign even before it got on its way.

As Foster shows in *The Great Steel Strike,* the First World War provided a golden opportunity for speedy organization of the steelworkers on a national scale. Uninterrupted steel production was imperative for imperialist war production; steel company profits were at a new high level and the companies strove to avoid a stoppage; the steelworkers were literally begging for organization.

On the basis of the successful organization of the packinghouse workers, under Foster's direction, "It was evident that in the proposed campaign radical departures would have to be made from the ordinary organizing tactics."

The first blow against the drive was struck by the reactionary AFL leaders. As Foster wrote many years later in *Unionizing Steel*:

> . . . The reactionary AFL leaders, however, with no real interest in the work, neglected this plan [for a national campaign], holding to the theory that the work must be begun in only one locality, gave the organizers but a few hundred dollars and a half dozen organizers to take up the work. This was a deadly blow.

Foster, who was elected secretary-treasurer of the organizing committee, was in fact the key figure from the first day of the drive. The National Committee for Organizing Iron and Steel Workers, which was set up at an AFL conference in 1918, embraced some two dozen cooperating AFL unions with a total membership of about two million.

The organizing campaign was viewed by all of labor as a great test of the "invincibility" dogma. The committee, under Foster's leadership, planned the campaign carefully and, with the limited funds and organizers provided, executed it master-fully. As a result, despite the abrupt expansion of the labor market with the sudden end of the world war and despite the continued sabotage by the AFL leaders, the campaign broke through in a brief matter of months. In the first 18 months, 250,000 steelworkers joined the union in the face of brute terror and murder, spying and mass firings.

Thousands of shopkeepers, professionals and other mid-dle-class people, as well as the whole corrupt hierarchy of lack-eys of the steel barons and outright underworld elements —in-flamed by the inciting stories in the venal press, by church ministers and by "law enforcement" authorities — were pressed into service as deputy sheriffs. They were armed, and given "open season" on strikers and their families. In Foster's words, "It was an alignment of the steel companies, the state, the courts, the local churches and the press against the steel-workers."

But the "impossible" was accomplished. The fairy tale that workers in mass-production industries "cannot organize a union" was destroyed. And William Z. Foster, despite the na-tionwide campaign of slander directed against him, emerged as the central figure in the labor movement.

ON SEPTEMBER 22, 1919, 365,000 STEELWORKERS WENT OUT on strike after fruitless efforts by the organizing com-mittee to get the employers (who were led by the noto-rious union-buster, E.H. Gary,[3] chairman of U.S. Steel Cor-poration) to sit down and negotiate. The demands of the workers were for: the right of collective bargaining, reinstate-ment of all men discharged for union activities, the eight-hour day and the six-day week, abolition of 24-hour shifts, an in-crease in wages, standard scales of wages in all trades and clas-sifications of workers, double pay for overtime and Sunday work, the check-off, seniority rights in hiring and firing, aboli-tion of company unions, and abolition of physical examination of applicants for jobs.

The steel trust used every trick in the book against the

steelworkers, who conducted a strike twice as big as any preceding one in the history of the country — a strike that was directed against the most powerful monopolists in the land. The steel towns were turned into armed camps as the federal, state, and city governments went all-out against the strikers. The bosses used machine guns on the workers, and the mounted state police played a particularly murderous role throughout the strike.

The reign of terror began to break the back of the strike, first in Gary (where federal troops under General Leonard Wood were used and martial law was declared), then in Indiana Harbor, South Chicago and the Chicago district generally, the Youngstown district, Cleveland, etc. By December 10 the number of strikers was down to about 110,000, almost all of whom held out for another month. But the situation was hopeless.

Finally, on January 8 the National Committee for Organizing Iron and Steel Workers, by a vote of ten to five, decided to call off the strike by authorizing the 100,000 men still out to return to work. At the same time the organizing committee declared: "A vigorous campaign of education and reorganization will be immediately begun and will not cease until industrial justice has been achieved in the steel industry."

The steel barons celebrated and rejoiced, announcing that unionism had received its "death blow" and would "never" rise again. Many of the class collaborationist labor leaders echoed these defeatist ideas.

In the welter of confusion that followed, there again came one clear voice. Immediately following the strike, Foster sat down and wrote his book, *The Great Steel Strike,* in which he drew the lessons of the struggle for the whole working class and outlined the next steps in the steel campaign.

The Great Steel Strike was, for tens of thousands of workers, an eye-opener about capitalism and the class struggle. It became a handbook of progressive trade unionism for a long time afterwards.

What were some of the chief lessons of the Great Steel Strike? Foster declared that although the vicious terrorism set loose by the steel barons and by the police and troops succeeded in crushing the strike, the organizing campaign and the direction of the steel strike marked a great advance in trade union tactics and output of effort. But this was not enough, for:

> . . . it represented only a fraction of the power the unions should and could have thrown into the fight. The organization of the steel industry should have been a special order of business for the whole labor movement. But unfortunately it was not. The big men of Labor could not be sufficiently awakened to its supreme importance to induce them to sit determinedly into the National Organizing Committee meetings and to give the movement the abundant moral and financial backing so essential to its success. Official pessimism, bred of thirty years of trade union failure in the steel industry, hung like a millstone about the neck of the movement in all its stages.

The failure to follow through the original organizing plan envisioned by William Z. Foster was a "monumental blunder" on the part of the participating unions. The number of organizers and the amount of funds provided could not possibly do the job required. This fact soon became apparent to all, and helped spread pessimism in the ranks.

As Foster strongly states, "Had it [organized labor] but stirred a little the steelworkers would have won their battle, despite all the Steel Trust could do to prevent it."

The whole organizing drive and the strike itself were conducted with virtually no aid whatever from the unions participating in the National Organizing Committee. They were sustained almost completely by the steelworkers themselves and by the organized labor movement at large. Moreover, the control of the organizing forces by the respective international unions comprising the National Organizing Committee itself, "tended to create a loose, disjointed, undisciplined, inefficient organizing force."

Foster showed further that the moral and material cooperation of the unions of coal miners and railroad workers was indispensable for a successful strike, but was not forthcoming.

Foster analyzed at some length the national origin and composition of the steelworkers, and exposed the vicious attempts of the bosses to pit native born against foreign born and one group of foreign born against another. These pernicious efforts were largely unsuccessful.

But what did achieve a considerable degree of success for the steel barons was the importation of Afro-Americans, from the South and elsewhere, on false pretenses and under constant guard, for use as strikebreakers. A number of the Black workers who discovered the facts heroically escaped the clutches of the scab-herders.

Where did the blame belong for the herding of Blacks as scabs in the Great Steel Strike? Foster showed that part of the guilt lay with the petty-bourgeois leaders of the Afro-American people's movement of that period, who permitted themselves to be used by Big Business for continuing Black-white disunity.

But the main responsibility for the success of the tactic of the steel barons in pitting Black against white workers, Foster showed, lay on the shoulders of the labor movement itself. In drawing this major lesson of the Great Steel Strike of 1919, Foster showed himself to be one of the pioneering fighters for full equality of the Afro-American people and the indissoluble unity of Black and white workers. He wrote:

> For the tense situation existing, the unions are themselves in no small part to blame. Many of them sharply draw the color line, thus feeding the flames of race hatred. This discriminatory practice is in direct conflict with the fundamental which demands that all workers be organized, without regard to sex, race, creed, politics or nationality. It injures Labor's cause greatly. Company agents harp upon it continually, to prevent Negroes from joining even the organizations willing to take them in. This was the case in the steel campaign. . . . Such a condition cannot be allowed to persist. But to relieve it the unions will have to meet the issue honestly and broad-mindedly. They must open their ranks to Negroes, make an earnest effort to organize them, and then give them a square deal when they do join. Nothing short of this will accomplish the desired result.

The essence of Foster's study of the Great Steel Strike is that only industrial unionism, based on nationwide, simultaneous organization in all plants, companies and areas, and on the organization of unskilled and semiskilled, as well as skilled workers, Black and white, can do the necessary job of organizing the steelworkers in the United States and leading them in militant struggles for their needs and interests.

In conclusion Foster showed that the steel strike was not a "lost" struggle. Writing even before the ultimate concessions granted by the steel corporations a few months later as a result of the strike, he showed the whole working class the significance of struggles like the Great Steel Strike:

> No strike is ever wholly lost. . . . An unresisting working class would soon find itself on a rice diet. But the steel strike has done more than serve merely as a warning that the limit of exploitation has been reached; it has given the steelworkers a confidence in their ability to organize and to fight effectively, which will eventually inspire them on to victory. This precious result alone is well worth all the hardships the strike cost them.

History has fully confirmed these farsighted words of William Z. Foster. The "theory" of the "invincibility" of the monopolies against unionism was destroyed forever. The lessons of the steel strike have remained with the working class to this day, influencing all the subsequent struggles of the steelworkers. The working class was now more confident of its own united power, more conscious of itself as an exploited class struggling for a better life. It gained a deeper understanding of the class struggle.

The Great Steel Strike, moreover, was not without material success. One of the direct results of the strike was the abolition of the 12-hour day for the steelworkers. The winning of the shorter working day was, however, accompanied by an increase in speedup and the mechanization of the industry. The unorganized steelworkers were not able to put up an effective fight against these developments. The years that followed were years of inhuman speedup, of a rising rate of exploitation and of growing intimidation of the steelworkers by the open-shop employers.

I N 1929, THE ECONOMIC CRISIS STRUCK ITS DEVASTATING BLOW. The unorganized workers in mass production industries were helpless victims of the great economic crisis of the 1930s. Giant monopolies maintained their high profits at the expense of the workers, who suffered indescribable misery. The majority of the steelworkers were laid off for long periods of time. Already by 1929 the wages of steelworkers were down 50 percent from 1927. In 1933 the U.S. Steel Corporation announced that it had no full-time steelworkers on its payroll.

The steelworkers were deserted by the misleaders of labor — but not by the Communist Party. In the absence of a steelworkers' union, the clubs and individual members of the Communist Party organized and led many limited struggles. The Communist Party shop papers in many cases exposed and stimulated struggles on various grievances, with many local victories. Considering the continued reign of terror, this pioneering was the work of heroes.

In 1929 the newly founded, Communist-led Trade Union Unity League (TUUL) organized the Steel and Metal Workers' Industrial League. Foster was on the job as ever. It was not the original purpose of the League to go into competition with the Amalgamated Association, but the League did take a forthright stand against the class collaboration policies of the AA. It carried on an educational campaign for militantly progressive class struggle unionism. The steelworkers responded very readily but the AA officials, as was to be expected, did not. The AA leadership reacted violently against the whole idea of fighting for the interests of the steelworkers.

As a result, the League reorganized itself in 1932 into the Steel and Metal Workers' Industrial Union (SMWIU). From the day of its birth this militant union was engaged in one struggle after another. The SMWIU quickly made a name for itself, especially in departmental struggles. The long list of militant strikes it conducted includes Republic Steel in Warren and Youngstown, Ohio, Empire Steel in Mansfield, Ohio, and many actions organized in Western Pennsylvania and in the region of Gary, Indiana. During its short life-span of two years, this small union left its mark in all the important steel centers, with its education of the workers in class struggle policies reaching numbers many times its membership.

The arrest of Foster and the other Communist leaders during the March 6, 1930 demonstration of the unemployed in New York had an electrifying effect on the unorganized and starving steelworkers. Unemployed Councils mushroomed in the steel communities, and soon grew into the largest organization of steelworkers in the country. The Councils organized the largest body of steelworkers in active struggle since the 1919 strike.

The Communist-led Unemployed Councils were militantly progressive, class struggle organizations. Through varied forms of struggle which received great mass support — hunger marches, demonstrations, delegations, etc. — the Councils were instrumental in winning the Works Progress Administration (WPA), the Civilian Works Administration (CWA)[4] and other federal, state and local relief. These struggles prepared the steelworkers politically and organizationally for the bigger struggles to come.

When the economic crisis began to recede somewhat, the workers who went back to work showed a strong determination to organize new unions. A new wave of militancy was sweeping the working class. The great strike struggles of the early and middle 1930s propelled masses of unskilled and semi-skilled workers, Black and white, most of whom had never before been union members, toward the organized labor movement. The membership of the trade unions began to grow.

In order further to unite the ranks of the workers and build the unions, the Communist- and Left-led TUUL industrial unions decided to send their members into the other existing unions, most of which were still headed by reformists and reactionary social democrats. The original formation of the TUUL in 1929, and of its affiliated industrial unions, had been made necessary by the outright betrayal of the trade unions and the interests of the workers in the 1920s by the reactionary, bureaucratic leaders, by the refusal of these leaders to organize the millions of unorganized, and by the terroristic and mass-expulsion practices of these labor misleaders against Communist and Left/progressive forces. By 1935, these policies had become bankrupt. The rank and file was in a mood for unity and struggle, and was eager to merge with the militant TUUL unions, which had amply proved their mettle in struggle.

The SMWIU decided to disband and join forces with the members of the Amalgamated Association. This was like an injection of vitamins for the membership of the AA. In spite of the actual resistance of its leadership, the union began to grow.

B Y 1935 THE WORKING CLASS HAD NOT ONLY SHOWN ITS DEtermination to organize trade unions, but also expressed in no uncertain terms its desire to organize industrial unions. The lesson had finally hit home. Ever since 1901, William Z. Foster and other militant trade unionists had been hammering away for industrial unionism. And ever since its birth, our Party had been teaching the workers the need for industrial unionism.

The growing rank-and-file sentiment for industrial unionism that had now become an outright demand resulted in the organization of the Committee for Industrial Organizations (CIO)[6] within the AFL. The Committee did not break with the notorious class collaborationist policies of the AFL officialdom, but it did see the need for the industrial form of organization. Step by step, growing rank-and-file pressure forced the Committee to move from mere education for industrial unionism within the AFL to outright industrial organization. Expulsion of the unions that made up the Committee brought the issue to a head.

While the CIO officials were still hesitating, a rank-and-file movement of steelworkers grew under the leadership of Communists and other progressives. Rank-and-file committees sprang up in most of the large steel centers, organizing and leading many struggles and carrying on an educational campaign for progressive unionism. This rank-and-file movement also published a weekly newspaper in Youngstown, Ohio, that was edited by Charles McCarthy and Joe Dallet.

The rank-and-file movement of the steelworkers sent dozens of delegations to pressure the CIO leaders to initiate an organizing campaign in steel. Thousands of steelworkers signed pledge cards and petitions to the same end, promising full support for such a campaign. It was only after this campaign of the rank and file that the CIO leaders in 1936 set up the Steel Workers Organizing Committee (SWOC).

It is a matter of record that the only workingclass organizations which had continued to provide genuine leadership to the steelworkers since 1920 were the Communist Party, the Communist-led Unemployed Councils, rank-and-file committees, and the SMWIU. The work of these organizations was also supplemented in the early 1930s by the Communist- and Left/progressive-led organizations of the nationality groups and the National Negro Congress.

Our Party was already engaged in mobilizing capable forces for the campaign long before the SWOC had established its offices or staff. It was inevitable, therefore, that the various district directors of the SWOC established close working relations with the local leaders of the Communist Party. Many leading Communists went on staff of the SWOC.

Almost without exception, the first union contact in the steel mills, the organizing core, proved to be a club of the Communist Party or individual Party members, an ex-member of the SMWIU, a reader of the *Daily Worker*, a member of the National Negro Congress, or a member or supporter of one of the Left/progressive-led nationality organizations. Many of these activities had also been the spark for the union in 1919 and 1930.

But the Communist contribution to the campaign did not end there. Before the drive started, Foster wrote two pamphlets addressed to the steelworkers: *Unionizing Steel* and *Organizing Methods in the Steel Industry.* These pamphlets reflected the rich, accumulated experiences of the working class in general and of the steelworkers in particular. They immediately became the guide for the work of all Communists in the steel industry, and especially for those of us who were on the organizing staff. Through us, the ideas and policies put forward by Comrade Foster were passed on to the whole staff. Foster also gave personal leadership to the drive. He spent many days and nights in meetings with those directly involved in the campaign. He met with Communists and non-Communists in the staff and leadership of the SWOC. In addition, the names of Jack Stachel, Jack Johnstone, Pat Cush, John Williamson, Joe Dallet, Al Balint, John Steuben, George Powers, Ben Carreathers, Dave Doran, Bob Burke, Abe Lewis and many other leading Communists are known to steelworkers for their effective leadership during this period.

The Young Communist League, as part of its work in helping to organize the steelworkers in 1936, published a popular pamphlet called, *Get Wise — Organize!* The *Daily Worker* and Communist and nationality-group newspapers were outstanding mobilizers and educators throughout the organizing drive.

The steel organizing drive broke all records. The campaign broke through a veritable "iron curtain" of corporation spy systems, intimidation and terror. In a few months 2,000 new members were joining the union daily. Whole departments of plants and groups of workers joined simultaneously.

The campaign very closely followed the proposals made by Foster in his pamphlets. The very heart of these proposals was the guaranteeing of full rank-and-file participation. On the basis of his experience, Foster recommended use of the "chain system" in which each union member signs up another member, the "list system" by which unionists provide lists of potential recruits to the staff for home visiting, the system of "key men" in each department, and the system of voluntary and part-time organizers. By using these techniques, the full-time staff became the center of a whole network of rank-and-file organization and activity.

The U.S. Steel Corporation recognized the new mood of militancy which swept the masses of steelworkers. U.S. Steel did not give up the struggle against the steelworkers when it signed a union contract in March of 1937; it decided to change its tactics. The house of Morgan, the real boss of U.S. Steel, decided to try to make the new steel union into another AA.

Led by Republic Steel, the "little steel" corporations (Jones and Laughlin, Youngstown Sheet and Tube, and Inland Steel) decided to continue the old head-on struggle against the union. Tom Girdler, the ex-police thug turned corporation president, sounded the battle cry: "I would rather go to the farm and pick apples than sign a union contract." Negotiations broke down over the issue of securing a contract.

On May 26, 1937, the SWOC was forced to strike the plants of "little steel" over this issue. The response of the steelworkers was 100 percent pro-union. Morale was high. All the plants were closed down. The steel corporations declared war.

After the strike, the LaFollette Committee calculated that the open-shoppers in steel had spent $178,138.65 for all types of guns and ammunition. Republic Steel admitted buying 552 revolvers, 64 rifles, 245 shotguns and 2,707 gas grenades. Youngstown Sheet and Tube admitted buying 453 revolvers, 369 rifles, 190 shotguns and eight machine guns. This does not include the arsenals of the state, county and city police. In addition, Republic Steel used two airplanes to fly strikebreakers into the Warren, Ohio, plant.

The strike started May 26. On Memorial Day the Chicago police attacked a peaceful union parade with rifles, revolvers, tear gas, etc., killing ten and wounding 90 strikers. Before the first month was over, six more strikers were killed by city and corporation police. The governor of Ohio called the National Guard out to break the strike.

After four months of sharp struggle, the union was forced to retreat. The strike was called off, but this time the steelworkers were not demoralized or disorganized. With very little help from most of the leadership, the workers in the mills showed remarkable ability to reorganize their ranks. The Communists and other militant and progressive unionists skillfully led the workers of "little steel" through these difficult days of temporary retreat. After a long period of court fights and NLRB elections, the corporations signed contracts.

Four months before the strike, Foster had written his pamphlet, *What Means a Strike in Steel*. It was clearly evident to all that here again was the voice of experience. I well recall the staff meeting I attended at which the strike call was announced. Not one word had to be said on how the strike was to be organized or led; the clear, masterful presentation in Foster's pamphlet made a deep impression on the steelworkers and the staff.

The entire Communist Party gave its very best in support of this struggle. Our Party can rightly be proud of its enormous contribution.

THE SWOC HAD FINISHED ITS WORK. THIS ORGANIZING COMmittee was transformed at the founding convention into the United Steelworkers of America. Now the steelworkers had a union.

This was a tremendous victory. The corporations signed yearly contracts. Workers could not be fired for union activities. A system of seniority was established. Wages were increased with each new annual contract. The union set up a grievance apparatus, and the steelworkers were in a position for the first time to do something about their extremely hazardous working conditions; they could now resist the inhuman speedup. Above all they were now united.

These were real advances for the steelworkers. But all was not well. At first unnoticed, later in the open, the poisonous ideology of class collaboration was infecting the USWA. The steelworkers wanted a militantly progressive, class struggle union. They had shown this time and time again on the picket line and at their meetings. But the leadership was taking the road of class collaboration. All unions whose leaders follow policies of class collaboration inevitably become bureaucratic, undemocratic organizations. It is the only way such leaders can force reactionary policies down the throats of the membership.

Were there some weaknesses in the work of us Communists that helped contribute to that state of affairs in the steelworkers' union? Yes, it is clear that there were.

Because of the policies of Browder revisionism,[7] we dropped our guard against the constant penetration of the ideology of class collaboration into this union. We did not expose, we did not sharply enough criticize and attack these policies when they appeared.

Our weakness was not that we worked with the present union leadership, but that while doing so we did not expose and criticize the treacherous, class collaborationist policies of that leadership. Our main effort should have been directed toward organizing and mobilizing a militant rank-and-file movement, activating and uniting the membership around a progressive program of action. Unfortunately, this was not at all times the case.

The clearest sign of this weakness has been the lack of sufficient understanding of the role of our Communist Party, the vanguard Party of the working class. As a result, the struggle to educate the workers to accept workingclass ideology was bound to be unsuccessful.

There were many tendencies to merge and "lose" the Communist Party in the general trade union movement. The seeds of this were already noticeable in 1937 when, in the midst of the organizing drive, we permitted Party sections and clubs to be stripped of leadership by giving these forces to the general union drive.

We further showed this basic weakness when we did away with all effective Party organizations in steel: shop clubs, shop papers, etc.

We did not fight vigorously enough against the policy of removing Communists and progressives from posts of leadership. Communists who were appointed to the staff and did not work to be elected by the membership were "easy pickings" for the bureaucrats.

We did not fight sharply enough against right opportunist tendencies and practices by our own leaders and members. Above all, this weakness showed up in our spotty and weak efforts to bring into the Communist Party the thousands of steelworkers who had learned to respect and accept its leadership. Where the efforts were made, the results were excellent.

The last 30 years have been a period of heroic struggles in the face of terror, killings, jailings, firings and blacklistings. It has been a period marked by many victories and advances for the working class and its allies.

The steelworkers have come a long way since 1919. Our Party has a magnificent tradition and record of achievement in these developments. The work of our Party is still marked by many weaknesses, but we can be very proud of the 30 years of dogged, persistent, skillful, heroic work and leadership exhibited by the Party.

The task of our Party is clear. Learning the necessary lessons from our experiences and analyzing them in the light of Marxism-Leninism, we must come forward boldly and courageously with the guidance and leadership which the masses are increasingly seeking. We can do this effectively if, in the process, we give greater attention to building our Party and our press.

On the occasion of this double anniversary of the Great Steel Strike and the founding of the Communist Party, let us confidently go forward to the fulfillment of this task. Let us be inspired by the leadership of Comrade William Z. Foster, Chairman of our Party, trailblazer for militant, democratic industrial unionism, pioneer organizer and fighting leader of America's steelworkers.

Big Business's Counteroffensive And the Anti-Communist Hysteria

[From an unpublished manuscript: "The Trade Union Movement: Review and Perspectives," written in 1967.]

THE STRUGGLE BETWEEN LABOR AND CAPITAL IS INBORN WITH capitalism. It is the sharpest manifestation of capitalism's most basic inherent contradiction. It is this basic built-in flaw that is the grave digger of capitalism. Whether one accepts or rejects this basic truth about capitalism is not simply of abstract philosophical importance. In a very basic sense it determines one's attitude to everyday trade union affairs.

Many top trade union officials have tried to live a denial of this truth. They have tried to cover up this inherent contradiction between classes by a hundred varieties of the "one big happy family" illusion. This has led to the concept of collaboration between the classes, to statements that the class struggle is outmoded or dead. But the truth will out, and with it the class struggle.

When the point of reference is history, there is no doubt: history is on the side of labor in this epic struggle. Progressively the working class gathers a consciousness and strength. The weight shifts against capital. But as is the case with all phenomena, within this longer range process there develop pressures periodically that can result in either ebbs or flows in the struggle. These pressures can feed either offensive advances or they can become a drag and thereby force periods of defensive struggles.

However, in human affairs the ebb and flow is not a mechanical motion like the pendulum of a lock. The ability of the human mind to reflect on and to influence our surroundings, to master the ways of nature, is what makes the difference. Thus in social affairs a conscious organized force can have a decisive effect on the patterns of these ebbs and flows of struggle. Because of this, an ebb can be merely a pause, a moment for regrouping of the forces, or it can develop into a serious setback. Also the nature of the period of advance can be greatly affected by the conscious human element. The advance can be just a step or it can be a qualitative leap forward.

Why is this so important? Because if one is to study the basic causes, the dynamics that propel periods of advance as well as the weaknesses in the ebb period, it is necessary to weigh both the influences of the objective factors and the influences of subjective human elements. It is easy to hide one's weaknesses behind a lopsided emphasis on the objective factors.

In the arena of class struggle both elements are always present. In social struggles the subjective influence is leadership — leadership that reflects the objective realities of the specific moment. Leadership can resist and thereby minimize and cut short an ebb period. But it can also miss the boat by not responding in time. A correct tactical policy must reflect the positive currents and embody the dynamics for a period of flow.

For U.S. labor the period of 1935-45 was a ten-year span of offensive victories. It was a period of flow. It changed the economic, political and ideological fabric of the USA. A very important result of these victories was the organizing of the mass production industries.

After repeated efforts that started with the genesis of U.S. industrialization, the working class finally broke through the most brutal system of terror, murder, blacklisting and rule by private but "legal" corporation armies, of spy setups, of terror by vigilantes and storm troopers who terrorized workingclass communities. The corporation executives who conducted the most brutal war against the workers and their unions made the most eloquent speeches about democracy. Thousands of workers gave their lives in this class struggle: the heroes, the casualties of the breakthrough.

This period of advance had its roots in the mass struggles of the unemployed during the Depression years. The economic crises and the struggle of the people resulted in a rise in political and class consciousness. The positive results of the upsurge included: the formation of a mass-based trade union movement, the emergence of trade unions on the electoral scene, a new level of Black-white workingclass unity, the emergence of a mass Left sector in the organized trade union movement, the establishment of a rank-and-file grievance apparatus, industry-wide contracts, retirement clauses in contracts, etc. The political waves from this forward sweep resulted in what are now called the New Deal social security measures, such as unemployment insurance, etc.

While the objective forces were all flashing "go," the conscious organized forces contributed greatly and thereby accelerated the scope and speed of the forward sweep. In this the members of the Communist Party played a key role. They were part of the leadership of the moment and the struggles. They helped create the forces and solve the difficult strategic and tactical problems of the forward sweep. They gave stability and foresight to the movement. This is important to recall as a backdrop when one reviews the tactics developed by Big Business for its counteroffensive against this progressive sweep by labor.

T HE COUNTEROFFENSIVE OF BIG BUSINESS WAS ONLY AS effective as the forces of labor were weak. Once the trade union officialdom began to retreat, the forces of reaction pressed for the kill and a period that could have been a pause turned into a serious setback for labor.

Drawing on the experiences of their German class brothers, U.S. monopoly capital found the weak spot in the ranks of the working class. The Achilles heel was in the political and ideological fiber. They could no longer win by directly attacking the right to organize unions. They could not win by an attack on the right to strike or to continue to reject labor-management contracts. Even Tom Girdler, former president of Republic Steel who publicly said he would rather pick apples than sign a union contract, signed on the dotted line. But they found an opening weak spot in the political-ideological fiber.

The weak spot was the fraud of anti-Communism. The cold war offensive for the "American century" of U.S. monopoly capital was now extended to the domestic scene. As Dulles[8] said: if there is no obvious external clear and present danger, you must create it. The Supreme Court accepted the fanatical ruling of Judge Medina in the Smith Act[9] case that thinking thoughts about organizing the forces opposed to capitalism constitutes a "clear and present danger" to U.S. capitalism.

The counteroffensive set out to establish two fraudulent positions that Big Business could use as a wedge to split the ranks of labor. The first was that "Communists" had infiltrated the unions in order to stir up struggles — not because they were interested in the welfare of the workers but for some ulterior purpose. This made all militancy, all initiatives of struggle, open to suspicion of being "Communist-inspired." All militant actions by workers were labeled "Communist-inspired." Actions by workers became "wildcat strikes inspired by Communists."

What was meant by "ulterior motives" of the Communists was set forth in the second of the ideological frauds: the idea that the Communist Party, USA is part of a worldwide godless conspiracy of foreign agents, a concept copied from the captured files of Hitler and Goebbels. In the public mind it is one thing to take part in struggles even if they were "Communist-inspired," and quite a different matter to think that these struggles are for "the ulterior motive of aiding a world conspiracy and a foreign power."

In this criminal travesty, the so-called "foreign power" manipulating the "world conspiracy" was the Soviet Union. Anti-Sovietism became the hysterical call of the witchhunters. Every militant worker was suspected of being "Communist influenced" and therefore at least an "unwilling dupe" of the "foreign power."

U.S. capitalism pulled out all Madison Avenue stops to put over this most criminal of all frauds. It became the ideological and political foundation for U.S. foreign policy. The cold war is based on this fraud. It became the political and ideological smokescreen for U.S. internal policy. It became the main instrument in the attack on the working class and especially its organized sector, the trade unions.

Once reaction was able to get its foot into the door by getting important sections of the labor leadership to accept this swindle, the skids were greased for attack. Once the concept that militancy and initiative in struggle were inspired by some foreign interests or for "political" reasons outside the economic self-interests of American workers, the stage was set to stifle the very spirit of trade unionism.

Big Business forces of reaction drove for a split in the CIO. The battle cry was the fraud of anti-Communism. This fraud became the umbrella for the passage of such open anti-labor bills as the Taft-Hartley, Landrum-Griffin and McCarran acts.[10] The acceptance of the fraud by leaders of labor had made their opposition to these anti-labor laws totally ineffective. They had become victims of their own trap. How could they mobilize against proposed laws that only codified the very fraud they were peddling themselves? Big Business moved to deport such Left militant trade union leaders as Harry Bridges.[11] The evidence against them was the fraud of anti-Communism.

The leaders of many trade unions made their contribution to the fraud by introducing anti-Communist clauses into their union constitutions. They grovelled at the boots of Big Business by repeating phrases from the big fraud. Once the groundwork was laid, the employers moved in. As if carrying out a decision that was arrived at centrally, plant superintendents in the basic mass production industries throughout the country made their declarations of class war. They all used one line: "This is a new day. From now on, all decisions affecting production schedules will be the prerogative of management. We are not going to stand for any interference from the union. We are going to stamp out Communist-inspired disturbances." All militant actions became "wildcat actions."

This was the attack of Big Business. They made this challenge at a time when they thought the poison of the fraud had done its work. The trade union movement was split and retreating. General Motors even became so bold as to distribute a pamphlet on the college campuses threatening students with ostracism for life if they dared to show militancy in their college days.

The gauntlet of Big Business was down. But most top labor leaders were in no condition to meet it. They had accepted the fraud. They were on record against militancy because it was "Communist-inspired." They had expelled militants because of the fraud. They had permitted the firing of militant workers as sacrifices on the altar of the Big Lie. Each step of retreat was only a new opening for attack by reaction. For many in union leadership the awakening came too late.

The wellspring of militancy in unions is the rank and file. The employers are well aware of this, so the main blows were directed against this lifeline of unionism. The most meaningful advancement during the victories of 1935-45 was the emergence of an active union rank and file in mass proportions. The structure of the new unions reflected this fact. The struggle for the daily grievances in the departments was placed in the hands of the workers employed there. The grievance structure reflected this relationship. During the period of advance the role of the "business agent" declined and the militant shop and department leaders became the key element in the unions.

The anti-labor drive has had a long-range negative effect on the role of the rank and file. Big Business has very cleverly demanded a payoff for the concessions it has been forced to give in wage increases and other fringe benefits. The payoff has been a slow but sure dismantling of the union apparatus that gave the rank and file a voice in the affairs of the union.

The corporations have been willing partners in creating bureaucratic, top-heavy setups both in the trade unions and in labor-management relationships. The grievance machinery based on the departments and shifts that gave the rank and file a say about the problems closest to their everyday self-interests has been slowly bargained away. It has been replaced by a system of full-time committeemen. As a result, labor-management procedures are piled up with hundreds of thousands of serious grievances that never get settled. The grievances tend to sink into legalistic bureaucratic mire. Thus the unions became largely ineffective in the struggle against speedup.

WHICH CAME FIRST IS DIFFICULT TO DETERMINE: THE NEW level of Black-white workingclass unity, or the unionization of the mass production industries. Because they are so closely interrelated processes, one could not have taken place without the other. They were two parts of one process. Taken together the two processes gave the working class and the trade unions a new dimension of strength. It was more than class unity. It was a process of class integration. This process became an important feature of the period of advance for the U.S. working class.

The process made great strides forward. But when the reactionary offensive of corporate power got under way this new unity, new level of trade union and class consciousness, had not yet overcome its most stubborn foe: the anti-union, Jim Crow, low-wage corporate sanctuary of the South. The CIO unions had been making headway in organizing the South. Jim Crow barriers were coming down.

Unions were eliminating the North-South wage differential, a struggle closely related to the struggle against inequality. This new dimension of class unity and class consciousness showed the explosive potential of labor's power. It was a real challenge to age-old policies of "divide and rule." Thus it is not surprising that the Big Business counteroffensive concentrated its blows on this sector.

When the witchhunt succeeded against Communists and other militant and Left elements in the ranks of Black and white unionists, it was a blow against the men and women who gave the leadership in the struggle to end the policies of discrimination. It weakened the struggle against racist ideas in the unions. In too many cases their posts were taken over by conservative, less class conscious people, who were also the carriers of racist ideology.

All this influenced the course of development of our trade unions. The drive to organize the South bogged down. The struggle to end the policies of discrimination in job advancement began to mark time.

It is not difficult to trace the weakness of the trade union movement in the Civil Rights struggle to the damage left by the McCarthyite witchhunts of the 1950s. This weakness of the trade union movement and the working class has been a source of huge extra profits for U.S. Big Business.

The counteroffensive of Big Business set out to undermine the position of strength labor had acquired during its period of advance. One of the very important areas of progress resulting from the period of labor's advance was its break with the antiquated, sterile policy of "elect your friends and punish your enemies."

The CIO set the pace for this new political course by organizing the mass-activity-oriented Political Action Committees (PACs). These played an important role in stimulating independent political thinking. They were an important influence in molding policies of the New Deal. The Wage Labor Act was a result of the upward curve in labor's new political initiatives.[12]

This new development did not reach the level of the trade union movement supporting a new independent political party of labor, although important sections of the trade unions supported the first Wallace Progressive Party candidacy.[13] But it did reach the point where it became a threat to the cozy tranquility of the two-party system.

Thus it was understandable why reaction made this the second front of its attack. Political action by labor was labeled as a Communist conspiracy. Laws were passed which turned the collection of dollars for electoral work into a crime.

The split in the CIO was an especially damaging blow to concepts of independent political activity. The retreat was toward political inaction. For many years labor's political action has been limited to the formalities of endorsing candidates. The curve of independent politics by labor has now turned upward.

The anti-labor drive based on the gigantic fraud of anti-Communism did great and deep harm to workers' spirit of struggle and militancy on a shop level. Big Business's offensive created confusion and divisions in the ranks of labor.

T HE FIRST BIG BREAKTHROUGH OF THE BIG BUSINESS COUNteroffensive was the organizational split in the CIO. This was quickly followed by a coordinated anti-labor offensive by industry, government and the press, assisted by the leaders of labor who had become instruments of the fraud. The federal government moved to apply the Taft-Hartley Act. Moves were made to place Left-led unions outside the law, which included denying bargaining rights guaranteed under the Wagner Act.

The House Un-American Activities Committee (HUAC)[14] set up scaffolds for its "hangings" in most of the industrial centers. The Committee ran short of hanging-congressmen from its own ranks so it had to use Committee employees. The so-called hearings consisted of releasing to the press lists of names of militant shop workers, including Communists. The lists were usually compiled by the FBI and corporation executives. Many of these "listed" workers were fired. Wherever they could the employers, with the help of ultra-Right elements, organized violent outbreaks against those named on the witch-hunters' lists at their place of work. The press, radio and TV gave prime time to "exposing" Communists in the unions.

By fraud and by intimidation local unions were pushed into disaffiliation from Left-led unions. Many top trade union officials gave charters of their unions to employers which were used to set up dummy union-busting, competing locals in their shops. The crusade of the big fraud reached fantastic hysterical levels.

I relate some of these details to caution anyone not to think in terms of over-simplified answers. The situation was very difficult. The task was to stop a reactionary stampede. There were no simple answers. Obviously it called for a many-sided tactical approach. In some cases it was correct for the Left-led unions to seek mergers with other unions. In other cases it was not possible, necessary or advisable. In some cases it was correct for trade union officers to avoid the non-Communist affidavits and remain in elected posts. In others, it was necessary to stay and to challenge the drive both by legal and political means. In general this was the tactical course followed by the Communist Party.

The Smith and McCarran Acts, Taft-Hartley and Landrum-Griffin in effect made membership in the Communist Party a "crime" — though these provisions were later nullified by the courts. But each of these fascist measures had special provisions against shop workers charged with being Communists. The provisions were so sweeping that participation in any militant action was evidence enough of Communist "affiliation." The accused were placed beyond the protection of laws and unions.

One should not underestimate the difficulties this created. We must keep in mind that for many years a Communist or someone accused of being a Communist faced not only the loss of their job, loss of seniority, Social Security benefits and black-listing, but also a prison term of up to life.

Flexibility in tactics was clearly called for. The overall tactical policy of the Party was correct. The Communist Party conducted a heroic and self-sacrificing struggle against this new phase of the onslaught. In spite of the extreme terror there were only a handful of defectors.

However, within this correct tactical policy of fighting the attack on the Party, some mistakes did appear, and in the effort to argue for the policy some erroneous rationales made their appearance.

There was nothing wrong with having flexibility in forms of Party organization, including the size of clubs, method of dues payment, etc. These were necessary for the protection of members who were the intended victims of the witchhunt. But it is a different matter when the rationalization is stretched to include a rejection, or at least a questioning, of whether there is a need for any kind of a Communist shop organization. Are there still influences of this rationale around? Yes, there are. And as ghosts are likely to do, they appear silently. When they are around long enough they become accepted as a part of the family, as it were.

No one openly argues against shop clubs. But not many have argued for them either. Not having them becomes an accepted fact without formal decisions. Part of the rationale even argues that Communist shop clubs tend to create obstacles between Communists and non-Communists. Of course, the opposite is true. A Communist shop organization can become the strongest influence towards a united, militant local union. Communists have always been the most effective fighters for trade union unity. This struggle for an effective militant trade union can best be carried out by an organized group. There is no contradiction between the self-interests of Communist and non-Communist workers.

Socialism is also in the self-interest of workers. There is no contradiction in the struggle or the advocacy of socialism and the struggle against speedup or for higher wages, or for an end to Jim Crow. Communist workers can contribute their best both in the struggles for the immediate issues and for socialism only if they have Communist shop organizations.

One of the shrill cries of the crusade of the big fraud was that the Communists organized fractions and caucuses in the trade unions. This cry went up in spite of the fact that caucuses in the trade unions are as old as trade unions themselves. To make the charge effective, of course, it was tied to the charge of "ulterior motives." Thus the caucuses became a part of the "conspiracy."

This cry became a weapon in the hands of any entrenched union bureaucracy. All opposition slates for union office were labeled "Communist influenced." The FBI secretly fed fraudulent material against militant office-seekers to the entrenched bureaucracy. Ex-FBI agents were hired as corporation personnel executives who used their past connections with the FBI to manipulate union affairs.

Here again it was correct to argue against the use of caucuses for unprincipled purposes. But it is a different matter when the rationale goes like this: Most, if not all caucuses in the union are organized only for the purpose of the "outs" against the "ins." This then leads one to conclude against taking part in any caucuses. In fact it leads to passivity about the activities of the rank and file in any form. Such a rationale does not reflect the realities of trade union life.

Most rank-and-file efforts, whether they be caucuses, clubs or committees are honest, sincere attempts to strengthen the union, to correct wrongs and defects. Caucuses develop because other avenues of democratic expression are blocked. Many union structures do not provide any other form of rank-and-file participation. Most caucuses in the history of our trade unions have played a progressive, healthy role. Anyone who has any acquaintance with the inner life of our unions, with tendencies of bureaucratic control, cases of strong-arm tactics, of racketeering elements and plain apathy by highly paid union officials can see not only why caucuses develop, but why they are a necessary feature of militancy and rank-and-file influence on the affairs of their union.

In the life of trade unions the concept of the caucus is not a dirty word except to those who fear an active rank and file. Of course, like with everything else in life, it can be misused. Our fight is for its correct use as an instrument to strengthen the fighting rank-and-file fiber of the union. What honest trade unionist would object to that?

I N A PERIOD OF EBB IN SOCIAL, POLITICAL AND ECONOMIC struggles it is not always easy to judge what are necessary adjustments in tactics. And it is not easy to separate tactics that correctly reflect the new problems, the new relationship of forces of the ebb period, from actions that are motivated by an opportunistic retreat from the difficulties of struggle of such a period. What adds to the difficulty is that there are pressures for both.

Opportunistic retreat and a shift in tactics appear simultaneously because they are reactions to the same realities. It is further complicated by the fact that in most cases the path of opportunistic retreat starts with very necessary and correct steps of tactical adjustment. Where one ends and the other begins is at times very difficult to determine because there also periods when one individual can reflect a mixture of both and also because the rationale for a retreat often sounds very much like the rationale for a tactical shift.

The key word in determining one from the other is "struggle." A correct tactical adjustment is not a shift away from struggle. It is a shift of tactics for and in struggle. Tactics after all have meaning only when they are an integral part of the struggle. On the other hand an opportunistic retreat is an edging away from struggle. It is a process of giving up positions, making unnecessary concessions, and all this without struggle. A correct tactical shift is to find a new path to struggle, while an opportunistic retreat is a way of avoiding struggle, and giving up positions, thinking this will placate the enemy.

During the anti-labor offensive of the late 1940s and 1950s both of these problems appeared. There were warranted tactical shifts. But there were also positions and actions taken by Communist and non-Communist Left people in positions of trade union leadership that were clearly in the nature of an opportunistic retreat. As is the case so often, in many instances this right opportunism was covered by radical-sounding phrases.

The Party was correct in its struggle against these errors of opportunism. But in the course of this correct struggle the Party leadership, or more accurately a section of the leadership, made some serious mistakes. It is necessary to say "a section of the leadership" because there were some sharp differences over these matters. The mistakes in this case were serious because they tended to drive a wedge between the Party and the Communist and non-Communist Left trade union leadership at a very crucial moment of the struggle.

This error was expressed in its sharpest form by the nature of a campaign in the Party and in the Party press, directed against some Communist and non-Communist Left trade unionists on the issue of "rank opportunism."

What was wrong with the campaign? The error was not that there was a struggle against opportunism. The error was in how this struggle was conducted. The struggle was not based on an examination of the new realities and new relationship of forces, and as a result an examination of tactics. There was not a recognition of the new problems. It was based on dogmatic abstract phrases.

The very heart of the error was in not carefully examining, and as a result separating, that which was a correct and very necessary tactical readjustment and that which was in the nature of an opportunist retreat. In fact, very often a position based on abstract phrases does not leave room for any tactical readjustment. The error was in painting everything with the brush of "opportunism." This weakened the Party's ability to work out realistic tactics in the struggles of the trade unions. Every suggestion of a tactical readjustment was blocked as being opportunism. The blanket charges of opportunism became a cover for an inability to work out tactics of struggle.

What are some of the conclusions from this latter error? First, it was not an effective struggle against opportunism. It gave opportunism a hiding place. The opportunist could hide behind the individual who was painted by the same brush but who was guilty of nothing more than making a correct tactical readjustment.

Second, you cannot effectively fight against the influence of opportunism with dogmatic slogans and abstract phrases. The only effective method is a discussion of the correct relationship of forces which, above all else, includes an estimate of the level of mass consciousness and a knowledge of the nature of the struggle the workers are ready to participate in. This can best be done by those who are in closer contact with the workers, by those who are willing to listen combined with an understanding of theory, the science of Marxism. A general struggle about general concepts, in a general way, does not get to the root of problems.

Third, because there was not a clear enough separation of that which was opportunism from that which was tactical readjustment, Communists were not able to make a full contribution in formulating the best possible tactics to meet the new and difficult problems. A precondition for devising new tactics is a recognition of the need for them because of a new set of circumstances.

Fourth, in some cases the error was sharpened by a bureaucratic style of handling of individual cases. Administrative measures were resorted to as a substitute for political and ideological dialogue. It is an interesting fact that so many of those in the Party who pressed for the sharpest administrative actions are among those who left the Party for the most obvious of opportunistic reasons.

This sharpness tended to further drive a wedge between the Party and its trade union members. Those influenced and motivated by opportunism very often used the sharpness of relations to separate themselves from the Party. The error in a way was an attempt at a shortcut. It was an attempt to formulate policy without consideration for the problems of real life. Such an attempt is possible for a short period, especially if you do not have to deal directly with the problems of that reality. It seems reasonable from afar, but not for long. Very quickly the problems of real life have a way of emerging, as if to say,

"Where the hell do you think you are going with such fancy abstractions?"

On a much larger scale similar errors are being committed by some world Communist leaders. The "big leaps," the plans for "worldwide countryside revolutions," the "go-it-alone" nationalist swings, are all conjured up plans with one basic flaw: they have very little if anything to do with the real problems, the actual forces without which all plans remain like paper dolls.

Our Party has long since taken steps to correct these errors. But we have not yet discarded the skeletons of the rationales. At times they still have some influence. We have not yet developed enough sensitivity. We do not even now give careful enough attention to specific tactical questions. This means we do not yet weigh and assess with enough "precision" the specific relationship of forces and the level of mass consciousness, mass trends and currents.

Even today there are cases where the abstract phrase becomes a substitute for careful examination of the factors of real life, where our hopes and desires replace a careful examination of all factors and a projection of tactics with the specific purpose of giving direction and building confidence that will lead to struggles resulting in forward motion.

THE RELATIONS BETWEEN CAPITAL AND LABOR CONTINUE TO move toward a qualitatively new level of confrontation. The forces that propel class relations toward this new sharpness stem, of course, from the development of the new technology. The crisis grows because monopoly capital stubbornly confiscates all of the benefits of the developing technological revolution. This results in the machine replacing people, without any special steps to take care of the person thus replaced.

Many of the unions have been wrestling and fighting with this problem. Some gains have been made, but by and large the question remains unsolved. The problems resulting from automation are of a new magnitude. They bring a new dimension to class relations. Their solution calls for new dimensions in trade unionism; new dimensions in unity, in militancy, in political and ideological understanding; new dimensions in the whole sphere of collective bargaining, in labor contracts, in grievance procedures.

A program of struggle must start with a recognition that the most basic and lasting reality in the relations of labor and capital is the contradiction of self-interests between them. This then results in an irreconcilable antagonism, and struggle. Thus the class struggle is not an invention of Marx, nor does it become outdated or old fashioned. It will be with us as long as capitalism remains. It acts as the mainspring of all social developments. This basic contradiction is the source of the perpetual renewal of class antagonisms.

The struggle over this issue runs like a thread throughout the history of our trade union movement. To one degree or another it has influenced every act. Those who refuse to accept the class nature of life under capitalism are at constant odds with reality. They have been forced to develop a philosophy of platitudes to cover up this discrepancy with the hard facts of life. They speak of "social peace" and "partnership." Big Business does not mind this kind of talk as long as it does not in any way interfere with gathering in the fruits of the labor of its "partners."

The "partnership" concept leads to wrong trade union practices. It is an obstacle to political independence by labor. Labor remains a tail-end "partner" within the two parties of Big Business. It leads to the illusion and apathy that the most one can expect from life can be achieved through a series of reforms. It hides the basic injustice of capitalist exploitation. It accepts as a matter of fact capitalism's practice of not accepting any social responsibilities.

This concept is now coming into a head-on confrontation with the effects of new technology. Machine is replacing human hands. The corporations are stealing the products of this new technology. They take no responsibility for human discords. All demands to safeguard the jobs of workers when the machines take over are labeled "feather bedding."

Trade union leaders who act on the basis of "partnership" are reluctant to say, "So what! Human rights must be placed above rights to profits. If humanity can produce machines to take its place, then let there be beds of feathers for our leisure hours. What's wrong with that?" The bargaining position of the trade unions would be greatly improved if their struggles would rest on a publicly stated concept: "If the industries in the hands of private owners cannot fulfill the responsibilities for society, then let us transfer them into the public domain."

Once the basic feature of life under capitalism is understood, then a vital, vigorous, progressive labor movement becomes an absolute necessity. It then becomes a vital instrument of the working class in the class struggle. To understand this is to be class conscious.

All the propaganda of how labor and capital are members of "one happy family" is an attempt to conceal this class reality of life. This leads to policies of making concessions to Big Business without a struggle. This old demagogic thought fits into the anti-Communist theme. They say, "Here we are, one happy family, and the Communists are trying to disrupt our tranquility for their own 'ulterior' purposes." It is the path of retreat. It is a path that leads to a weakening of the labor movement.

This is the very heart of the lesson all must learn from the experiences of the big fraud. This does not mean to say that a trade union leader cannot oppose ideas or concepts put forward by Communists. We do not have all of the answers. And, as history shows, we can also be wrong.

What it does mean is that when one conjures up a fraudulent, caricature image of the Communist movement and then fights it as if it was the real thing, one becomes a victim, an instrument of the fraud. There is one truth no one can now deny or evade. Anti-Communism based on the big fraud is above all else an anti-workingclass, anti-union weapon. It is a poison that saps the fighting spirit of the unions. This was the soft spot through which the forces of reaction penetrated. This was the beachhead for the anti-labor McCarthyite crusade.

To move labor onto the path leading to a higher level of

struggle, a level that measures up to the problems of today, dictates the closing of the beachhead of Big Lie anti-Communism. If this is not done, the poison causing divisions, confusion and disorientation will continue to flow into the ranks of labor. Whatever one thinks of Communist ideas is not the issue here. The question all must face squarely is that the trade union movement cannot effectively chart a new course so long as it is boxed in by the fraud of Big Lie anti-Communism.

Trade union leaders can break with the dead-end policies of class collaborationism only by rejecting the fraud of anti-Communism. We Communists are not saying: "You must agree with us on all matters." What we are saying is this: When you disagree with us, do so in a responsible way, do so on what in fact are our ideas, concepts and thoughts, but avoid becoming an instrument of an anti-labor drive that uses Big Lie anti-Communism as a smokescreen.

OUR WORKING CLASS AND OUR TRADE UNIONS HAVE A glorious and militant history. In struggles on the economic front, U.S. unions are at the head of the line. The weaknesses have been in the political and ideological sphere. Whenever the working class has suffered a setback, the initial breakthrough against it has always come on this political and ideological front.

The class struggle takes place within the framework of one's own capitalist society. Our unions and our class have been molded by the class relations that have developed in the specific circumstances of U.S. capitalism. Now U.S. capitalism is entering a new epoch. It is faced with a new set of circumstances.

One-third of the world is socialist. Industrially and technologically the Soviet Union is reaching the point of running neck and neck. No people in the world will now remain in the status of a gold mine for some imperialist power. All this is having its impact on the home front. This is going to further sharpen class relations. When one adds the problems arising from new technology, it spells an historic class confrontation.

Communist Approach To Building the Unions

[Excerpts from: "The U.S. in Today's World," report to meeting of national Communist Party leadership, 1961.]

WHILE PREPARING THIS REPORT, I TRIED TO TRANSFER MY thoughts back to the local union halls of the steelworkers, miners, structural iron workers and lumber workers — the locals where I used to be active in past years. I tried to visualize myself giving leadership and understanding to their problems, not in general terms but by focusing attention on the specific problems and issues facing the working class and the trade unions of the United States today. And this reflection had a sobering effect.

One need not dig deep to realize that we do not have all of the answers to some very serious and difficult problems that are facing the working class and the trade unions today. There are many new, complicated questions to which the old answers, some of which we repeat so often, are really no solution.

So I saw myself out there with these workers, blasting away at the leadership of the unions. I called them "seat warmers," "class collaborationists," "bureaucrats" and "swindlers." The workers did not get angry, but they said the following: "Alright, wise guy, we will go along with you and maybe even add a few juicy adjectives of our own about the leadership. But what is it that you propose to do?"

Ignoring this, I continued to speak about the need for rank-and-file committees, about the need to kick out the old leadership, etc. But the workers countered by saying: "We did that last year. But how do you see our difficulties? Concretely, how do *you* propose to solve them, because if our local and district leaders had the answers, they would do something, and if we the workers had the answers, we would be the leaders and we would not be asking you for the answers. So, concretely, what do you propose to do? We are willing. Go ahead and lead us."

So I became concrete. I spoke about the 50 percent reduction in steel production, about the fact that there is unemployment not only in Ohio but in Pittsburgh, Chicago and elsewhere. The workers answered: "We know that. We read the same papers. But what is it you had in mind?"

They continued: "We know we are in trouble and to tell the truth we can't figure out exactly why and we do not know what to do about it. We are willing to listen to anything that sounds realistic and responsible, but please, no lectures or general advice. We get enough of that from the so-called labor experts. Further, you say our union is bankrupt and in a crisis. We get the same line from the reactionary press every day. So why should you add to it? And frankly, before you get so critical about our unions, what is it you have in mind? What is it that you propose to do?"

As a Party and as individual Communists in the unions, we must say exactly what it is we have in mind, how we propose to lead and to find solutions to these questions. But before we go on it is necessary to note that these workers said something else. They said, "And don't say socialism is the answer. It is a nice idea. Maybe it works in the Soviet Union. Maybe it's something to think about, but anyway the American people are not ready for it. So in the meantime, what do you propose?" I replied: "Yes, it's indeed worth thinking about. It's the final and only complete answer. But I will agree it is not the immediate one."

I know some of our comrades will say, "That sounds like an introduction to a policy of pure-and-simple trade unionism." I don't know about the "pure" side of it. But I do know that this is an introduction to the need for a fresh Party policy and a basic shift towards work that starts from the practices and the problems, yes, of everyday unionism. This is an introduction to a sharp turn of emphasis, to a policy of concentration on working with the working class and trade unions and giving specific as well as general leadership.

Because of certain shortcomings in our work we must, in a fresh way, fight to give life to some elementary Marxist concepts. We are a workingclass Party. The working class —

white, Black, foreign-born, American-born, old, young, men, women — should be the very center and heart of all our work, our activities and our thoughts.

On the other hand, in the years of its greatest advance, our Party did center its work on the unions and shops. The whole Party engaged in this work. Community organizations helped in concentration work and distribution of material, and every Party leader was familiar with developments in the unions and shops. Now this has been reduced to a mere departmental activity.

The problems and difficulties and weaknesses of the working class are our difficulties, the difficulties of our class, of our family. We are going to work with them on these problems. We are not working "for" them or merely preaching, lecturing or advising them.

We are not a built-in opposition. We are not professional cranks, gripers and bemoaners. We are for rank-and-file movements, but not as ends in themselves. And we will not reduce our relations with the labor movement to the level of automatically and always being for a policy of the "ins" getting out and the "outs" getting in.

If we do not have all the answers, to say the least it is unbecoming to behave as if we do. There are some tendencies in our ranks to assume a literary critic-to-author relationship in our attitude to the unions and their problems. The literary critic in many instances blasts away at the author unmercifully while knowing that he or she could not even do as well. Our relations, on the contrary, must be partisan, warm, frank and modest.

We do not have all the answers but we do have full confidence in this fact: if we work with workers and honest trade union leaders we will not only make an important contribution, but we will find answers and solutions to the many vexing problems that now plague them.

We also know from experience that for labor to meet the new offensive of Big Business, there is an absolute need for a fresh look at the problem of unity within labor's ranks as well as at Afro-American/labor unity. The labor movement must understand that the challenge places before it the historic task not only of uniting its ranks to fight for its very life but also of taking the initiative in uniting all the victims of monopoly oppression in a general offensive against it. There is a need for militant leadership. There is a need for an active grassroots movement bringing together union members, their families and communities.

W E ARE NOW IN A PERIOD OF SHARPENING CLASS STRUGgles. The need for militant, forward-looking leadership and organization of these struggles will become ever more urgent. This challenge is not only a test for the trade unions; it is a test for our Party. The objective developments and the subjective attitudes which exist are both very favorable.

Wherever union members have been given any leadership and real demands to fight for, they have demonstrated militancy and determination and a readiness to strike and hold out for a long time, both to defend their existing gains and to fight for new gains. Workers have demonstrated great courage and perseverance in bitterly fought strikes. Even under bad leadership and conditions of disunity, workers have shown a readiness to fight. This was true even in General Electric. The defeat of the 1960 General Electric strike[15] certainly cannot be attributed to any unwillingness of the workers to fight.

The strikes and struggles of the past year show that we must not overestimate the persistence of the effects of corruption in the ranks of the working class. It is the readiness of the workers to fight for their unions, for their gains, and for better conditions which is the dominant feature of this period. The militant strike of New York tugboat workers in 1957[16] and the solidarity of labor behind it should dispel any lingering doubts on this score.

It has been shown that when workers are in a fight, are united and are demonstrating determination and militancy, they can reduce to a minimum the damage of incompetent and even corrupt leadership. Further, though restrictions still exist, it has been shown that it is easier than before for progressives and Left workers to be active in the unions and in strikes, and to play an important role in cementing the unity and determination of the workers and to influence events in their unions, provided only that they work correctly.

The most important thing is to build, unite and enlarge the family of active, progressive unionists who display independent initiative towards influencing others and affecting events and policies. It is also important for the Party as such to issue more material on its views on important questions. Of course, neither task can replace the other.

The progressive forces naturally must take a critical attitude to class collaborationist leaders, particularly cold war anti-Communists. But Communists and progressives must be distinguished first of all by the proposals they make on what is to be done and by their efforts to win the membership for these proposals. That is the best way for the members and lower leadership to change policies and where necessary to change leadership.

We must educate and help our trade unionists to be dedicated union members, active pluggers for the interests of their fellow workers and their unions, staunch and selfless fighters for the grievances of the workers and in strike struggles, trained and skillful and informed about the problems confronting workers, good friends with the workers in the shops and also outside of the shops. All of that is basic and absolutely essential.

But if we stop there, we stop short of being Communists. A Communist must be something more than that. He or she must provide the workers with perspective and with political understanding. To do that he or she must find a way to circulate the Party press and literature. We need more pamphlets. The Party outside the shop must help our comrades in the shops. And these shop workers must recruit others to the Party. They must raise the level of political understanding of the workers on the basis of their experience.

Under present conditions, however, Communists cannot

go around doing all that and retain their jobs. But they can and should become intimate friends of the more advanced workers inside and outside the shop. They should develop relations in which they visit each others' homes, go out together with their families, discuss questions together, and exchange literature. They should introduce their friends to our ideas. At first they will have a group of progressive friends, and later a group of Communist friends within the shop.

At the same time the Party itself, through its press, articles, and leaflets, must carry on a steady campaign of explanation and activity on the most important issues facing the workers today. Our Party and the press in particular must react and reflect every struggle, no matter how small.

One word of caution is necessary in regard to emphasis at the present time. While it is essential for our Communist trade unionists to take up both economic and political questions, they must not leave political questions such as peace to times of national emergency, or the question of independent political action to election time. That's often too late. Such questions must receive year-round attention so that the workers are prepared for times of crisis.

Yet, important as the political questions are, the greatest weight falls on the union and economic questions — jobs, wages, relief, union rights, strikes — which are becoming increasingly acute. Communists must be resolute, outstanding fighters for these. Without this stress as a foundation, work on political issues is difficult if not impossible.

Economism has been an evil in our trade union work. But the charge of economism has also been thrown about loosely and very often unjustly and in a way which has lessened our effectiveness in day-to-day union activities.

This concept must not be treated dogmatically. At a time of sharpening class struggles, when the working class is under attack on the economic front, our major efforts must be directed toward winning the battles immediately at hand. Such efforts at this time are not economism but correct Marxist-Leninist policy. To do otherwise is to miss the boat. Because of the nature of the problems of the new period, there is a close interrelationship between economics and politics, and one leads to the other.

The problems of the working class and the trade unions must be brought to the top of the agenda in all meetings of clubs, sections, and all state and national bodies of the Party.

back to basics

Fighting for Class Struggle Trade Unionism

Labor in the Post-McCarthy Period

[Excerpts from: "Labor — Key Force for Peace, Civil Rights and Economic Security," report to meeting of national Communist Party leadership, 1966.]

I THINK ALL OF YOU WILL AGREE THAT THE TIME HAS ARRIVED when it is vitally necessary for our Party to make a sharp break with past practices and, once and for all, place the question of the working class, the trade unions and the related problems into the very center of our work. We cannot any longer postpone this change of emphasis.

The future — and I mean the immediate and the long-range future — of all social progress, the future of the Left upsurge, the future of our Party is decisively bound up with this question. All subsequent developments in the struggle for peace, for civil rights, as well as in the youth upsurge will, in a critical measure, be determined by what the working class will do, how it will react to coming events.

We are dealing here with one of the most fundamental laws of social development under capitalism. The position of the working class doesn't necessarily determine how struggles and movements will start. But it does determine how far they'll develop, how much and how lasting the gains will be and, above all, what the political content of the victories will be.

With this in mind, I want to discuss some questions, both as to content as well as to approach and attitude. The working class of the U.S. is up against some very difficult and perplexing problems. In spite of the industrial boom, the movement towards a sharp class confrontation continues apace. The economic factors propelling this movement are many. But the central factor is the creeping effects of the new technology. This has now raised the questions of job security and speedup to the very top of the grievance list.

There is great concern and uncertainty about job security in the ranks of the working class. This is at the bottom of every sharp labor struggle. Most labor contracts have sidestepped or else dealt with the issues arising out of automation only indirectly.

While for the present the boom in war production and the drafting of young workers who have no draft deferments temporarily ease the problem, the effects of the new technology will remain one of the central, long-term economic problems from now on. It will remain a serious problem permanently, and will become critical immediately during cutbacks in production. There are repeated efforts by private and government researchers to minimize and sweep this problem under the economic rug.

A corollary of this development is the sharpening of class relations. There is a noticeable increase in the attacks on labor and on the trade unions. This increase in anti-union attacks is Big Business's way of preparing for the developing confrontation. In this sense, the strike this year of the New York transport workers[1] has again exposed how close to the surface is the nerve of class antagonisms and class struggle in our society. The veneer of "classlessness" went up in smoke. The staid *New York Times* completely lost its self-control and went into a class rage. The *Times* warned that the days of "old fashioned cynical trade unionism must never be permitted to return."

In the militancy of the Transport Workers Union the *Times* saw the handwriting on the wall. The *Herald-Tribune* joined in the chorus and declared that there is no absolute right to strike or right of revolution in the United States. What is interesting is that they have a premonition about the close relationship between the right to strike and the right of revolution. In their book the workers have the right to strike only if the government and the employers extend that right to them. Or you have the right to strike or revolt as long as you don't use that right.

There are also great pressures for new anti-labor laws in all centers of political power. One of the most dangerous among the anti-labor measures is the proposal, in fact the campaign, for compulsory arbitration. These, like all of the other proposals, basically chip away at the right to strike and at the right to unionism as such.

In fact the proposal for compulsory arbitration would replace the right to strike. The rest of the trade union movement — and I must say this includes us — did very little when the coal miners were cited for contempt and when large fines were levied against them for striking. They were saddled with high fines. Now it should be clear that the use of courts, of injunctions, of contempt citations and large fines, or the threat of such actions, is becoming a major updated anti-union weapon. But, of course, as we know, this is not the only feature of the government's anti-union activities. The gimmick of using the government as a "third party," allegedly representing the public interest, looms as a real threat to the trade unions.

The federal government has a policy against cutting working hours even as a measure to offset some of the effects of automation. But it has no policy against laying off workers because of automation. The right to a job — the right to a livelihood regardless of technological changes — a right to be guaranteed by labor/industry contracts and by the government, is slowly emerging as a new concept.

The government throws its weight around in situations where unions are strong and in a position to win concessions. But it remains silent — this "third party" sees no public interest involved — where the unions are weak and the employers use terror, murder and frameup to discredit unions and to keep wages and working conditions down. As you know, this is still an everyday occurrence in large sections of our country, especially in the South.

The 1965 steel settlement was an example of settling labor disputes not by collective bargaining but by presidential executive edict. This is a dangerous pattern. The full danger of this pattern emerges when one grasps that these edicts are made by a government of state monopoly capitalism. In fact, that is why this danger appears now.

Tears by government officials about the "public interest," "public health," or the "national interest" are in fact crocodile tears. Such officials oppose the public and national interest; they serve only the self-interests of Big Business. If one puts together compulsory arbitration, collective bargaining by government and presidential edict, use of the injunction, contempt citations and the levying of large fines, it becomes a very dangerous anti-labor package. But this is what we have in the making. These anti-labor tools of the open shop days are now being resurrected as anti-labor tools of today. More and more the government is resorting to direct interference in labor relations.

This is a path that leads to the sapping of the strength of the trade unions. This is a path that leads to unions that are prisoners not only in economic matters, but to unions and to union officers who are prisoners of the political machines and government officialdom.

Once the framework for bargaining by government edict in the so-called public interest is accepted there is no end to its use. There is no strike where it cannot be used. We must seriously take up the task of exposing this anti-labor gimmick. The government sees no "public interest" involved in speedup, layoffs, low wages, etc., but when the workers go on strike to correct these abuses, then the "public interest" comes in.

We must raise the question of why are not higher wages and shorter hours in the public interest?

During the New York Transport strike Meany,[2] as was to be expected, echoed the Big Business fraud about "public interests." A week later Walter Reuther became the belated "Little

Sir Echo" by voicing his support for the campaign to pass new anti-labor laws behind the smokescreen of public interests.

Some say, "But is this opposition to the intervention of government not in contradiction with our demand for government intervention in some cases?"

We are for anything that is in the interests of labor. We are against everything that is against the interests of labor. This concept applies to the role of government. To get government to intervene on the side of labor is a part of the class struggle. Thus we are for laws that help our class. We are against all anti-labor laws. It is a contradiction only for those who do not have a class understanding of capitalism, not for partisans of a class.

These are the types of questions we can make a contribution to, because these are also the questions that lend themselves to mass class education, questions through which workers can learn class consciousness, the nature and role of the state.

IN THE FACE OF THESE DIFFICULT PROBLEMS THE TRADE UNION movement suffers from a number of serious internal problems and weaknesses. These problems must become our deep concern. In the very center of these weaknesses is the many-faceted problem of unity. In many ways this is the key question.

I want to propose that we take this as our central point of departure, that we make workingclass unity a continuous long-term campaign, not haphazardly and not as an abstract slogan but as a political concept around which we build our trade union policy. On this basis I also propose that we center the campaign around three specific areas:

1. The unity of the existing trade unions;

2. The unity of the working class, especially Black and white unity;

3. And unity of the organized and unorganized, by means of organizing the unorganized.

A few words about these areas. It is not necessary to argue with you that the need to bring the Teamsters, the Mineworkers, West Coast Longshore, Mine, Mill and Smelter, and Electrical unions into the AFL-CIO is not a matter of bigger numbers (although that is not unimportant). Much of the really meaningful benefit that should have accrued from the unity of the AFL and the CIO was dissipated because it did not include these very important unions. An immediate, basic and qualitative change in the relationship of forces within the AFL-CIO and within each union would take place once these militant sectors of labor were in again. It would change many of the forces now in the AFL-CIO.

The question is all the more important now because there is movement in this direction on top, and pressure from the ranks of the trade unions could have an escalating effect. The fact that objective and subjective conditions are changing makes this area of the struggle for unity a realistic possibility now. There is the need to raise this question in both the unions that are in and those that are out of the present structure.

The push for trade union unity must include the question of labor solidarity, including such questions as support for strike struggles, organizing drives and political action. It is interesting that the press is angrier about the labor leaders' support to the TWU than it is about the strike itself. The campaign for trade union unity and labor solidarity touches on every basic question of class education and class consciousness.

The second area where we can play an important role is in the crucial struggle for Black-white unity. This affects both the unity of the class as well as the unity of the trade unions. The basic source of the weakness in this area, as we know, lies in the refusal or the slowness of the trade unions in taking up the struggle for equality, although there is movement here also. This requires a consistent struggle on all fronts. And who else but ourselves is equipped to give the lead on the ideological front in this struggle?

On this we can make rapid headway if we relate it to the concrete issues, to concrete steps in the fight for job equality and promotions. What is needed now is to raise the level of this fight among the rank and file of the unions. There is a need for a campaign to convince union members that the just system of seniority, which was and is an important victory in the struggle for job security, cannot be used as a system that perpetuates 300 years of injustice.

What is needed now is leadership that stirs up the membership on this issue. What is needed now is leadership that can explain both the justice and the workingclass self-interest in putting an end to all forms of discrimination. What is needed is the election of local presidents, shop stewards and grievance committeemen, including progressives and Communists, who can and will give leadership in the struggle for equality on the shop level. A few local presidents and shop stewards who understand this question can make a qualitative change in an international union.

Only we Communists can give the conscious ideological ingredient for this kind of class unity. Only we can give the unique leadership in struggle against the poison of the mind: white chauvinism. Only we can expose the class basis for this racist ideology. This struggle also goes to the very heart of class education, of class consciousness.

The third area of critical weakness is the division between the organized and unorganized sectors of the working class. This has become even more critical during the last years. The gulf has widened. This division is further reflected in the division between the workers of the North and of the South, between Black and white workers, between the employed and the unemployed, between white collar and the rest of the labor force, and between the youth and the older workers. This is so because it is the workers of the South, the unemployed, the white collar, Black and young workers who tend to be the unorganized workers, which therefore adds a special quality to their status. So the question of organizing the unorganized becomes a key question of the unity between key sectors of the working class.

There is some motion on this front also. What is needed is the political mobilization of the rank and file of the organized sectors. We know from experience there are no better or more effective organizers than the organized workers in the shops. There has been and there remains some suspicion about the motives of full-time official trade union organizers. The great majority of workers in the mass production industries were signed up by organized shop workers. No organizing drive can be successful without the mobilization of the organized rank and file. This mobilization also goes to the roots of class education and class ideology.

These are the three key areas where the lack of workingclass and trade union unity shows up in its sharpest form and this is the key to any major new advance for labor and for our people. This rounded campaign for unity can encompass and be the basis for our overall trade union policy.

I think it is also clear that in the solution of these problems we necessarily must put the major emphasis on the mobilization of the rank and file of the trade union movement. I will speak about that further.

Now what are some of the overall arguments that we have to nail down, first within our own Party and then within the ranks of labor, in arguing for these policies?

First and most obvious, of course, is that the working class cannot effectively meet the confrontation of the new technology without such unity and the campaign for such unity. Second, the working class cannot become an independent political class force without such unity and the campaign for such unity.

Third, the working class cannot build alliances, it cannot become an effective partner in the Afro-American/labor alliance, it cannot build its alliance, electoral or otherwise, without such unity and the struggle for such unity.

Fourth, it cannot make any meaningful political breakthroughs in any field, economic or political, without such unity and the struggle for such unity. Fifth, it cannot play its historic role as the leading class in society without such unity and the struggle for such unity.

I have repeated the phrase, "and the struggle for such unity" because the campaign and the struggle for unity are as important as the unity itself. The struggle for unity can become the instrument by which we can raise every important political and ideological question. It is the means by which to raise the consciousness and understanding of the class. It is the means by which we can then also erase the weaknesses in the labor movement. This will give us the right approach, the right attitude. It will give us the necessary leverage to move our class.

W E MUST DEAL WITH THE QUESTION OF THE AFL-CIO leadership and the policies it follows. There can be no argument about the fact that the Meany-Lovestone[3] axis that dominates the basic policies of the AFL-CIO has in many ways reached a new political low. They have become partners in the policies of U.S. imperialism.

They, and the most reactionary sectors of the political spectrum, are the only vocal, consistent and unqualified supporters of the aggression in Vietnam. Their support is not the result of confusion or lack of information. They are not misled, they are misleading. Theirs is a policy of conscious support to imperialism. They are willing tools of the forces of imperialism.

The Lovestone apparatus has been and is the CIA's labor arm. It is an arm in the services of U.S. corporations at home and abroad. This service is in the interest of imperialism and runs counter to the interests of the workers in our country as well as of the workers in all other countries. This has become an important feature of the monopoly state capitalist apparatus for the sole purpose of helping U.S. corporations in their drive for greater private profits.

The argument that the Meany, Lovestone and Dubinsky[4] forces are trading their support of the war for favorable consideration on economic questions does not hold water. Furthermore it takes them off the hook with politically backward workers who would agree to such an exchange.

The actions of the Johnson administration on economic questions do not justify the validity of such an argument. The anti-labor laws, the refusal to abolish section 14-b of the Taft-Hartley Act, the anti-labor actions of the government in all major struggles — all argue against any such conclusion. Meany and Lovestone's support for the policies of aggression follows from their support of capitalism — not capitalism in general but U.S. capitalism, their immediate master.

The Meany-Lovestone axis has given lip service to the civil rights struggle only because of the great pressure of the Afro-American people's struggles and especially because of the pressure of the Black trade union membership. But they have put up no fight within the ranks of labor to eliminate the bars to Black workers. There are problems of chauvinism, but it is this conservative leadership and not the membership that stands as the main obstacle to the unity of Black and white workers, to an alliance of Labor and the Afro-American people.

Problems of bureaucratic structure, the inability of the rank and file to influence policies, have become a more critical problem during the past ten years. Some of the more democratic former CIO unions have taken on some of the anti-democratic ways of the old AFL unions. The changes in leadership of a number of international unions are in fact a revolt against this stifling atmosphere. Abel[5] won the election in the Steelworkers union mainly because he promised "to restore rank-and-file control over basic policies." He spoke against "tuxedo" leadership and class collaboration.

The national and industrywide contracts, check-off of dues, the practice of sending all grievances to top committees — were important victories in winning economic concessions, but they have had the additional effect of stripping the locals and members of leverage in their union affairs. The full-time officials and top committees have replaced the locals in many unions.

Corrections do not have to come only by removing the leadership. In fact the campaign to restore union democracy and membership participation must start without any such outlook. Our problem is not to find the reasons for blasting the leadership. The question is not even whether we should or should not do so. We do have some problems on how to do it. We must criticize the leadership and the wrong policies in such a way that, in doing so, we win over the membership and strengthen the unions, in such a way that no anti-union elements can exploit our criticisms for anti-union purposes, and in a way that deepens the concern and loyalty of the workers for their unions.

As a part of our increased activity we must take on the task of exposing wrong policies. I think there are some ground rules for this task.

What is the problem of tactics? That we expose wrong policies and the leaders who carry them out, but we do so without falling into the camp of the anti-workingclass or anti-union crowd. We cannot even permit ourselves to be in a parallel position with these forces. There are tactical ground rules:

First, we can be fully effective only if we have won our rights. This we can do if we are involved and rooted in the solution of the problems that the working class faces.

Second, we must be concrete both as to the wrong policies and the individuals we criticize. To lump all leaders together gives the bad apples a cover. When we are critical of a policy we should have an alternative policy to propose.

Let me give one example. The average worker does not see the question of his or her self-interest, or class interest, and the policy of aggression in Vietnam as having much to do with each other. Workers, like other Americans, are for peace. They do not condone imperialist aggression but this is not enough to get them to fight against that policy of aggression or to reject Meany's support of such policies. For some time we have complained about the lack of labor support in the peace struggle. But what have we done to convince labor?

Third, we must master the art of taking what is positive, using it and building on it. This is such an important tactical element because it is almost a law of political advancement that organizations and individuals are ready to express a more advanced idea in general and on paper, in a resolution, long before they act on it. Our task is to give expression to these more advanced ideas by transforming good resolutions into guides to action, to struggle.

A few days ago Meany stated that the poor must not be made to pay for the war. The President echoed it. These were empty platitudes by both. But they can be handles of struggle for us. What is one person's demagogy is another's weapon of struggle. One of the most effective ways of exposing a faker is to fight for what he has demagogically promised.

I HAVE DISCUSSED ALL QUESTIONS FROM THE VIEWPOINT OF moving the rank and file of the trade unions. If we are going to be effective, this is where our emphasis must be. If we are going to make a change in our trade union work it will come about only by this emphasis. It is the only way we can help to correct wrong policies of the leadership. It is the only way we can move the leadership that wants to or can be moved. Every honest trade union leader will welcome our help in mobilizing and educating his or her members — if they feel it is not directed against them. There are thousands of trade union leaders and activists who will not only welcome our help, but will join us in our efforts.

We do not need a blueprint on forms of rank-and-file activity. In general, where the members can express their ideas and influence policies through the regular democratic channels of the unions, that is how our work should be organized. Here we must become a factor, together with others, in changing the inner life of such unions so that they do become the centers of membership participation.

In unions where this is not possible we should take the initiative to create other forms of rank-and-file participation. Such rank-and-file forms must service the interests of the members and the union. For example, it seems clear from the attitude of the membership that in Dubinsky's union, the ILGWU, and in the industry, the Black and Puerto Rican workers and union members need forms of organization in their struggle to break through the barriers set up by the union leadership and the industry. They can have leverage, they can break through only if they have an organized voice.

Even the best of unions need new additional forms for membership participation, including sports and social activities, and conferences on specific issues. New forms must break through the barriers of Robert's Rules of Order. Very often a bureaucracy maintains its grip on a union through a bureaucratic interpretation of such rules.

There is a Left sector in the trade union movement. This is going to develop further. We must help to find organizational expression for it. But this must be reflective of specific developments. How things are happening in the peace movement and the civil rights movement can serve as a guide. The forms must be a logical and natural byproduct of whatever level the rise of the Left current is at.

Our emphasis on the working class must start with a campaign in the Party to convince all Communists who can that they must become members of trade unions, and all who are members must become active members. While doing so we should keep in mind that many things have changed. Some of the old ways of doing things are not going to work now.

However, this emphasis raises anew some old questions such as shop papers, shop leaflets, shop gate distributions, etc. It raises the questions of shop clubs, industrial clubs, shop concentration. These are old methods, old concepts that now must be revived in a new setting. Emphasizing our work on the working class is not only a task for our workingclass members — it is a responsibility for the whole Party.

The emphasis on the working class in all of our work must not be narrowly limited either to economic problems or to trade union organizations. Let me remind you of a very fitting statement by Lenin on this question:

> However much we may try to "lend the economic struggle itself a political character" we shall never be able to develop the political consciousness of the workers . . . by keeping within the framework of the economic struggle, for that framework is too narrow.
>
> Class political consciousness can be brought to the workers only from without, that is, only from outside of the economic struggle, from outside of the sphere of relations between workers and employers. The sphere from which alone it is possible to obtain this knowledge is the sphere of relations between all the classes and strata and the state and the government, the sphere of the interrelations between all the classes.[6]

Considering the nature of the problems the working class faces in this age of new technology, the problems arising from the development of state monopoly capitalism, this advice is a thousand times more applicable.

With this in mind, let me give one example. The crisis of the big cities has become a serious problem. Within these cities in crisis the situation in the ghettoes is explosively critical. When we say this, we are talking about the place of residence of the working class. It is the working class, Black and white, that make up the people in these, the cities in crisis. It is a workingclass crisis.

This is the angle from which we must approach the crisis of our cities. Our approach for a solution must include the demand for workingclass and Afro-American representation in the running of those cities. We must dramatically raise the question of Black community and workingclass power as the solution to the crisis in these cities. To raise the crisis of the cities from this viewpoint is to help bring class and political consciousness from "outside of the purely economic struggle."

Throughout these remarks I have placed emphasis on the rank and file and on the necessary political and ideological content in everything we do. We will not be able to convince our Party members of the importance of this shift unless they can see clearly that we as Communists have a unique and a vitally necessary contribution to make. We are trade unionists, but with a difference.

Our contribution is not only unique, but without it the working class will not play its role. There is no purely spontaneous political or ideological growth.

Finally, let us not get into the bind of saying: "Does this mean we do not believe work in other areas is as important?" All work is important. Some demands special attention. But this is the key.

The Rank-and-File Movement and the Emerging Left

[Excerpts from: "On Course — The Revolutionary Process," report to the 19th National Convention of the Communist Party, 1969.]

THE ACCELERATION OF THE PROCESS OF RADICALIZATION NOW evident in the working class is the most significant development of this moment. The effects are showing up everywhere. It is reshaping and revitalizing the trade union movement. In its train it is bringing a new level of trade union and class consciousness.

This process takes different forms in the ranks of the working class than among other groups. Here it is more closely related to economic issues and struggles. Here it is the reaction of a class that is the direct victim of exploitation. Here it is the response of a class that is at the dead end of a class society.

The new factors that feed radicalization are the new forces in the class structure, the new elements in today's drive for maximum profits. In the old boss-worker relationships, militancy against a particular boss served the purpose. Now the growth of multinational corporations and conglomerates have raised new problems for the working class. The open, brutal use of the machinery of state as a class instrument in the drive for bigger profits has further complicated the struggle.

The criminal misuse of technological breakthroughs by the monopolies solely as a means of speedup, layoffs and a higher rate of exploiting the workers has also added a new dimension to the class struggle. Job insecurity, speedup, the menace to life and limb on the job, the extraction of 40 to 50 percent of workers' wages in taxes, mounting inflation — all for the sake of the policies of imperialism — have likewise added to the class struggle.

This has resulted in a sharpening of class contradictions, a sharpening that gives rise to the process of radicalization. This process is also a reflection of the changes in the makeup of the working class. It reflects the large number of young workers, Black workers and women who have entered its ranks.

The process of radicalization is also a reaction to the increasing attacks on labor. The escalation in the rate of exploitation has been accompanied by the escalation of a reactionary, anti-workingclass drive. Legislative hoppers are full of anti-labor bills. The courts grant anti-labor injunctions for the asking.

These new problems and developments have further widened the gap between the top labor leaders and the masses of organized and unorganized workers. This is not an age gap, rather it is a class gap. The rank and file is moving toward policies of class struggle, and the top echelons of leadership more and more openly toward class collaboration.

Never in the history of our country have the dominant sections of the trade union leadership been so completely and openly in the camp of the class enemy. It is a millstone around the neck of the working class. In the real sense of the class struggle, there is no national trade union center. The meetings and deliberations of the Executive Council of the AFL-CIO are irrelevant to the class struggle. They go through the motions, they issue statements, but they do not give leadership to any of the struggles. They do not even constitute a good labor lobby in Washington.

T HE QUESTION OF WORKINGCLASS AND TRADE UNION UNITY is as critical as at any time in history. It is a difficult problem. The path to trade union unity is now open and it is not only a matter of affiliation and paying per capita dues to the AFL-CIO. Big sections of the trade union movement are today unaffiliated. This includes the two million members of the Teamsters, the more than one-and-a-half million autoworkers, the coal miners, the West Coast longshoremen and the electrical workers of the UE.

The struggle for workingclass and trade union unity must be related to the struggle for class struggle policies. "Unity" based on accommodation to the class collaborationist and racist policies of the Meanys is empty and sterile.

The merger of the AFL and the CIO was a historic step toward trade union unity. It had great promise, but the experience since the merger argues for stronger guarantees against the organization being co-opted by class collaborationist elements. It argues for a firmer struggle, which would include the rank and file, to guarantee a class struggle program. In such unity moves, the progressive forces and the rank and file must retain positions of power. Unity is not a thing in itself — it must serve the ends of the class struggle. It must strengthen the class struggle character of the trade union movement.

The most dynamic and potent expression of the radicalization process is the rapid growth of organized rank-and-file movements. The quantitative political shift on the American scene finds expression in these rank-and-file caucuses, leagues and clubs. The most dynamic of all the expressions of this upsurge are the caucuses of Afro-American members. Black caucuses are now an active force in hundreds of shops and locals.

Motivating this rank-and-file upsurge are the new problems of the class struggle, the special problems of Black workers, and the desire to reshape and retool the trade union movement as an instrument of class struggle so that it can meet the problems of today. The workers who make up the rank-and-file movements are the shop militants, the radicals, the Left and the Communists.

This development is the key link in the class struggle. Moreover, it is the key link in the struggle for social progress. It is the developing, growing feature of the American scene. History will forget or overlook our missing some political buses, but it will never forget or forgive if we miss this bus of the class struggle. We can be aboard from the very first stop. Indeed in many areas we already are. For us, the greatest danger in this area is the failure to see what is happening, the failure to see the new possibilities — in short, our danger is that of conservative hangups, of underestimating the process of radicalization.

Rank-and-file movements can develop in various ways. Those with the greatest vitality start with the problems of the workers at the point of production. Rank-and-file movements whose primary thrust is against the monopolies are less apt to degenerate into sterile political pawns of inner-union factions.

Rank-and-file movements must concern themselves with

the quality of trade union leadership. They fight for democratic unionism and a program to advance the interests of the workers. They are a means of pressure on conservative union leaders to become more militant or face removal. They are the surest safeguards against corruption and opportunism in leadership.

Rank-and-file movements are a prerequisite to healthy union practices in Left-led as well as in conservative-led unions. They are a source of strength and support to militant Left union leaders who come and will come out of rank-and-file struggles against the corporations. Such leaders must retain their ties to the organized rank and file, responding to its demands and giving it leadership.

Rank-and-file movements can develop around problems at the point of production as well as around the problems of an industry: the struggles of Black workers for equality, invigorating the shop steward system, trade union control over automation, the six-hour day, fair tax laws, the issue of peace. Consolidation of rank-and-file movements swells their effectiveness and is important to the revitalization of the labor movement.

Rank-and-file movements democratize and revitalize the labor movement, making it a militant instrument of the workers against the monopolies and developing a leadership that rejects class collaboration policies and fights for basic needs.

THE RISE OF BLACK CAUCUSES IN THE SHOPS AND UNIONS IS a militant response to the racist practices of the employers and their influence on the life of the trade unions. We must see the Black caucuses as an important special form of the class struggle, one which has added a new dimension to it. We are for class unity. We are for trade union unity. But these cannot become a reality on the basis of accommodation to racism.

The struggle for unity of Black and white in the labor movement is on a new level. "Don't-rock-the-boat unity" is out. Unity based on full equality and representation is in. The high level of struggle of the Black caucuses against racism is in the interests of the whole class. Their struggle against speedup and poor working conditions raises the job standards of all workers.

With two million Black workers in the AFL-CIO, the fight for Black participation at all levels of trade union leadership is fundamental to the fight against racism. The fight to expand and to change the system of electing the top leadership of the AFL-CIO must include the fight to multiply the number of active Black trade union leaders.

To put an end to discrimination against Black workers in union leadership is going to rock the boat — it means extensive changes, both in personnel and structure.

Collaborationist leaders accuse the Black caucuses of "dual unionism." The old chestnut has been dredged up from the fights for industrial unionism of a generation ago. The Black caucuses are not "dual unionism." They are attempts to substitute class struggle unionism for do-nothing unionism; equality unionism for racist unionism.

"Black and white class unity" is and has been a basic concept of the Communist Party from its earliest history. We strive for this unity in the labor movement. We continue to struggle to end all restrictive admission practices in the craft unions and support the demand that they be opened to all workers, Black and white, able and willing to do the job. We condemn most examinations for apprenticeship training as nothing more than racist instruments to block the admission of Black and other minority groups, and we demand their elimination.

A major aspect of the ruling-class drive to split the working class through the use of racism is the attempt to convince white workers that they have a stake in white supremacy. While Black and other minority workers are the worst victims of racism, the disunity it creates weakens the fighting ability of the whole class, permitting the intensified exploitation of both Black and white.

Wherever capitalism has been able to split the class there is a general deterioration in living standards. Up to now the ruling class has used racism in the South to restrict trade union organization and has used the resulting lower wages as a threat against workers in all parts of the country, while permitting the South to remain a base for the nation's most racist, anti-labor and reactionary political forces.

We condemn the current propaganda campaign being spread among white workers that "the Blacks are after your jobs" as racist-inspired and unfounded. Millions more jobs are needed to meet even the minimum needs of the American people for homes, schools, hospitals and other necessities. In the fight for these jobs we support preferential job training and hiring of Black and other minority workers as necessary to the success of this struggle and the strengthening of class unity.

Racism is not inherent in white workers. It emanates from capitalism as a foul instrument to divide and weaken the working class. The Communist Party must constantly expose white supremacy, anti-Semitism and other aspects of racism as capitalist ideology that is a threat to all workers. We must make the workingclass slogan "An injury to one is an injury to all" an all-embracing slogan for Black-white unity. Our aim must be to direct the struggle against the real enemy.

Our Party must build confidence that the fight against racism can be won — toward this end publicizing the frequent manifestations of Black and white workingclass unity.

COMMUNISTS MUST WORK FOR UNITED FRONT POLICIES AT all levels of the trade union movement. Our basic orientation is toward building the unity of workers at the rank-and-file level. The most effective Communist leadership of a local union is through a united front of Communist, Left and progressive forces.

But we reject limiting our work to "united fronts from below." It is a misconception that we are interested only in challenging union leaders or having an undifferentiated approach toward them as totally corrupted individuals living off the backs of the workers.

Of course, there are opportunistic and corrupted union

leaders — the dominant leadership of the AFL-CIO gives ample proof of that. But historic experiences prove the error of lumping all trade union leaders together, or failing to see the positive effects of rank-and-file struggles on even some of the most conservative officials. John L. Lewis's role in the leadership of the CIO is a case in point.[7]

There are two tendencies that hamper the united front in the labor movement. One is an uncritical attitude toward centrist leaders as a mistaken way of building unity, of tailing behind particular leaders who have a good position on certain issues. The other is refusal to compromise on tactical or peripheral issues. A cardinal principle must be: don't break up the united front on such issues.

Building a successful united front is frequently a complex task. Some trade unionists will lead long, hard-fought strikes, project health organizing drives, attack the war in Vietnam, make general statements against racism, and call for making Dr. King's birthday a national holiday. The same leaders will redbait if they think they can get away with it, let the grievances of their members accumulate, make racist attacks on Black members who demand that these leaders fight racism "at home." Yet these are among the elements who help make up a united front and we must master the ability to work unitedly with people with whom we take issue on specific questions.

The surest way to build a united front at higher levels of trade union leadership is to base it on the militant movements of the rank and file. The united front approach is not at all old hat. It is the key that opens the door to unity of struggle at all levels. Rank-and-file movements are basically united front movements. Our united front concept must be geared to the process of radicalization taking place.

The term "radicalization" is a broad and sweeping one. It is related to other processes; it influences, and is influenced by, many currents. All these factors have created a new basis for a Left current in the workingclass movement. These objective developments have made a Left current a necessity. But objective developments have never by themselves organized anything.

We have to take the initiative. Together with other militants on all levels, we have to probe, bring the movement together and give it form.

What the struggles make necessary is an organized Left current based on a Left program of struggle. There is no other reason for an organized Left.

What is needed is to develop and give the class struggle perspective, to give workers a more conscious class outlook. What is needed is to present a class viewpoint. What is needed is to develop militant tactics. What is needed is to develop a struggle against the Meany-Lovestone anti-labor conspiracy. What is needed is to raise the struggle against racism in the production process and in the life of the unions.

All this is needed as a form of unity of shop militants and activists, of Black and white, of Communists and non-Communists — as a force for class political consciousness, for class electoral independence, to give leadership to the rank-and-file movements. It is needed as a force on the path to socialism. A Left as a form of united front of the more advanced sector of the working class in relationship with Center forces in the trade unions on any level is on shifting sands unless there is an organized Left current. It is the only way to influence the Center. It is the only way the Center can be separated from the Right elements.

Because of the new problems of the class struggle the Left can become the dominant influence in very short order, but it cannot do so if it does not reflect today's level of struggle and today's problems. It can be a factor only if it is related to the rising rank-and-file movements. The Left cannot become such a force on the basis of past performances or positions. It must fill the vacuum created by today's developments and by the refusal of the class collaborationist leaders to respond to them.

The Left must undertake the task of returning the base of union power to the rank and file. To democratize and revitalize the trade union movement is to assure the power of decision to the workers in the shops and departments. The shop steward system must be revived and built as an instrument of the rank and file. The right to strike must be firmly established as an inherent right of the shops and departments. The Left must lead in the new areas of the class struggle. It must break new ground for the class.

For many years we Communists were alone in the USA in pointing up the harmful effects of modern imperialism on the working class. Now consciousness of this is beginning to penetrate through the class, as bitter experience shows how the giant corporations are able to play off workers in one country against those in another.

Some of the "Left intellectuals," who themselves have finally discovered the existence of imperialism, have been downgrading the American working class as "bought off" and "welcomed" by the imperialists into the ranks of exploiters. But this nonsense is the exact opposite of what is happening in real life. The development of an anti-imperialist consciousness in the workingclass movement has become an acute necessity.

And that consciousness can come, but only in the course of struggles to develop unity of action of American workers with workers in other countries who are exploited by the same multinational corporations. The task of stimulating the organization of such joint struggles, of instilling the workingclass internationalism and anti-imperialist consciousness that go with such struggles — that is the task of the Left. The forces of the Left and, first of all, the Communists, pioneer in this major area of struggle.

A S LONG AS CAPITALISM EXPLOITS WORKERS, WORKERS and their unions will and must conduct strikes and struggles for higher wages and related demands as necessary protection against being driven into the most degrading conditions of life and work. And they must keep fighting to restrict management prerogatives.

But there are some yardsticks. The main one is that making capitalism operate better is not our business. Capitalism operates better only for bigger profits, only in squeezing more out of the workers, only for the greater domination of capital over labor.

Our interests are a one-way street. We are totally onesided and incurably prejudiced against anything in the interest of the capitalist class. We are interested only in how to get more for the worker and how, as quickly as possible, to release the rich of all responsibilities — including ownership. We will stay away from anything that even sounds like class partnership.

The unions must confront the employers on such issues as automation and other production techniques. They must strive to limit introduction of such techniques to situations and on terms that improve the wages and employment of workers, and not the opposite. The unions must be definitely opposed to technical improvements which throw workers out of jobs. For every technical improvement, the trade unions must fight for a commensurate cut in the workload without a cut in wages.

The unions must confront the corporate giants on such issues as the location of plants — whether within this country or abroad. They must strive to compel the corporations to negotiate on all such questions. They must aim to develop the power to be able to say to the employers, "You may not shut down this plant where 5,000 of our members are employed, and move output to a government-subsidized, substandard-wage open shop in this country or in one of the new colonies of U.S. imperialism like Taiwan. And if you try to do so, we will shut down the whole chain." They must develop relations with all the working people of the community, so that the entire community fights for the rights of its people.

Yes, the working class must fight to extend the range of its influence over the affairs of employing corporations, but always as an independent force in confrontation and struggle against the capitalist class.

The employers try to sidetrack this drive into various partnership schemes. We have seen plenty of such schemes in the past. Sometimes they were profit-sharing schemes. Sometimes they were union-management boards who were supposed to strive for higher efficiency, or to battle imports, or to cover a wide range of problems cooperatively.

Inevitably such arrangements worked only to the advantage of the employers. They proved to be means whereby union leaders, wittingly or unwittingly, helped the employers to increase their profits at the expense of the workers. When trade union representatives take positions on corporate boards of directors under these conditions, they end up merely as rubber stamps for the owners, helping them to enforce their will on the workers and to increase corporate profits at the workers' expense.

We must remember that the state remains a capitalist state. Labor participation at a policymaking level cannot be achieved until the working class creates the political conditions for it through its part in a victorious anti-monopoly coalition. Short of that, the working class inevitably finds itself in confrontation with the state, although the conditions of that confrontation, the possibilities of winning concessions, etc., are different than in such confrontation with separate employers.

We are for any demand that cuts down on profits, ups wages, cuts down on speedup, shortens hours, protects workers' health. We are for any and all controls to guarantee such agreements. Whatever adjustments have to be made, for whatever reason, we are for such changes taking place at the expense of the employer. Take the money from where it is at and not from where it is not.

There are many adjustments and plans dealing with new technology. But in the end there is only one qualitative concept for labor — to cut down the hours of work with no cut in take-home pay. This can be achieved in numerous ways: a six-hour day, annual two-month vacations, retirement at age 50 with full pay.

We must avoid any demand that even inadvertently slips into a position of class partnership when the industry is being run for profit. We are for controls, we are for nationalization, but only as a way of eliminating private profit and turning the money over to the workers.

This question comes to the fore today because of the development of the people's political struggle against monopoly capital in all industrialized countries. This struggle is still at an early stage of development in the U.S, but it is not too soon to look ahead. Certainly the demand will grow, and grow soon, for more labor representation in the regulation of the economy, for more restraint by labor on the operation of the giant conglomerates. And demands for labor representation, a labor voice in decisions, must be supported and encouraged. But always from the class viewpoint, always along the lines I have indicated.

TO SUMMARIZE, IT IS A PRIME TASK OF THE RANK-AND-FILE movements, of the Black and progressive caucuses, to see to it that their unions are not permitted to become collaborators with capitalism under the slogan of labor participation and labor influence on economic affairs. True, it is necessary to fight for representation, for a voice, for positions from which to fight for the advantages of the class. But this must not be used to create illusions of "partnership." The exploiters remain the exploiters and the exploited remain the exploited — we cannot stress this too often.

Neither labor representation nor even government ownership of this or that industry can be regarded as steps towards socialism. But they can all be used as positions in the struggle of the working class for immediate demands, as means for strengthening the anti-monopoly coalition. The lessons of such positions can and must be used to show the need for exclusive workingclass power which assumes all the decisive positions in the economic life of the country, rather than "partnership" in which the capitalists continue to hold the whip.

The fight against government regulations and state monopoly capitalism in general must always be conducted from the viewpoint of strengthening the forces of the ultimately necessary socialist revolution, and never from the viewpoint of stabilizing the system.

It is clear that there are new problems in the class struggle. But if we see only this and do not also see the new opportunities that are present, we will miss that bus. And to be on this bus of history is our cardinal task.

Hard Hats and Hard Facts:
The Vietnam War

[From: "Hard Hats and Hard Facts," written in response to a staged march of construction workers in New York City, 1970 — slightly abridged.]

DEAR FELLOW WORKERS: I WANT TO ADDRESS YOU AS A FORMER steelworker. I also wore a hard hat. I was a member of the Structural Iron Workers Union in Ohio. It happens that I am also one of the founders of the United Steelworkers Union. I know your life. It's no cinch.

I know the high injury rate on high-rise construction. Nobody need tell me about the tough physical requirements which end the working life of construction workers after the age of 45 or 50, if not sooner.

The hard hat is a trademark of the hard job. It should protect you from falling bolts, etc., but in addition it should help safeguard you against phony ideas.

I want to say a word to those of you who were in New York during early May and maybe took part in the actions and marches in Wall Street and at City Hall which were called to back up Nixon. I am sure many of you are thinking hard about the action because involved in what you did is the question of your children's future — whether they will live or die on some remote battlefield in a war they never declared.

It may not appear so but your bread and butter, the life of your union, your democratic rights were directly involved in your march in support of Nixon.

A large part of the population of our country, most of the working class and most of the youth, feel that when you march supporting Nixon's war policies in Indochina you are marching against your own best self-interests as workers. As sure as the sun rises, this is most totally a rich man's war and a poor man's fight — a poor man's burden.

Let us face some hard facts. The United States flag is not the issue of this struggle. Don't be misled by this outcry. No sensible person is out to tear up the flag or spit on it. Anybody who does that is either an agent provocateur in the ranks of the peace marchers or truly some mentally deranged or irresponsible person who wants to see workers fight workers.

When this march was organized I know many of you did not have a chance to think the question through. You are not for the war — you've got too much at stake: your kids' lives, your family's future, the nation's well-being.

Many of you took the time off simply because you got paid for it, right? After all, it is easier than working on the steel beams. And I know fresh beer on a hot day is plenty refreshing. Then others of you were locked out by your bosses for the two hours. There are cases where, when workers refused to go out, the bosses refused to pay for the time involved. That was nothing more than a lockout for war.

Let's look closer into the facts and what's behind them. There were men behind the scenes who secretly organized the march, for their purposes. As workers we need to find out what purposes such people have. They told you the issue was the American flag and they knew pretty well what they wanted. They knew what the political effect of the march would be.

Some of those secret operators were big real estate operators who put big money into organizing these marches. Do you really think they have your interests at heart? Do you think the blue-blood John Birch Society that is mixed up in this up to its neck is your true friend? Or the ultra-Right fascists, or the racketeers who did the real organizing behind the scenes? Tell me, do you really think they have your interests at heart? They are campaigning to destroy your unions.

You know what, fellow worker? They are using you. They used your demonstration to help Nixon go even farther than he has in invading Cambodia.[8] They use your demonstrations for purposes different than you conceived them to be.

Since you marched the Nixon Administration has backtracked from its announced plans to get out of Cambodia. They hint there will be other invasions. Now the U.S. has pushed Thailand into the mess. Next, U.S. troops will have to go in and save their fascist government. Your march is used as a support for the war — a war that cannot but end in a disaster for the United States.

No one wants to be another's stooge. But that's what these behind-the-scenes operators propose to do with you. Fighting words? Listen to these facts.

The big-time operators are organizing for higher profits against the interests of the country. They do so by wrapping themselves in the flag even as they are betraying their country. It was a wise man who said, "Patriotism is the last refuge of the scoundrel." So they appeal to you, using your sense of patriotism, your pride in the hard hat.

They are using your hard hat symbol to mobilize a force that in basic essence is against labor, is against democracy, and is racist to the core. They seek to divide labor, break its unity — its greatest defense — by pitting white against Black and Black against white. They are out to destroy everything the United States flag stands for.

Ask who bought the hard hats that were worn by marchers in business suits who never climbed the ladder on a construction job in their lives. There were plenty of them, as you have learned.

As you know from your own life, often things are not as they seem. It is necessary to look beneath the surface of things. To give support of any kind to the policy of war against the people of Indochina is not only morally wrong, it is not in the best self-interest of the people of the United States. Therefore such an act is not patriotism.

Some say the issue is a defense of democracy. They are right — but not in the way the *Daily News* presents it. The U.S. is militarily and economically supporting and keeping in power the worst fascists, such as Ky and Thieu.[9] It is the people of Vietnam who are fighting against U.S. aggression, who want to get rid of the fascist, anti-labor butchers, and to establish a government of democratic self-rule. Any support of the Nixon policy of imperialist aggression is support for the fascist puppets of South Vietnam.

W E ARE IN ANOTHER DEPRESSION. THE U.S. ECONOMY IS
in the beginning stages of an economic crisis. All of
Nixon's policies are geared to bring on an economic
crisis for the workers while helping the big corporations to continue making big profits. Unemployment has now climbed to
over five percent while taxes, prices and rents go up.

You do not want to support such policies. But when you are
either silent or when you take part in pro-Nixon marches, this
action by you is turned into support for Nixon's policies in all
areas, including his policies that propel an economic crisis for
you. The slogan "USA — all the way" means all the way for
maximum profits. It has the same meaning as "What's good for
General Motors is good for the USA." If the corporations are
"all the way for USA," why don't they give up some of their
billions of dollars they make in profits? Why should you, as a
worker, be forced to pay for the war in high taxes and prices
while the rich get richer from the same war?

The issue is not the defense of the United States. The people of the United States supported the actions of the government during the Second World War because the struggle
against fascism involved the independence and democratic
rights of peoples, including ours. I volunteered and served in
the U.S. Navy. Now it is the United States that threatens the
independence, the democratic rights and lives of people the
world over.

What does this war — this aggression against the people of
Indochina — mean to America, to you as a worker?

First let's examine the reasons for this conflict. You have
been told that Communism is the issue. The reality is that it is
not. Remember that Richard Nixon said he inherited the Vietnam war from Lyndon Johnson, and Johnson said he inherited
it from John Kennedy who said he inherited it from Dwight
Eisenhower. Well, it would be good to look at what Eisenhower said about it in 1953: "Now let us assume that we lost
Indochina," Ike said. "If Indochina goes, several things happen
right away. The Malay Peninsula, the last little bit of land hanging on down there, would be scarcely defensible. The tin and

tungsten we so greatly value from that area would cease coming. . . . "

Eisenhower was even more explicit than that, for he continued: "All of that position around there is very ominous to the United States, because finally if we lost all of that, how would the free world hold the rich empire of Indonesia?"

Hold the "rich empire of Indonesia." Know what that means? It means trying to take into tow the fifth most populous country in the world, Indonesia, which has a population of 100 million. Most people don't know that. It means to police —with our boys in uniform — so vast a place.

Ike went on:

> So when the U.S. votes $400 million to help that war, we are not voting a giveaway program. We are voting for the cheapest way we can to prevent the occurrence of something that would be of a most terrible significance to the USA, our security, our power and ability to get certain things we need from the riches of the Indonesia territory and from Southeast Asia.

Where is all the talk about "helping democracy," etc., etc.? The lowdown, fellow workers, is as Eisenhower puts it, "to get certain things we need from the riches of the Indonesia territory and from Southeast Asia." Later in his book Ike added "prodigious supplies of rubber and rice," and the countries of Thailand and East Pakistan to what's at stake.

Is that wholesale hijacking of tin and tungsten for your benefit, for the people of the United States? Hijacking it is, for the corporations pay the workers out there starvation wages of a few pennies per hour and charge fat prices for manufactured articles containing tin and tungsten.

Who is all that shooting and killing for? All those raw materials are designed to go to Union Carbide which gets the tin of Thailand, and Standard Oil which gets the oil of Indonesia. The war is not over but the big oil monopolies have already divided amongst themselves not only the land area of Southeast Asia but the continental ocean shelf as well. A division of labor: you supply the boys to kill and get killed so that the big corporations get the supply of cheap raw materials. That, in sum, is the reason for imperialist wars to which our rich man's government ships our troops, our sons, all over the world for every other reason except to "safeguard democracy."

American corporations dream of using the Vietnamese to exploit for $15 a month just as they now exploit the South Koreans and the people of Taiwan. Listen to the *New York Times* which said not long ago, "South Korean workers work long hours for little pay under harsh and sometimes dehumanizing conditions." And for whom? You guessed right: big American corporations.

Already in South Vietnam, you especially will be interested to learn that billions in construction contracts went to the RMK-BRJ syndicate. Probably some of you have worked for Raymond International, or Morrison and Knudsen. They pay their Vietnamese workers 14 cents an hour — $35 a month for a 60-hour week. They pay American foremen 43 times as much. But first they bomb the Vietnamese peasants out of their rice paddies and herd them into concentration camps, then make them work or starve.

It's a war to get cheap labor — first them, then you.

The profits, as you might guess, are fabulous. *Fortune* magazine, organ of the biggest financial interests here, tells of the promoter Herbert Fuller who wants to put up a $10 million sugar mill in South Vietnam and is waiting for troops and the napalm treatment to open up the territory for him. *Fortune* says about Fuller:

> When the troops arrive to clear the area, as they sooner or later must, this American capitalist will literally be one step behind them. . . . "I am in it for the money," Fuller says. "We could get back our investment in two years."

Now does this serve your interests? Or the national interest?

It does serve Mr. Fuller. It serves American Big Business. Jobs by the thousands are folding up in the United States — in electronics, auto, textile, apparel, machinery — as the giants of American industry move the work to the new-type colonies of the Pentagon where they can escalate their profits ten times.

That, fellow workers, is why the war is escalated. What I described above is what is meant by the military industrial complex.

War is good weather for the military industrial complex — even if it benefits nobody else. Biggest among the financial elements in that complex are the big-money men, the kings of finance capital: Chase Manhattan Bank and the Rockefeller interests. They have, believe it or not, a real day-to-day relationship with you, they have an effect on what goes into your pay envelope; therefore, they have a mighty impact on how you and your family live.

Hardly a piece of major construction takes place in Manhattan without the financial involvement of Chase or the Rockefeller interests whose representatives are on the boards of directors of the corporations paying for the buildings you work on.

Well, the Vietnam war profits swell their bank accounts; but let's see what those profits do for you.

Last year your trade's average pay was $210 a week. Right off the bat, $45 to $60 was deducted for federal, state and New York City taxes. That left you a take-home of $150 to $165. Then another $40 was taken in what are called hidden taxes, which are included in the prices and the rents you meet, or in real-estate taxes if you own your home. That means that only $110 or $125 out of the $210, or barely half, was actually available to you to pay for goods and services.

But let's look at the Rockefeller family for a moment. John D. Rockefeller III testified before the Ways and Means Committee in Washington, February 1969, and said: "Although I have qualified for the unlimited deduction privilege during every year since 1961, I have deliberately paid a tax of between five and ten percent of my adjusted gross income each of those years."

For construction workers — 40 to 50 percent of their income in taxes. For the Rockefellers, with a combined family income of $5 billion, each enjoying tens of millions of personal income yearly — a "voluntary" "tax" of five or ten percent, just for "appearances."

That's the kind of freedom this war is about: freedom from taxes for the billionaires!

SOME OF YOU MAY THINK THE STUDENTS ARE GOING "TOO far" in their actions. First, don't blame the students for the few individual acts of violence. Second, their militancy is understandable. It is the youth who are being killed in this war. It is their lives that are being disrupted. The youth are not ready to accept a lifetime of barely making ends meet. They are not ready to accept a life of constant worry about layoffs, high taxes, prices and rents.

They feel life should offer more. They are probing for a more sane, just and equitable social system. They want a life without wars, a life without racism, a life without economic recessions or unemployment. They cannot understand a system where a few get rich and live like kings by exploiting the great majority. They want a more humane system. Now what is wrong with that? Such desires have always been the propellant behind human progress. The youth are not the problem. They are not the cause of the present crisis or the issue that should divide us.

Some of you are joining pro-war rallies because you are against Communists. But Communism is not the issue in Vietnam any more than it was the issue when the Japanese attacked Pearl Harbor or the Nazis attacked France in World War II.

Aggression these days always uses the pretext of anti-Communism. The issue in Vietnam is nothing more or less than U.S. military aggression. The issue is national liberation, the unconquerable will of the Vietnamese people to be free, to be able to govern their own land, the right to be masters of their own destiny. Their goal is no less just than the goal of our forefathers in the struggle to be free from England.

That's why this relatively small number of people in distant Asia has been able to confront the might of the richest country in the world, which has dropped more bombs on them than were dropped on all of Europe in the Second World War. During World War II the Vietnamese people fought against Japanese invaders. Afterward they fought against French colonialists. They were able to deliver French imperialism its most disastrous defeat at Dienbienphu.[10] They withstand everything the U.S. has been able to send against them: from napalm, which burns everything it falls on, to fleets of helicopters carrying infantry, and weapons from submachine guns to cannons.

Most observers know that the Vietnamese cannot ever be defeated, that we get deeper into the quicksand with every escalation of the war, as in Laos and Cambodia. We face military and political defeat of the first magnitude. Yet Nixon continues to expand the war, knowing full well the majority of the country is against him.

That is why two days before he revealed to the country and Congress that the U.S. invasion of Cambodia had begun, he told a secret meeting of the leaders of ten military-linked groups that he would soon order action "on the Cambodian side of the border." These groups included the National Rifle Association, the Reserve Officers Association, the Navy League, the Marine Corps League and the American Ordnance Association. Big-time, big-money outfits.

He exhorted them to help build public sentiment behind him when the action in Cambodia would be announced. He felt he needed support from these ultra-Right fancy Dans who are no friends of yours. He needed them because he was bypassing Congress, bypassing even some members of his own cabinet.

Why does Nixon do all this, risk so much? The answer lies in the ledgers of Nixon's bosses — the industrial and financial complex that is in partnership with the military.

According to government statistics, corporation profits after taxes in the five years of 1965-1969, the years since we started bombing North Vietnam and sending in hundreds of thousands of troops — in those five years U.S. Big Business profits totalled $244 billion.

Yes, that's it: $244 billion!

And that's after taxes. And that's just reported profits.

There is much, much more hidden in expense accounts, depreciation and other trick items. In the five previous years, 1960 to 1964, corporate profits after taxes totalled $157 billion. The increase during the Vietnam War was $87 billion or 56 percent.

Now listen to this: they call Vietnam a "limited war." World War II cost several times more than the Vietnam war. There was plenty of profiteering then too. But corporate profits after taxes during the five years of 1941-1945 came to $51 billion. In other words, profits during this war, the Vietnam war, are five times as much as during World War II! That's why they will pay your time off to demonstrate for continuing the war in Vietnam. Right?

These are the reasons that impel me to address myself to you. These are the real issues of this war in Vietnam that threatens to throw us all into the holocaust of World War III.

No, Communism is not the issue. It is military aggression in the interests of Big Business in the USA. As a worker, don't let yourself be misled about Communism. As a worker, I have no interest that is different from yours. I am a Communist because I am a worker. I believe the workers and all others will be better off if the industries are publicly owned, if we, the people, own and control the natural resources of our land.

As a worker you have no interest in making profits for the rich. Socialism, which I believe in, will put an end to this madness that kills our sons (50,000 dead; over a quarter million wounded) and the sons of other peoples for the sake of Chase Manhattan Bank, the Rockefellers and all the other big interests.

As one worker to another who wears the hard hat, I ask you to consider these hard facts. When you look beneath the surface of things, it becomes clear. We must build the movement that will force the Nixon Administration to end the aggression and to bring the armed forces back home.

It is necessary to build a new people's alliance: an alliance that will challenge the political and economic power of the military industrial complex, an alliance that will shift national priorities in a basic way, an alliance that will fight to end racism, that will safeguard democratic institutions, an alliance that will fight for job security and union scales for all workers. We need a new people's alliance that will place the interests of the people — the interests of working people — at the very top of the list of priorities.

fresh winds

The Class Struggle Today

Beat the Steel Crisis
Save Every Job

[From: "Beat The Steel Crisis! Save Every Job!" speech made in Youngstown, Ohio, 1977 — slightly abridged.]

COMING TO YOUNGSTOWN IS COMING BACK HOME. BUT THIS TIME, because of the closing of steel plants and the laying off of steelworkers, it feels like coming back to visit and help an old friend that is ailing.

But let me say: Mahoning Valley,[1] like Buffalo, Bethlehem and other steel centers, is not terminally ill. There are effective remedies. The ailments can be cured.

For the 60,000 permanently laid off steelworkers and the quarter million members of their families, for the construction workers, service sector workers and for small-business people in these steel communities life has turned into a disaster, a nightmare. For those who are able to collect unemployment benefits or still have some savings, the full impact of this disaster is like waiting for a flood to crest before relief arrives. Like all crises, these tragic developments in the steel industry are a moment of truth for all institutions and organizations.

This crisis again puts the spotlight on the bestial, anti-human and brutally criminal nature of the profit-hungry steel corporations. It also exposes the subservient, captive and lying nature of the mass media, especially the press. It exposes the "elected representatives" of the people in government, who sit in silence or make asinine excuses for the reckless actions of the steel companies. And it puts a spotlight beam on the bankruptcy of apple-polishing trade union leaders who are caught with their class collaborationist pants down. Strictly on merit, instead of $90,000 salaries the George Meanys and the Lloyd McBrides[2] should be given the pink slip.

I landed in Mahoning Valley in the middle of another disaster: the economic crisis of the 1930s. Life then was raw and brutal. Hungry families were evicted from their homes. There were soup lines. Death from so-called natural causes — of people weakened by hunger — increased dramatically. There were no unemployment checks, relief checks or old-age pensions. And there were no welfare systems people could turn to for emergency relief.

But, in spite of the hunger and misery there was hope because there was a fightback.

There were strikes, and not a week passed in Youngstown without some mass demonstrations, petitions, hunger marches. For some of us the county jail became a second home. It was a common sight to see the marshals coming to evict families from their homes, the neighbors getting together, taking the furniture off the street and putting it back into the houses.

Because of the militant fightback the federal government was forced to take emergency measures and appropriate money for programs like Works Progress Administration (WPA), Public Works Administration (PWA), etc.[3] Because of the fightback movements we now have unemployment benefits, Social Security and welfare systems.

When the economic crisis of the 1930s was over, aside from some of the skilled workers in the hot rolling mills, most steelworkers were still unorganized and did not have the protection of trade unions. In those days, if workers even whispered complaints about low wages and working conditions or the need for unions, they were fired without recourse or appeal. I was fired by both Youngstown Sheet and Tube and Republic Steel for union activities.

Each steel corporation was a power unto itself. Besides the FBI and the city and county police departments, each corporation maintained its own armed police force and its own secret stoolpigeons as well as an industrywide blacklist.

But again there was hope. The workers saw a glimmer of light at the end of the tunnel because there was a rising mood of determined struggle and fightback. Against all obstacles the steel unions slowly took root: first as a secret, underground force, later as open, fighting, United Steelworkers locals. The lessons are obvious. Without struggle, without unity and organization, millions would have died of starvation during the Depression. Without organization and united struggles, steelworkers would still be working ten to twelve hours a day for 30 to 40 cents an hour. In fact, without struggle, there would be a system of slaves and slavemasters and we would still be a British colony.

Unity in mass struggles is the only weapon the people have. As history is witness, people have a choice: either to remain on their knees begging for crumbs or stand up and fight for what is rightfully theirs.

NOW STEELWORKERS FACE A NEW CRISIS, A NEW DISASTER. Who today can seriously challenge the fact that without struggle, without organization and unity, cities like Campbell, Struthers and Youngstown, Ohio, will go down the drain, down the polluted Mahoning River? Today it is the Campbell Works and tomorrow, when U.S. Steel completes its new mill in the Ashtabula-Conneaut area, it will be the Ohio Works and McDonald. Without struggle the Mahoning Valley, and many others, will become ghost valleys.

The question is: what and who is destroying this once busy, green valley? Why is there a crisis in the steel industry?

As usual, the captive mass media and the steel corporations, in a conspiracy to hoodwink the people, are deliberately pointing the accusing finger in the wrong direction. They are lying through their teeth. It is a calculated, dirty falsehood when they claim that the causes of the crisis are high wages, steel imports, high taxes and too-strict pollution controls.

It is true that U.S.-made steel is not as competitive as it used to be. But the main reason for this is not the wages of U.S. steelworkers, but because the steel corporations in Japan and Western Europe are ready to accept a profit margin of 8½ percent while the U.S. corporations, in their boundless greed, skim off 12 to 18 percent in profits. In the last ten years, the U.S. steel corporations have more than doubled their profits and their executives' salaries.

It is an unmitigated, bald-faced lie that the cause of the problem is that the steelworkers' wages are too high.

The hard facts are that ten years ago in 1967, steelworkers' wages accounted for $16 of every $100 worth of steel shipped. By 1976, wages accounted for only $12 of every $100 worth of steel. In other words, the corporations are getting a bigger share and the steelworkers are getting a declining piece of the total steel pie. And in the same period of 1967-1977, the steel corporations increased the price of steel by 150 percent.

Ask any steelworker's family how much they have managed to save — how rich are they after the 25 percent tax bite, escalating rents, rising mortgage payments, interest rates, utility bills and the inflated cost of food and clothing.

Ask any steelworker whether they should voluntarily take a wage cut because they are too well off, too affluent. Steelworkers' wages are not the cause, and therefore cutting wages is not the solution to the crisis. And look who's complaining about the high wages of steelworkers!

The Lykes Corporation[4] is a bank president's dream. The 18 directors and officers of Lykes and Youngstown Sheet and Tube admit to a take-home pay of $1,300,000 last year. They are the most successful pirates in all of history. A man named Cleary, a vice president of both corporations, has an annual salary of $130,000 plus $90,000 a year in retirement benefits, plus the coupons he clips from 3,000 shares of stock. Joseph T.

Lykes gets $135,000 a year in salary, $100,000 in annual retirement benefits, and the coupons on 380,000 shares of stock. Randolph Rieder, another vice president of Youngstown Sheet and Tube, gets $155,000 per year, and $45,000 in yearly retirement benefits. After all this legal robbery, Lykes, the parent company of Youngstown Sheet and Tube, admitted it made a profit of $20 million last year.

These leeches whose productivity is zero have the brazenness to speak about steelworkers' productivity! The gall of these degenerate embezzlers — to complain about workers' wages! And these same corporate pirates have now forced the coal miners in the mines they own to go on strike.

These corporate vultures have the audacity to complain about taxes. They are the biggest tax swindlers in all of history. Last year the U.S. steel corporations' tax swindle was over $273 million in taxes they should have paid. For closing the Campbell Works, the Lykes Corporation has reported a $138 million loss and filed for a $20 million tax credit.

This is proof positive that crime does pay — but only if the crimes are committed by the big corporations.

It is also a complete fraud and falsehood to say that one of the reasons for the present steel crisis is that workers in Japan and Western Europe work harder and are more productive than U.S. steelworkers. The hard fact is that there are no steelworkers in the world who are as exploited as are U.S. steelworkers. In fact that is one of the problems. Fewer and fewer steelworkers are producing more and more steel. There are 100,000 fewer steelworkers today producing much more steel than ten years ago. Last year U.S. steelworkers produced as much steel in 30½ hours as they did in 40 hours in 1967. That is a 25 percent leap in productivity.

Now, the critical question is: Are there solutions to this crisis?

Without any question there are both immediate and long-range remedies. But you can bet that the steel corporations are not going to like our solutions. They did not like our solutions to the Great Depression or the drive to organize steelworkers.

They do not like our solutions because of the unavoidable fact that any real solution is going to demand changes in priorities. Any real solution is going to affect the corporate sacred cow — namely their profits.

W HAT ARE SOME REAL SOLUTIONS AND REMEDIES? THE real solution must start with an immediate, right-to-live, emergency appropriation by the U.S. Congress that will provide a decent standard of living for every laid-off steelworker for the duration of the crisis. There must be a demand that the senators and members of congress from the steel-producing areas get off their fat behinds and, for once, fight for the interests of the people.

Such an emergency appropriation is absolutely necessary for steelworkers. And the fact is that it would cost less than the cost overruns of corporations doing business with the federal government. It would cost less than the interest that bankers get on the national government debt, and less than what the U.S. government spends to bolster the military, racist, fascist dictatorships in countries like Chile and South Africa.

Such an emergency appropriation must be based on the concept that for society there should be only one priority, the most basic of all human rights — the right to live.

Now the question: is there a potential domestic market for steel? Yes — and the potential is bigger than ever. A few examples will be proof enough.

The Federal Transportation Department reported that out of some 750,000 steel bridges in the country, 110,000 are collapsing and in need of replacement. One-half of the bridges in Pittsburgh are now limited to 3,000 pounds. The Department reports that a steel bridge collapses every other day in the United States.

A program of rebuilding and replacing these bridges would keep the Campbell Works in operation full-time. In the big cities water main breaks in the water systems take place every other day. Most of the water mains are over 50 years old. It is estimated that New York City alone needs $2 billion worth of steel pipe to replace a 100-year-old system. This could keep the pipe mills running year-round.

The cities badly need transit systems. The building of such systems would keep the Ohio Works, and my old stomping ground Briar Hill Plant, going at full steam.

There is a housing crisis in the U.S. There is a crying need to tear down and replace the slums with modern, liveable apartment complexes. This would create a large market for structural steel and the steel that goes into manufacturing pipes, stoves, refrigerators, etc. This by itself could easily add an additional 60,000 jobs in steel. So when you add to this the steel that goes into the manufacture of autos and badly needed railroad tracks, it is obvious there is a potential domestic market for steel.

The obstacle is priorities. The top priority of the Carter Administration is the $130-billion, totally wasteful military budget, and the doubling of corporate profits every five years. Therein lies the problem.

Dollar for dollar the military budget — the production of weapons, arms, missiles, etc. — results in the least number of jobs and uses very little steel. Something like two to three percent of the steel produced in the USA is used in the production of arms. The military takes up $130 billion when only $25 billion of that would be required to replace all the 110,000 rickety steel bridges.

Besides, the military budget is promoted by a campaign of flagrant falsehoods and fakery. For 60 years the Pentagon has demanded bigger and bigger budgets behind the cry that "The Russians are coming." Well the Russians have not come, and they are not going to come. It is a fraud.

So the simple transfer of 50 percent of the Pentagon budget and a cut in the enormous corporate profits would open up the domestic market for steel. A cut in corporate profits would make steel more competitive. But again, this means a change in priorities — from our dead-end, war-oriented economy to a peace-oriented economy.

There is also a great potential foreign market for steel and steel products.

The facts are that while the older capitalist countries like Great Britain, France, West Germany and Spain suffer from a chronic crisis of stagnation and therefore do not provide a potential market for steel, the socialist countries and most of the developing countries are in a long-term historic period of growth and construction. They are in a period of an economic boom. They want to buy steel and steel products.

So again, what is the obstacle? The hangup is U.S. foreign policy. A policy of aggression has become counterproductive for the U.S.

For example, the people of Angola are now entering a historic period of construction and industrialization. But they cannot forget that U.S. imperialism was the main supporter of the colonialist, racist oppressors of the people of Angola. How can Angola (or for that matter other countries like Angola) think about buying U.S. steel or steel products when the Carter Administration to this very day refuses to give up its policies of aggression and will not establish diplomatic recognition of Angola, while continuing to give support to the main enemy of all national liberation movements — the fascist, racist regime of South Africa? This is the obstacle to trade with the developing countries.

The socialist countries are a huge potential market. But again, there is an obstacle. The Jackson-Vanik amendment to the 1974 trade bill,[5] by Senator Jackson of Washington and Congressman Vanik of Ohio, places a special discriminatory tariff on imports from most of the socialist countries. And the amendment by Senator Stevenson of Illinois actually cuts off ordinary business credits to the socialist countries that are used by all countries who import and export.

These discriminatory amendments have no other effect than to wipe out 60,000 jobs of U.S. workers.

The simple removal of these special discriminatory amendments would open the markets in the socialist countries to U.S. steel and steel products. There is an accepted rule of thumb: every billion dollars of exports creates 60,000 jobs for one year.

So it is clear: a change in priorities, and a change in the foreign policy that cuts off the United States' nose to spite its face, would open up both domestic and foreign markets for U.S. steel and steel products. The military industrial complex is against these measures because they would then not be able to play around with military budgets of hundreds of billions of dollars. But, for the steelworkers, for the people and for the steel communities, these measures are becoming historic necessities.

And a six-hour day without overtime or cuts in take-home pay in the steel industry would create approximately 100,000 new jobs. That by itself would be more than enough to put every recently laid-off steelworker back on the job.

I N THE PAST YEAR THE STEEL CORPORATIONS HAVE CONdemned and banished 65,000 steelworkers' families to a life of pain, insecurity and suffering. By any yardstick of human rights, this is a crime. These criminal actions should be proof enough that these corporations cannot be permitted to continue to dominate and be in charge of such an important and vital aspect of life, one that in so many ways directly affects the lives of the majority of people.

There is no crisis for the big stockholders of steel corporations. Five years ago the stocks of the eight largest steel corporations averaged $12.30 per share; last year the shares averaged $23.40. And no one buys shares without expecting big dividends.

How can the steel plants be left in the hands of people who pick up a phone and cut the lifeline of a quarter million people with no thought, compassion or concern?

There is an effective remedy and in a sense it would be just punishment for the crimes of the steel corporations. The time has come when in the U.S. we are forced to consider the nationalization of a number of industries. We simply are not going to be able to solve the serious problems of energy, steel, coal, housing, mass transit and pharmaceuticals without nationalization.

Why not relieve the Lykes Corporation of all the Youngstown Sheet and Tube plants by means of nationalization?

Nationalization means that these industries would be taken out of the system of corporate profits and would then be democratically operated and controlled as public properties by elected representatives of the workers and the public, and run for the benefit of all the people. Such industries would then dispense with private profits and corporate executive salaries.

It is unrealistic and illusory to think this can be done by some committee passing the hat and collecting $50 million to buy the Campbell Works. This idea becomes a diversion. Such dreams turn into nightmares. Many of the people who are pushing this idea are well-meaning but not very realistic.

The federal government has a special fund for small plant takeovers. It is called ESOP (Employee Stock Ownership Plan). It could be better known as "Aesop's Fables" because there are a number of pitfalls. Such takeovers are a trap, because the federal government insists that the corporations and the old management hold on to key positions.

Senator Long of Louisiana,[6] the open corporate stooge, said of ESOP: "It is better than Geritol — it will increase productivity, it will save this (capitalist) economic system." The Youngstown *Vindicator*, the oldest corporate stooge, rushed in with its anti-labor editorial: "Productive changes in work rules will require officials of the United Steelworkers Union to take a new look at their adversary relationship with steel management. Realistic concessions may well be the order of the day. . . . " There is only one concession that must result from plant takeover: the elimination of corporate profits.

In the ESOP takeovers the workers become patsies. And the concept of paying the corporations for the closed industrial plants is itself a fraud. Why not give the Lykes Corporation a dollar bill? The Youngstown Sheet and Tube Company is closing the Campbell Works, laying off 6,000 steelworkers, and the federal government is paying a bounty to the corporation in the form of a $20 million tax writeoff. Therefore the takeovers must take place through and by way of the federal government. But after the takeover the workers and the people's representatives must then be permitted to operate these plants.

The argument that workers and people's representatives

are not capable of running such facilities is sheer nonsense. After all, who runs the plants now if not the workers? Most of the present stockholders of Youngstown Sheet and Tube and Lykes don't know a rolling mill from a gin mill.

Like vultures waiting for the kill, there are "fast buck" con men also getting into the act. The people of Mahoning Valley had better be on guard against swindlers.

The talk of reopening the Campbell Works under new corporate management is accompanied by a barrage of propaganda about a cut in wages, deferment of wage increases, about speedup of production, about postponement of pollution controls. There are powerful corporate forces who would like to see a pilot plant — without a union, with lower wages. They see this as a wedge, a way of destroying the effectiveness of the Steelworkers Union in all of the plants.

The solutions and remedies I have presented are realistic, necessary and possible. However, these solutions will not materialize without mass pressure and mass struggles.

And this is no time for union leaders to sit in warm-cushioned chairs and play footsie with the corporations. This is a time when union leaders and members must raise hell all over the place. There is no other way.

The key to mass struggles is workingclass unity. And the main ingredient of steelworkers' unity has always been the unity of Black and white workers. This question has now emerged as an integral part of the present crisis in steel because steelworkers cannot win without unity.

And there can be no solid unity without a struggle against racism — racism that the steel corporations have fostered and practiced for over a hundred years.

The bottom line in the struggle against racism in the steel industry is the struggle for economic parity for Black, Puerto Rican and Chicano workers with their white class brothers and sisters. Therefore there is a need for an affirmative action plan in the steel industry, a plan that will eliminate the unequal status of Black steelworkers and others through adjustments in hiring, upgrading and layoffs.

There is a solid basis for unity in the struggle to raise the economic status of the 40 percent of Black Americans and the 16 percent of white Americans who are now forced to live below the official poverty level.

I N HIS BETTER DAYS ERNEST HEMINGWAY ONCE WROTE: "THE world is a fine place and worth fighting for." Yes, it is a fine place. But it is also true that without struggle, and if the corporations continue to have their way, it can be a nightmare.

Through struggle it is possible to win reforms. But the long-range truth is that no matter how many short-range victories and remedies are won and put into effect, the basic pattern, the source of the problems, will remain. As long as private corporations have control over industries such as steel and other basic industries, there will be crises and disasters for the working people.

The only way to put an end to the crises and disasters is for the people to take over the industries, the banks and the government. Only then is it possible to put an end to the evils and insatiable greed for private profits, and proceed to set up an economic system that will operate the mines, mills and banks solely for the benefit of people.

One-third of the world's people are doing just that. Socialism has become the wave of the future.

Steelworkers in the socialist countries not only do not face disasters because of layoffs; their bill of rights guarantees each worker a job — a job at his or her highest skill. In the socialist countries there are no high-paid executives, no corporate coupon clippers. The steelworkers own and operate the steel mills. They are the sole "stockholders."

It is obvious that when people themselves run the industries, they are concerned about people. No one in the executive suites of the Lykes Corporation knows or cares about the laid-off Campbell workers. All they care about is their profits. For them, the closing of the Campbell Works is nothing more than a $20 million corporate tax writeoff. Left to themselves the corporate executives will never care about people.

But there is a way to make them take notice. There is a way

to force concessions from them. And it is the only way. That way is militant, mass struggles.

If my visit here has helped stir things up, and if my being here has raised some fears in Washington and in the corporate offices — a fear that if they do not respond the steelworkers just may join the Communist Party and opt for socialism — then I am happy to have made that contribution.

Why a Left-Center Coalition

[From: "Why a Left-Center Coalition," talk to the staff of the Daily World, *1978 — slightly abridged.]*

IN GENERAL TERMS, THE TASK OF THE CENTRAL COMMITTEE OF our Party is to analyze developments and to formulate our policies and tactics in response to these developments.

Left-Center unity is a term applied mainly in the trade union movement and the workingclass movement in general. There are similar concepts of unity in other areas of mass work, but they usually have other designations. In the struggle for peace, against racism, against regressive taxation, a Left-Center concept may be too restrictive.

The Left-Center concept is a guide for building united front formations and relationships within the working class and trade union movement. It is a response to the changes that are taking place in the ranks of workers and the trade unions.

We say "Left-Center" and not "Center-Left" for a reason: to give the proper emphasis to the role of the Left as the initiating force. In other periods when the same concept was emphasized, some drew the conclusion that the Left was an unimportant afterthought, or the tail to the Center forces. We want to emphasize, therefore, that we are not giving up the idea of working for Left unity or building Left formations. The Left-Center concept does not replace any other organized forms. It unites them.

The Left-Center concept is not a new idea. This is not the first time our Party has projected this concept. It was a guide for united front movements in other periods, reflecting other realities. It is not new, but it is also not simply a return to the old; in concepts and tactics "you can't go home again" because "home" keeps changing.

The class struggle, the objective processes and the nature of class political currents of today are different. Left-Center alliance is now projected under today's conditions and relationship of forces. It is projected in its own unique historical framework.

I would like to emphasize that we have now placed this concept as the centerpiece in our trade union work. It is now the key to our trade union policies, tactics and overall approach to workingclass movements. We do this because the relationship of forces within the working class and the trade union movement has changed. It would have been a wrong emphasis in the recent past, and it would be an error now not to project it. It comes up now because it reflects the new reality and the new relationship of forces in the trade union movement, including the fact that important trade union forces are moving from Right field to Center field. This is the broadest and most significant political motion that is taking place.

One of the most serious setbacks of the McCarthy period was the destruction of the Left in the trade union movement. I considered whether the word "destruction" is too harsh. It is not. This was the most damaging development in the McCarthy period. The destruction of the Left in the trade union movement took place on all levels. And once the Left was destroyed the Right-wing elements became the unchallenged leading influence in the trade union movement and for a long period remained so. The Left was shattered and the Center was demobilized and scattered.

The Party also suffered great losses in that period. Again, the greatest losses in the Party were in the industrial areas. This also helped to create a situation where the Right was in an unchallenged position.

Because of McCarthyism and also because of some internal

weaknesses, the Party for some time did not pursue a policy of industrial concentration. Now we can fully appreciate what a weakness that was. We also had almost no shop clubs and for a time there were no shopgate distributions of leaflets or our press. This was the period when the Left was disorganized and therefore not an effective force in the trade union movement. There were of course some Left forces, but they were not organized.

The Center forces, when they did not have a Left to gravitate towards or be influenced by, were pushed to the Right. The Right influenced the Center, and in many cases the Center forces simply went along for the ride with the Right. Many became silent and passive.

After the McCarthy period the Party, with other militant trade unionists and workers, had to face the problem of how to pick up the pieces as far as the Left in the trade union movement was concerned. As the crisis of capitalism deepened and as policies of class collaboration became more evidently bankrupt, the process of radicalization shifted into higher gear. This gave impetus to a Left current. In the beginning it was a grass-roots development, in the form of rank-and-file groups.

It is a long process. The Party had to reestablish the policy of industrial concentration, which meant reestablishing shop clubs, circulating the Party press at shopgates, etc. Slowly, step by step, the Party has become an organized influence in the shops and trade unions. The Party's industrial concentration has influenced the reemergence of the Left.

The work of the Party, at each stage, has been based on the changes in the outlook and thinking of workers. The process of radicalization called for an emphasis on organized rank-and-file groups. That was a very important historic step in the process. It was based on the truth that there was no other way of basically influencing the trade union movement. It was not possible to influence or change it from the top. The rise of rank-and-file movements was a historic development because they made possible establishment of a mass base for the Left trend. Now the rank-and-file movements and groups have become the grassroots base for the Left trend on all levels.

With the development of a grassroots movement the Center elements in local and secondary leadership began to feel that there is some hope after all. They began to respond and develop a sense of confidence and to move in a more militant direction because they had a new mass base. So the development of a grassroots Left has played a very important role in creating conditions for the emergence of the broader and bolder Center forces that we have at the present time.

THE DEEPENING CRISIS OF CAPITALISM HAS GIVEN RISE TO the growth of a Left, and following that, the development of an active Center force in the trade union movement. As the crisis deepens so the policies of class collaboration go into deeper crisis. It is much more difficult for Right-wing elements to put over their ideas. As a result, the Right has been losing its influence on the Center forces. The Right has become more isolated and the Center has become more active. These Center forces have started to look for alliances and relationships with the more Left forces. This has been going on for the last number of years. Important sections of the trade union movement have separated themselves from the *status quo* of class collaboration and will not return to the old position.

A weakness becomes evident as a result of this development. The weakness showed up as reluctance and hesitation on our part to establish relationships with Center forces, both on a leadership and grassroots level, based on fears resulting from old experiences and a lack of confidence in the Left forces. This more than anything else forced us to reformulate our trade union policy more basically and to project the idea of Left-Center unity.

We felt that it was necessary for the Party and Left forces to say to the Center forces, "You're welcome. We want to work with you." And we have to say it boldly. I think we are still hesitating. The hesitation leads to sectarianism.

The reason for this hesitation is a lack of understanding of the historic moment, a lack of understanding that things have changed and that we must actively reflect this change and react to it. Everything in life must be seen in transition, including political forces and trends.

Who are the Center forces? They are honest, militant working-class trade unionists. This is true also of those on leadership levels. They are honest trade unionists. They are the largest sector in the trade unions. They are in transition from Right to Center, moving toward the Left. Therefore they must be worked with. They must be encouraged to move further from one position to another.

They most likely will not agree with the Left on all immediate questions and certainly not on a specific program. But they will agree in specific areas with the Party and with the Left, and they will work together with the Left. That is what the idea of Left-Center is all about — it is a united front between forces who agree on some questions, but disagree on others.

Center forces are in the process of becoming radicalized. The Left-Center concept is a united front policy with forces who are in transition from Right to Left. I want to emphasize this because there are historic moments when the transition is not in that direction.

This was not the case during the McCarthy period. That is a very important distinction. This is why our policy of Left-Center unity is realistic today while it would not necessarily have been realistic in other periods. We could not project this kind of program if the tendency were in the opposite direction, from Left to Right, from militant actions to passivity, to class collaboration.

I WANT TO EXPLORE THE CONCEPT OF LEFT-CENTER UNITY IN relation to the steel industry. Clearly in the steel union there are different kinds of forces. There are the Right forces — McBride, Abel, the top leadership; there are the Center forces; there is a growing organized Left force and a Communist Party.

The contest in the 1977 election campaign for the steel union leadership was between the Right forces and a Left-Center coalition. In this case it was a loose Center-Left coalition of forces. There were three organizations involved: the McBride Right-wing organization, the Sadlowski Fightback organization,[7] and the Steelworkers Rank-and-File Committee which is a gathering of numerous Left and Center rank-and-file movements and groups.

This Left-Center, rank-and-file movement plays a very important role in some specific struggles, for example in the 1977 iron miners' and taconite workers' strike in Minnesota.[8] This is a most important strike. It is a direct challenge to the anti-labor policies of Big Steel and the no-strike, class-collaborationist policy of the Right-wing leadership of the Steelworkers union. The Right-wing leadership of the union does not attack the strike, but neither does it give much support.

To get clarity it is necessary to make a more concrete assessment of which forces are Center and which are Left. And it is necessary to make this assessment by analyzing the positions of the different movements on specific issues — the economic struggles, the struggle against racism, independent political action and many others.

Examining the forces involved and their positions, it is clear that the Center forces have an intermediate position on economic struggles, not consistently militant; a Center position on the struggle against racism sometimes seeks opportunistically to get around the issue; and on political action they are moving in a Left direction but have not yet reached the level of the Left and broken with the two old parties. They are honest, positive, militant forces, often influenced by Left concepts and ideas, but they have some limitations.

Left-Center unity is designed to influence the Center forces on specific questions, but in most cases that does not mean they are therefore moved to a Left position in general. Very often there are no solid walls between the Left and the Center. There is always a mixture of Center and Left ideas that overlap. Once the correct assessment is made it becomes clear there is no contradiction between building the Steelworkers Rank-and-File Committee and working with the Center forces and Sadlowski's Fightback organization.

For example, the Left had a fundamental influence on the

Center forces on the question of the struggle against racism. This could not have been done without two things: shop clubs of Communists and a Left-Center movement like the Steelworkers Rank-and-File.

The correct assessment is important because if one thinks the Center forces are a Left force, one will expect to work with them on that level. And one can be disillusioned very quickly when they do not respond as the Left does on many burning questions of the moment. They will go only so far at a specific moment and no further.

Let's take the issue of affirmative action. The Right wing, including the Right social democrats, take the Bakke position in full support of racism.[9] That remains a serious problem. The Center forces, while taking positions against racism in general, sometimes say affirmative action is no solution but that the solution is "full employment." Under pressure from the Left they vote in favor of resolutions for affirmative action, but do not agree on measures to force its implementation. And while this position is not the same as the Right's, it is both demagogic and opportunistic. It is even self-contradictory because the working class cannot fight for full employment if it is divided, and affirmative action is a means of uniting the working class.

We have reached a point — not just in steel, but generally — where concrete plans to eliminate inequality have become a must. The plans must include adjustments in hiring, upgrading and all the other questions that arise. The plans must concretely propose adjustments in the seniority system to do away with inequality.

Such adjustments will not destroy the seniority system; on the contrary, refusal to make adjustments will destroy the seniority system. The seniority system must serve the purpose of uniting the class. Put in the context of an overall plan, white workers will understand it better and can be convinced that the adjustments in seniority, upgrading, hiring, etc., are necessary. So on this issue it is clear why a Left voice is essential. This is true of all situations. Life has proven that the Left can influence the Center, as demonstrated especially in steel.

We must guard against any error of seeing the Left as only

the Communist Party or the Communist Party as the Left. The Communist Party is very much a part of the broader Left, but there is a Left that is not Communist.

The Left-Center concept cannot be limited to actions in common. It is a much more basic concept. It cannot and should not end with a single action. It is the basis for continuing actions. And it is the basis for continually bringing Center forces toward the Left position.

The Left-Center approach in the present context means a broadening of the united front.

While developments differ in other unions, they all move in the same direction. There are parallel developments in the Machinists, Autoworkers, Longshore, Electrical and in some of the construction unions. The hold of the Right-wing forces is loosening and the Center forces are gravitating more toward Left positions. The Left-Center concept is a viable united front policy of struggle.

To conclude, the struggle to build Left-Center unity is to concretize, to give expression to the new level of political and ideological currents in the ranks of the working class and the trade union movement. It is a guide to building a broad-based unity of struggle.

The Old and the New

[Excerpts from: "The Decline of Reaganism," report to meeting of national Communist Party leadership, 1985.]

WHEN DEALING WITH DIFFERENT SECTORS OF THE PEOPLE WE must always keep in mind that they are constantly in motion, in the process of change. They move with and create new political currents. They change in an ongoing ideological process.

As a result they respond differently to events today than they did a year or five years ago. Their priorities change. When we do not take these changes into consideration, we tend to tail movements and struggles and to misjudge the thinking and mood of the masses. We become tactically stagnant. We cease to give vanguard leadership. Therefore it is necessary constantly to update our assessments and refresh our tactics.

It is always important to be alert to what is new and growing. There are situations in which the new should still be dealt with in the framework of the old. But it is most important, from a tactical viewpoint, to be able to recognize when there is a qualitative change in the relationship between the new and the old, a point when it is necessary to see the new as the dominant factor. Then the new must be seen as the framework in which we must deal with the old.

One of the new and growing factors in this period is the overlapping of issues and struggles. The objective developments bringing this about are the three layers of economic crisis: the cyclical, structural and general crises of capitalism.

This is especially true of the effects of the structural crisis. When a plant shuts down it affects all workers, all families, all communities, all small-business people.

The overlapping also holds for the fear of nuclear war. There are no hiding places from a nuclear war for any section of the population. How this issue overlaps other questions is evident in the scope of the Nuclear Freeze movement,[10] which tends to cut across all sectors of the population. The struggles that are taking place over the federal budget in a new way bring together the overlapping issues of Social Security, farm loans, interest rates, the military budget and many others.

This does not mean all the effects are equal. For instance, it does not mean there is no need for special demands and struggles against the special effects of racism or for women's equality. What it does mean, however, is that we have to take into tactical consideration that concepts like an all-people's front against Reaganism are much more in tune with these new overlapping developments. These developments create objective factors that make possible a many-sided struggle and emphasize the need for all-around unity.

A NOTHER AREA OF MASS TRENDS WHERE THE NEW MUST increasingly be taken into consideration is the maturing of class consciousness. The objective conditions that give rise to class consciousness in the ranks of workers are the experiences and struggles at the point of production.

There is a coming together in broad circles of class consciousness and rising consciousness of the role of the class struggle and the role of the working class. This creates the objective conditions for broad anti-monopoly coalitions and alliances between the working class and its allies. The maturing of class consciousness influences all sectors of the multiracial, multinational, male-female working class.

The maturing of class consciousness brings with it a deeper sense of class unity. For white workers, class consciousness becomes a stronger barrier against the influences of racism and other bourgeois influences. They see more clearly the monopoly corporations as the enemy. For Black workers, class consciousness develops to where the primary identification is with the class, leading to strong anti-capitalist sentiments. This does not mean class consciousness replaces identification with race and nationality. But the new and growing identification is with the class.

The same process is taking place in all sections of the class. The growth of class consciousness in the ranks of Mexican-American workers, including workers in agriculture, leads to a growing identification with the class. For Puerto Rican workers the dominant identification is with the working class. For other workers who have national and cultural ties with the people of other countries there is a growing identification with the working class in general, but the trend is toward identifying with the U.S. working class in particular.

With their entry into industry, there is also a new growth of class consciousness in the ranks of women. Because of the experiences of struggle and the need for unity, the class consciousness of male workers becomes a factor in eliminating male supremacist influences.

The same process takes place among the unemployed.

This maturing of class consciousness is a critical historic process, a dialectical process that takes place alongside many other developments over a period of time. But at a certain point the change becomes more obvious and operative. It has an effect on objective developments.

As the working class becomes more class conscious, its influence grows because the source of its influence is its greater unity and strength. This is also true for the different sectors: their influence grows as they become more class conscious.

This process of change should be reflected in how we approach the working class. It should determine the level and the framework in which we deal with issues.

We underestimate the level and the rate of this process. Even our description of a multiracial, multinational, male-female, young and older working class is misused. The intent was to place the emphasis on the oneness. But some place their emphasis on the separate sections. We have to be sensitive to this process, but always keep in mind that the molding and maturing will continue. Based on these concepts of what is new and growing we have drafted the new Party Trade Union Program for discussion and adoption. This new program is in response to the changes in the working class and trade union movement.

Changes are taking place because of objective developments in the class struggle. They are a response to the effects of the three-layered economic crisis, especially in response to the structural crisis. They are reactions to the Reagan/corporate offensive, to the cutbacks and concessions. They are reactions to the nuclear war danger and the escalating military budgets.

A NEW TREND TOWARD POLITICAL INDEPENDENCE IN THE trade union movement emerged in the 1984 presidential election. This new trend has surfaced on the picket lines and arrests at South African consulates. The new is emerging in the struggle against further concessions, in the fightback against the two-tier wage swindle, in the new level of class unity, of class solidarity.

The new is making its appearance in the decline of anti-Communism in the unions. It makes its presence felt in the growth of the broad Left sector, in the growth of the Party's influence within the movement. The new is strongest in the rank and file. But it is also making its way into the higher levels of the trade union leadership.

The draft Party trade union program is in response to all these new developments. The program discusses the older negatives and weaknesses. But it does so in the framework of what is new, not the new in the framework of the old. That's because of the qualitative change that is taking place.

Some comrades have difficulties with this. They tend to dismiss the new, placing an emphasis instead on the weaknesses, in the framework of the old. This leads only to pessimism and to increasingly defensive tactics. For example when we judge the labor movement, even trade union leaders, without taking into consideration the objective situations that the working class faces, our estimates are often not in accord with reality.

We have to see the trade union movement in the proper framework of today. The corporate/Reagan offensive is having its effect. The main emphasis must be on this offensive. But we have to place the trade union movement not only in the context of this offensive but also in the context of what the structural crisis has done.

This presents the working class and trade union movement with more difficult problems. We must not put the blame on the trade unions.

The major problem is the nature of the objective situation because of the structural crisis. This is what we have to deal with. We cannot deal with the unions without taking into consideration the times and the objective situation. We even have to deal with class collaboration in the proper framework.

Especially if we do not have solutions, we should be very modest with our criticisms. We must at all times be partisan to our class and to the trade union movement. It is easy to sit on the sidelines when you don't have to deal with the specifics of the corporate offensive, the structural crisis, the Reagan Administration, the new Right-wing network, the professional anti-union outfits, etc.

We must not even inadvertently undermine, underrate or attack the trade unions. We must at all times take their point of view into consideration, defend them and refuse to be critical in any way that is destructive.

Not seeing the significance of the new — the independent role of labor in the presidential elections —has already led some to draw wrong conclusions from the 1984 elections. Because they did not see the new independent role of labor they did not see the damage done by Gary Hart's anti-union "special interest groups" campaign.[11]

Of course it is possible to overstate what is new. But it is much more damaging to continue dealing with questions as if there is nothing new, because that leads to stagnant thinking and inaction.

THE STRUCTURAL CRISIS IS CAUSING DRAMATIC CHANGES IN the overall industrial complex. Industries have declined. Industries have disappeared. Some new ones have made the scene. The industrial complex is being decentralized. Of some 60 steel minimills, eight are in Florida, seven in Texas, five in California, four each in South and North Carolina, Tennessee and Georgia and two in Hawaii. It is difficult to think of Florida and Hawaii as steel centers. This is a new concept.

High-tech industries are spread throughout the 50 states. The same is true of the electrical, auto and aerospace industries. These new plants now stretch along the freeways outside the industrial centers and along the U.S.-Mexican border. Most of them are unorganized. This dispersal presents a serious problem for organizing the unorganized.

The redistribution of the industries creates new problems, but in no way changes some basic concepts:

1. It does not affect or change the nature of the class struggle;

2. It does not cut down the size of or eliminate the working class or the industrial working class;

3. It does not change the role of the working class;

4. It does not eliminate or change the basic role of the trade unions.

Because the redistribution of industries does not change our basic concepts, it does not change the need for the Party to pursue our policy of industrial concentration.

It does mean, however, that we cannot continue to put all our efforts into the older, basic industrial centers. It means we must pay more attention and put more of our human, financial and political resources to work in the new industrial states, without cutting back in the older industrial centers.

There are also changes in the old industrial states. New industrial centers have emerged in Ohio, Illinois, Michigan, Pennsylvania, California, Massachusetts and others.

Therefore, district Party organizations must also make some structural changes. Party state organizations and the clubs in the states that have recently become industrialized must now give a much higher priority to industrial concentration.

New Framework for the Class Struggle

[Excerpts from: "The Party in a New Framework," report to meeting of national Communist Party leadership, 1986.]

SINCE OUR LAST MEETING IN JUNE, 1985, SOME IMPORTANT CLASS battles have taken place — on the picket lines, at the negotiating table, on the shop floor and the assembly line.

An example of the activity and militancy is in Chicago where, besides the *Chicago Tribune* strike,[12] on any given day in October, 1985 there were 20 strikes in progress.

The strikes by Wheeling-Pittsburgh steelworkers, A.T. Massey coal miners, Bath Ironworkers, Watsonville cannery workers, Chrysler autoworkers, United Airlines pilots, Morrell and Hormel meatpackers, Pratt & Whitney aerospace workers, and the three-year-old strike by the Phelps Dodge copper miners in Morenci, Arizona, were all pattern-setting.

Each of these strikes took head-on basic anti-labor, Reaganite/corporate policies such as concessions, Chapter 11 bankruptcy,[13] two-tier wage structure, contracting out and union-busting. Many of these were strikes to save the union, the shop steward system, health care, and strikes against speedup and elimination of established health and safety regulations and work rules.

And the corporate/Reagan anti-labor union-busting drive goes on. They keep coming up with new union-busting tactics. At the Hormel plant in Austin, Minnesota, it is the old "smash the picket line and run in scabs." So far they have failed. The monopolies have been able to do away with industrywide bargaining. The steelworkers, the non-ferrous metal and American Can workers all face the coming negotiations one corporation at a time.

The attitude of American Can Corporation is typical. The company recently threatened, "Either the union agrees to a $4.50-per-hour cut or we will sell five of our 21 plants and close five more and leave the union with half of its membership to deal with." Given the new mood of militancy and fightback, this approach will never wash.

INDEPENDENT POLITICAL ACTION AND THE LABOR POLITICAL Action Committees (PACs) played an important role in the 1984 presidential elections. Trade union leadership participation on picket lines at the South African embassy, missions and consulates, as well as the longshore boycott of South African ships, marked a new level in workingclass solidarity. As John Sweeney, international president of the Service Employees International Union (SEIU), said: "It is just as much union business to support working people and trade unionists in South Africa as it is union business to support working people and trade unionists in south Alabama."

The struggles of South African labor and the widespread support from American labor came together in a new level of anti-racist, anti-apartheid positions at the AFL-CIO convention.

Twenty-two international unions joined forces with the Nuclear Freeze movement; 26 internationals took a stand against U.S. policies in Central America. As a result, U.S. aggression in Central America became a key foreign policy issue at the AFL-CIO convention.

All these activities and events reflect changes taking place in the thought patterns and mood of the rank and file. This changing thought process has been going on for some time.

All these actions are workingclass responses to the structural crisis and to the Reagan/corporate anti-labor offensive. Anger and frustration have been building against the concession policies of some union leaders. Rank-and-file militancy has been growing in the face of the ten-year decline in real wages.

A new generation of leaders has emerged in locals and central labor bodies. More militant rank-and-file leaders are being elected, as was the case in the 1985 New York teachers union elections. Interwoven with all this is the growth of a Left trend and Left forces, on both rank-and-file and leadership levels.

Some advances in the struggle against racism have been achieved, expressed in closer working relations between the trade unions and leaders of Afro-American organizations. The fires of the class struggle in South Africa, in Central America, and at home have further deepened the class consciousness and international class solidarity of our multiracial, multinational working class.

The AFL-CIO has put out a very fine pamphlet marking the birthday of Martin Luther King, Jr.: *Labor Honors an American Hero.*

There is growing concern about the growth of the non-union sector of the workforce and the decline of the workforce in the organized sector of the basic industries. When we speak about the decline in trade union membership we have to note the big layoffs in the organized industrial sector. We have to be very careful not to fall into the trap of thinking that the trade unions are in a total membership crisis. Of course there is a decline. But it is basically associated with the demise of the organized basic industries.

T HE 16TH AFL-CIO CONVENTION, HELD IN OCTOBER OF 1985, had a new tone. There was a new sense of militancy. The focus was sharply anti-monopoly, anti-multinational corporation.

Class collaborationist sentiment was on the defensive. Anti-Reagan sentiment, especially on domestic issues, was strong and militant. Anti-apartheid expressions were sharp, based on the activities of the past months. Anti-imperialist sentiment was sharp, especially in regard to Central America and South Africa.

A new anti-racist position emerged and went even further than expected. On affirmative action, it addressed the problem of changing seniority rules to ensure affirmative action.

The convention expressed an even higher level of political independence and political action, especially aimed at the 1986 congressional elections.

Some of the new tone was already reflected in the Officers' Report, which as a rule is the most conservative, even reactionary document. This time it expressed the pressures of the rank and file, central labor bodies and some internationals.

The changing labor scene made its appearance in the remarks of William Winpisinger[14] at a National Lawyers Guild convention:

It is rather amusing to note how most labor historians choose to ignore what was probably the real impetus to form the CIO and to pass much of FDR's New Deal. The major impetus was the formation of unemployment committees and councils in practically every major city in the U.S. during the 1920s and the early 1930s. Spearheading those local drives to organize the unemployed and educate them toward egalitarianism and socialism, invariably were local Communist Party organizers . . . who survived the Red Scare and smashing of the Socialists in the '20s. Many of them were intellectual-activists, like John Reed. Others were just street-smart and mule-tough veterans of union organizing drives.

On foreign policy the AFL-CIO convention positions, in general, were better than before. For example, the convention welcomed the 1985 Reagan-Gorbachev summit meeting in Geneva and called for a mutual reduction in arms. It endorsed the concept of a nuclear freeze and the easing of tensions between the U.S. and USSR. This is a setback for the anti-Sovieteers in the trade union movement. Also, the UAW introduced a resolution calling for ratification of the SALT II treaty.

The Officers' Report called for a cut in the military budget. The last Executive Council meeting talked about this but the convention endorsed it. NAACP president Benjamin Hooks got a standing ovation when he called for a cutoff of the trillion-dollar Star Wars budget.

The UAW and the AFL-CIO Industrial Union Department introduced a series of powerful resolutions on the economy, all based on cutting the military budget and converting to peace-time production. The Officers' Report condemned the KKK, the Nazi Party and the John Birch Society. This is a big step away from its cold war positions of placing both the Nazis and the Communists in the same bag.

After a bitter battle, the convention rejected the proposition as stated in the Officers' Report and voted for a compromise resolution calling for a political solution in Nicaragua and El Salvador. This was an unprecedented action. This was the first debate on foreign policy since the debate on the Marshall Plan after World War II.

There is a contradiction in the AFL-CIO policy toward Central America. On the one hand is the new convention resolution. But there is also the support for the old American Institute for Free Labor Development (AIFLD) which, in the name of the AFL-CIO, operates as an arm of the CIA and the State Department.

This outfit has over 200 full-time CIA operatives in 22 countries. Their main function is to train counterrevolutionary cadre. Their main tactic is to split the ranks of labor. Right-wing social democrats have been a leading force in these operations from the beginning. We must do more to expose these forces.

T HE INFLUENCE OF THE PARTY'S POSITION ON MANY QUES-
tions was obvious in the deliberations, the debates, speeches and resolutions. The status and influence of the Party is growing and is greatly enhanced by our new draft Trade Union Program.

There is growing desire by trade union leaders to meet with Communists. There is less redbaiting and anti-Communism. The lack of anti-Sovietism and anti-Communism in the convention was a rejection of that part of the Officers' Report.

Some of the new quality was expressed by Richard Trumka, president of the United Mine Workers Union, who said:

> U.S. foreign policy aims to make the world safe for corporate profi-
> teering. It backs any dictator of any stripe who will maintain a "good
> business climate" by keeping wages down and keeping workers
> from organizing.

Totally out of step with the mood in the convention, the international section of the Officers' Report was CIA-dictated. All the more important was the resolution passed on El Salvador and Nicaragua which rejected that section of the report. This resolution became key long before the convention itself. The 26 unions who supported and advocated it were challenged by the Shanker-Kirkland forces[15] before and at the convention.

As a writer in the January issue of the *Nation* magazine wrote, "The consensus behind the traditional Meany-Loves-tone-Brown[16] foreign policy is clearly breaking up."

One Hundred Years of Heroic Class Struggle

[From: "May Day: 100 Years of Heroic Class Struggle," speech to Political Affairs conference, 1986 — slightly abridged.]

ALTHOUGH BORN IN THE UNITED STATES, MAY DAY SPREAD TO ALL corners of the world and has become a truly international day to express labor's strength, solidarity and victories.

In the million year span of human history, 100 years is but a brief moment. The 100 years since the class battles that gave birth to May Day have been filled with great victories and achievements of the working class.

In these years of pitched battles and hardship, and through hard work and union organizing, the American working class fought its way from a downtrodden, dispersed and oppressed laboring mass to the most organized, central driving force for social progress in our capitalist society. More than ever the class struggle is the jet stream of history.

The victories of the world revolutionary process are monuments to the prophetic speech of August Spies at the opening of the Haymarket kangaroo court:[17]

> In addressing this court I speak as a representative of one class to the representative of another class. And if you think that by hanging us you can stamp out the labor movement, if this is your opinion, then hang us. But here you tread upon a spark. But there and everywhere flames will blaze up. It is a subterranean fire. You cannot put it out.

Clearly, Spies had the class struggle in mind.

The years of workingclass victories are also a grand tribute to the last words of Albert Parsons before his hanging: "There will come a time when our silence will be more powerful than the voices you strangle today." Parsons, too, thus spoke as one with the class struggle.

Because of the class struggle, the "subterranean fires" have continued to flare everywhere in class battles and the silence from the Haymarket gallows has become the loudest and clearest workingclass voice the world over. The heroic class struggle achievements are also monuments to the farseeing Karl Marx, who was able to make the connection between the Haymarket era and May Day, and the connection between history and the class struggle:

> Out of the death of slavery a new life at once arose. Thus the first fruit of the Civil War was the eight-hour struggles that ran with seven-league boots from New England to California.

Here too, Karl Marx saw the class struggle as the driving force of history.

Thus, when we pay tribute to labor and its achievements, it is the class struggle that we are honoring.

T HERE HAVE BEEN OTHER HOLIDAYS SET ASIDE TO RECOG- nize and pay tribute to the achievements of working men and women. In fact, this was the original meaning of the Fourth of July. In the early years after the American Rev- olution and until the end of the nineteenth century, July 4 was set aside to honor labor. But for one hundred years only May Day has retained the unique, radical, militant, class-struggle character of mass protest, of marches and demonstrations for workers' demands, a day to display labor's strength, unity and international solidarity.

The half-million workers who downed tools and walked off jobs to march on the first May Day set the pattern, the theme and tone that has been expressed every May Day since. What has given May Day this unique character is the fact that it was cast in the furnace of the class struggle and through the years it has maintained this inherited characteristic.

May Day serves the purpose of paying tribute to labor's heroes and heroines. But its greatest significance is in restating and reasserting the centrality of the class struggle. It restates something that would seem to be obvious — at least it should be the most obvious characteristic of capitalist society, because it is the main irreconcilable contradiction of our class society.

Unfortunately, it is not so obvious to the many who are confused. And it is all too obvious to those who deliberately distort this central fact of life under capitalism. It is not obvious because there has been and continues to be a most persistent and elaborate campaign to deny its existence, to cover it up, to downgrade and to bury it.

It is possible to do this mainly because the working class is often not seen as a class. For example, the class composition of a demonstration is not visible to the eye, even though the majority of demonstrators are trade unionists and workers. Although the majority of civil rights and anti-war demonstrations were made up of working people, most often the speakers were professionals or intellectuals — the visible ones.

However, the reality is that the vast majority at demonstrations are working people, trade union activists, men and women, rank-and-file, trade union leaders, working, laid off, on strike.

To deny or cover up the centrality of the class struggle is to deny the very existence of the main mover of history. Denying the centrality of the class struggle is to deny the root cause of all forms of oppression. This is the source and mainstay of all forms of class collaborationist sellouts.

Denying the reality of the class struggle is the polluted fountain head for all brands of Trotskyism, Maoism, Eurocommunism and, of course, Browderism. The demarcation line, the dividing line in all fields of thought, including philosophy, has its source in the class struggle.

To deny or downgrade the class struggle is to accept the concepts inherent in the phony ideology of a classless capitalism, classless politics and classless philosophy. To push a classless capitalism, classless politics, classless philosophy and culture is to run interference for monopoly capitalism. It is a way of defending the indefensible, or justifying the unjustifiable.

Some advocates of a classless world no longer feel they can say it outright, but instead hint at it with phrases like: "As a philosophical and economic theory Marxism has had its golden age." Or "Concepts of class struggle and revolutions are today no more than echoes of a great, age-old myth."

Another American professor argues: "The scientific revolution has made the exploitation of nature so effective that the exploitation of man by man has become unprofitable and obsolete." The main problem with this is that computers and the unemployed are not paying customers.

Out of these conjured-up theories one is supposed to draw the real-life conclusion that the class struggle itself has become obsolete — has, in fact, disappeared. Then we are supposed to draw the logical conclusion that if the class struggle has become nothing more than an old myth, the working class has been so transformed that it has joined the ranks of the exploiters and is no longer a class unto itself and thus has no independent class positions. Then we are irresistibly compelled to draw the conclusion that trade unions are disappearing or losing their place and role in society.

The final conclusion in this illogical sequence of deductions is that because of all these changes — because the class struggle has disappeared, because trade unions are outmoded — there is, therefore, certainly no need for a revolutionary workingclass party like the Communist Party, USA.

From their nitpicking dream world the anti-labor forces conjure up the ultimate fantasy: that there never has been anything to echo or to become obsolete because for them the class struggle never existed. Thus the ideological trap is sprung. This is the main aim and the ultimate result of rejecting and denying the very existence of the class struggle. Fortunately, the direction of history is not determined by the negative, anti-labor nitpickers.

The truth is that, in spite of the rhetoric from these nitpicking anti-labor forces, it is not the class struggle that is "an echo of an old myth." It is not the working class and revolutionaries who are "obsolete."

The class struggle is in the very center of the law-governed process of socioeconomic development. And this process of history, this law-governed process, moves irrevocably in a forward, progressive direction. The propellent, the moving force of this progressive direction, is the working class on the winning side of the class struggle.

S INCE THE FIRST MAY DAY, THE CLASS STRUGGLE SCORE-board has recorded setbacks and lost innings. But in the total games played and won, the working class is in a world-class all by itself.

The establishment of socialism in over one-third of the world is the greatest of all workingclass victories. The 27th Congress of the Communist Party of the Soviet Union, held in February of 1986,[18] was a reflection of the crowning achievements of workingclass economic and political power. One can say that for some 68 years socialism has won the class struggle world series every year. This is the result of better planning, better coaching and management, better pitching, more home runs and superior teamwork.

The working class was the main force in saving the world from Hitler fascism. The working class has been the dominant force in the victories of national liberation. And after liberation, it is the decisive force in choosing the new direction of the country.

This is demonstrated in the present debate over what the developing countries should do about the trillion-dollar debt owed to imperialist banks and governments. Because of their class viewpoint, workingclass organizations generally take the position that these loans should be cancelled because the imperialist banks and governments have collected more than the trillion dollars in unjustified interest payments and unfair trade relations.

The working class has become the main force in the struggle against all forms of imperialism, oppression and aggression. The struggle for peace and the effects of the devastating military budgets on economic conditions has moved the issue of war or peace into the arena of the class struggle. On critical flashpoint issues such as Central America, Nicaragua, El Salvador and South Africa, the working class has moved into leadership.

In the capitalist countries, including the United States, the working class has become the most consistent anti-monopoly force. The rise of monstrous multinational corporations, whose tentacles reach across national boundaries, has given these corporations new sources of extra profits and new maneuverability. These multinationals and the internationalization of capital and production present the working class and the class struggle with a new kind of challenge. In a sense, this dictates the need for internationalization of the class struggle.

As a minimum, this calls for new kinds of international class unity, for new tactics, such as multinational-union strikes against the multinational corporations, worldwide boycotts of products, and international labor contracts.

On this one hundredth May Day anniversary, the U.S. working class and the class struggle confront the challenge of the continuing Reagan/corporate anti-labor racist offensive. The labor movement has to find ways to go from defensive struggles, from policies of taking cutbacks and concessions, to offensive fightback struggles.

The trade unions face the problems resulting from the fusion of huge corporate galaxies. The mergers of RCA with GE and Hughes Aircraft with GM produced trillion-dollar monsters. The multibillion dollar military monopolies like Boeing, Lockheed, General Dynamics and McDonnell-Douglas have developed into the corrupt, reactionary core of the military monopoly complex, corporations making most of their profits from military production.

The emergence of new technology is also creating new problems for the working class. Here again the anti-labor nitpickers make their appearance. They agree there have been objective developments such as new science and technology. But like a broken record they keep repeating: "The new technology has so changed production that the working class has ceased to exist."

It is true that there are technological changes taking place in the kind of work that workers perform. But this in no way changes the basic essence of class exploitation or the class struggle.

On the U.S. class struggle scoreboard there have been innings lost, but mainly games won. The right to organize legal unions was a battle that lasted for 100 years. Labor lost many players and innings. But the game was finally won. The battle-ground was the shops and picket lines. And finally, in 1935, Roosevelt signed the victory into law.

IN THE FOUNDING YEARS OF THE AFL THERE WAS A CONSTITU-tional bar against racism. Affiliated unions had to remove all "color bars" before they were given an AFL charter. However, after the rise of the big corporations which put tremendous class collaborationist pressures on the unions, the constitutional bar against racism was put on the shelf.

There were other restrictions. The corporations barred Black workers from learning skills and from entering apprentice programs. And state governments barred Afro-American workers from obtaining trade licenses. The early trade union leadership used these discriminatory practices to bar Black workers from unions that were organized along craft lines. The craft unions were based on racist discrimination.

In 1902, based on a study, Dr. W.E.B. DuBois[19] concluded that the AFL's policy regarding racism had "regressed." This report stated that 43 craft unions had no Black members and that one-half of the 40,000 Afro-Americans in the unions were members of the coal miners' union. Thus, the official union policy became total racial segregation and organizing Black workers into separate locals. This policy remained intact until the organizing drives of the CIO.

The trade union movement has traveled a long road from the total acceptance and practice of racial discrimination in the workplace and within the trade unions to an anti-racist position at the AFL-CIO's 16th Convention just a few months ago, which passed resolutions calling for adjustments in the seniority system in order to ensure affirmative action.

Thus, while there are many miles to go in the road to full equality, the class struggle has made significant progress.

The new patterns and the new direction do not, in any way, change or moderate the class struggle. In fact it is sharper, more on the surface and more focused on the class enemy.

The new challenge that the class struggle must take on is

the deepening and widening crisis of everyday living: 30 million of our people live below the poverty level. At the height of an economic upturn 20 million are unemployed; five million people, many of them children, are homeless and hungry; 250,000 farm families are evicted each year.

The sharpening struggle against the increase in racism across our land is having a deep effect on the working class and class struggle. This is also changing the thought patterns of the working class and the essence and forms of the class struggle. These new thought patterns were reflected in the 16th AFL-CIO Convention.

WHILE WE RECOGNIZE THE RISE IN CLASS CONSCIOUSNESS and criticize its sometimes slow development, we must also take note of the many factors in U.S. history that have slowed down the maturing of class consciousness, the many factors that often flattened the sharp peaks with valleys.

U.S. capitalism had the best of all conditions for its development and growth — rich in natural resources, a big supply of immigrant labor and skills. In later years there were the profits from foreign, imperialist exploitation. Add to this the racism, transferred from the slave market, that has been and continues to be a special source of superprofits and capital accumulation.

These unique features have been slowly deteriorating, and with this deterioration the class struggle has sharpened. In turn, the sharpened class struggle has brought in its wake a growing class consciousness. The class struggle creates new material for the development of class consciousness.

But the human brain is not a clean sheet on which you can write whatever you like, as Mao Tse Tung once thought. To make room for new class struggle concepts it is necessary to remove some of the old, class collaborationist anti-workingclass ideas that surround workers — ideas that justify class exploitation. Workers are told every day in many ways that nothing can be done, that this is the way it is and the way it will always be. To help develop class consciousness it is necessary to fight against wrong concepts and at the same time inject new ideas to replace them. Such a process is a most important feature of class struggle.

It is only the Communist Party that can bring to the working class a consciousness of itself as a class. It is the party of the working class. This is the main leadership role of the Communist Party. It helps the working class to recognize the need for its own political party. It translates the experiences of workers into class conscious concepts. It helps to transform trade union consciousness into class and socialist consciousness.

This is an important aspect of May Day events. It is the process of replacing old ideology with new ideas that support and fortify the working class in its daily battles with the class enemy.

The class struggle will go through changes in form, but it will be around, influencing events and the course of history, so long as there are classes of exploiters and exploited, so long as there are two world socioeconomic systems. Those who ignore the centrality of the class struggle will not only lose their direction but find themselves in the swamp of opportunism.

To ignore the centrality of the class struggle is to knowingly or unknowingly be on the side of monopoly capital. Ideological clarity and firmness is possible only if it is rooted in a clear understanding of the class struggle. It forces one to take sides. One cannot sit on the fence between two opposing classes in a class battle.

For example, taking the side of socialism in the world arena is taking the side of the working class — as one would support a strike struggle. A deeper understanding of the class struggle is necessary to have a deeper understanding of the role of the working class in history.

Such is the main lesson and meaning of 100 years of May Days, the Haymarket history and the class struggle.

This is where the science of Marxism-Leninism and the indispensable role of the Communist Party comes onto the stage of history. The Communist Party is itself a product of the class struggle. Its roots are in the strike struggles, the unemployed marches, the organizing drives, the struggles against racism and for women's equality. The Party is the most consistent force for class unity.

Marxism-Leninism makes it possible to understand the whole picture, not just passing scenes. The Communist Party helps the working class to see where we have been, where we are, where we are going and how to get there.

On this 100th May Day we are very proud to announce that with the help of thousands of trade unionists, peace fighters and fighters for equality we are going to start the publication of a new, national daily newspaper that will be published simultaneously on both coasts, East and West.

Our new *People's Daily World* will give life to August Spies' prediction that "everywhere the flames will blaze." It will help fulfill Albert Parsons' defiant prophesy, "The voices you silence by strangling us here will grow into a powerful mighty voice heard the world over." The new *People's Daily World* will be just such a flame, just such a voice.

The class struggle takes no time off. It will play its role to the very end. And when the working class leads the struggle that will finally put an end to the capitalist system of exploitation, when it retires the old capitalist class, as a final glorious act it will collectively proclaim its own end. For there will no longer be a need for workers to act as a class.

Ironic as it may seem, in the end the anti-labor nitpickers will be right — the class struggle will wither away, the working class will have fulfilled its historic role. All the future May Days will celebrate the advances and achievements of communist society. Future May Days will pay tribute to the new victories of humanity in its total mastery over nature and the cosmos.

Basics of the
Class Struggle

laws of motion

The Science of the Working Class

The Working Class

[From an unpublished manuscript: "The Working Class," written in 1966.]

WHENEVER A ZIG OR A ZAG IN THE REALITIES OF LIFE DOES NOT correspond to a straight and narrow preconceived and shallow concept of a theory, the theory itself comes under question. That theories and basic concepts are being challenged is healthy and necessary. Theoretical concepts develop in the process of being measured and tested against realities and new experiences.

But each of these new challenges must be put through the most thoroughgoing examination because a zig or a zag does not make a new reality, nor does a challenge necessarily disprove or add to an old theory. General basic concepts have earned acceptance because they have been proven correct by a long historic train of life's zigs and zags.

The realities of life very often do not unfold in the exact pattern of a theory. That is why a theory cannot be compared to a blueprint. But this in no way reduces or minimizes the role of theory as a guide to the understanding of the unfolding of reality and as a framework for judging new experiences.

Because theory is the purified and tested guideline of human wisdom resulting from human experience, challenges to the theory based on evidence gathered from relatively limited activities and studies must of necessity get a close scrutiny.

Social, political and economic theories are not neutral or indifferent to the issues between contending classes. They rise from and reflect a class point of view: the theories either challenge or they apologize for the class in power. Theories that have challenged either the permanency of capitalism or its right to continue are under constant attack. Of all the theories challenging capitalism, Marxism is the most consistent and rounded-out. It has "staying power" because it is a science.

I N THE USA, ANY THEORY THAT EVEN RECOGNIZES THE SIMPLE idea of classes and class struggle comes under the heaviest ideological barrage. I believe this is the only country left where Marx is still seriously charged with the crime of inventing the working class and the class struggle.

The attacks on Marxist concepts are insidious and indirect as well as direct and open. The open attacks are geared to discouraging any newcomer from studying Marxism. The indirect and insidious, especially the attack with a "radical" or "socialist" cover, is geared to confuse, to divert those who are already influenced by Marxist concepts.

It is within the context of overall sharpened ideological struggles that one must deal with the new challenges to Marxist concepts arising within the growing Left movement in our country. One of the basic theoretical concepts that has of late come under question and suspicion, and is in fact being openly challenged, is the Marxist concept that the working class is the only consistent progressive and revolutionary class in our society — that all social progress must of necessity, and increasingly so, lean and depend on this class as the basis of advancement. Marxism holds that the working class is the only class whose long-range self-interests are not tied to the *status quo* of capitalism but whose class interests necessitate the advance of all society through the elimination of capitalism and the construction of socialism: a system whose ultimate purpose is ensuring a life of abundance and of creativity for all the earth's human inhabitants.

The challenge is, first, whether the working class is in fact politically living up to its advance Marxist billing, and second, if the working class is not disappearing altogether because machines are replacing it.

Here is how the challenge is formulated by one writer: "What I am trying to suggest is that an examination be undertaken from a socialist viewpoint of the proposition that the unions in America may play a progressive role at some points in history but that normally they are neutral and sometimes even reactionary because they operate within the framework of a *status quo* they accept."

The writer continues, "This proposition leads me to the second, even larger and more troublesome question. Is it possible that the role assigned to the working class is also fallacious?" And further, "Why is the working class assigned this role? What is there about the working class that makes it uniquely fitted for such a task?" And, accusingly, "The question of the role played by the working class in general is one which socialists might reexamine with reward. It would be interesting, too, to study, for example, the role played by the working class in the rise to power of European fascism and the annihilation of the Jews."

More than a question, this is a condemnation before a study. Or even worse, this is a refusal to accept the conclusions of studies that have been made and which prove that within the context of the level of the overall struggle, the working class is the one class against which such an accusing finger cannot be pointed.

And a husband-and-wife team proclaims, "We submit, however, that the cybernation revolution poses an impasse for socialists also: it presents us with nothing less than the liquidation of the working class as a significant component of society." And, "It is now a rapidly declining class. Its most skilled and adaptable members are recruited into the lower ranks of the lackeys." Continuing, they say the working class is "no longer subjected to homogeneous conditions of life, they no longer have the basis for a common philosophy; workingclass solidarity has become a nostalgic legend."

Here the fondest dream of capitalist ideologists becomes a reality at the stroke of a Trotskyite pen. But it remains a mirage.

Others argue that the Cuban and Chinese Revolutions prove that the working class or a workingclass party are not necessary for the establishment or the building of socialism, when in fact the Cuban and all socialist revolutions and the building of socialism in these countries is proof for just the opposite conclusion.

When pondering these challenges, one must keep in mind that they are voiced by people who claim they are in the workingclass/socialist corner. The above examples are open challenges. But these ideas are also reflected in many undercurrents, of honest questioning and doubts, about the role of the working class.

On the surface these concepts would seem to question only the role of the working class. But in reality the challenge goes much deeper because it is impossible to deal with such a basic element as the working class as if it were in a vacuum. You cannot remove half of the foundation of a building and pretend it will have no effect on the building. So, in a further sense, it is a challenge to the basic class character of capitalist society. It is a denial of classes and the class struggle.

Where these theories about the disappearance of the working class lead its proponents is shown by the second article which states, "In the United States the current revolution calls not for socialism, but something beyond it." It follows: once you eliminate the working class, you also eliminate socialism. How much more nonsense can there be in one sentence? The working class and socialism are banished and excommunicated in the name of radicalism — but only between the covers of certain journals of the so-called New Left.

This is an extreme example of the political dead-end to

which such theories lead. But there are many milder variations of this same theme peddled under many different guises. Their net effect is to confuse and discourage, and to undermine confidence in the working class and in socialism.

I WANT TO DEAL SEPARATELY WITH THE MAIN ARGUMENTS AS they are presented by the "liquidators" of the working class. The first school sees the working class actually disappearing because of automation and cybernation. The second, and possibly the most prominent of all these schools sees the working class disappearing as a "political factor," as a "social force" of "any consequence."

In dealing with these challenges, let us keep in mind some of the facts. The USA is the most industrialized country in the world. When compared with the rest of our population, the U.S. working class is the largest in the world. In total numbers and in relation to the rest of the population, our working class continues to grow.

The number of our people who make a living by working for someone else, and are therefore the victims of exploitation, has now reached the figure of 75 million.[1] With their families, they are about two out of every three of our people.

Both groups of "liquidators" of the working class, but especially the first one, accomplish their objective by scaling down, by narrowing the concept of what or who is the working class. This is not always done openly. The narrowing-down mainly takes place when the working class is put on the scales of: "What is the working class doing?"

As a rule, in these considerations some or all of the following sections of the working class are left out: unorganized workers, Black workers, white collar workers, unemployed — especially the young unemployed — workers, retired workers, agricultural workers, students who are workers or who come from workingclass families, professional workers, workingclass women and wives of workingclass husbands, and workers from automated departments or industries. Then, of what is left the question is asked, "What is the working class doing?"

Such a concept is narrow and does not reflect reality. The working class is not all of one identical mold. There are workers in basic industries, there are manual workers and white collar workers. These differences are of significance, but in a fundamental assessment of what is the working class, all of its components must be thrown onto the scales.

Then there is another side to this narrowing concept. In arguing about what the working class does not do, they refuse to consider as workingclass activity any but that which is taking place strictly through the trade unions. But the lives of workers and their relationship to society is much more than trade union activity. It is a weakness, but American workers tend to view the trade unions as a factor only in relation to their jobs. If trade union activity was the total field of workers' participation, then this weakness could be used as an argument in the assessment of the overall activities of the class. But workers are active and influence their surroundings in many other places and ways. They are an overall community force.

Within the context of the overall prevailing level of political activities of the American people, the words and deeds of the working class have always been progressive and are heavily weighted in that direction. The working class was the center for the defeat of Goldwater and the ultra-Right in the 1964 elections.[2] Workers are active in churches, in fraternal organizations, social clubs, political organizations. They leave their class trademark in everyday activities as a part of a community. They are the mainstay of the senior citizen movement and of the campaign for Medicare, as well as for public education and all social legislation.

In a broad sense, how these organizations which are not considered workingclass organizations react to events can very often be traced to their class composition. The greater the workingclass component, the more likely they are to take a more progressive position. So again, one cannot take the narrow and limited approach of weighing only that which the workers do in and through their trade unions.

Of course it is also true that, on some issues and under certain circumstances, even workingclass organizations may take a backward position — but this only reflects anti-workingclass influences in their ranks or pressures from other classes or social strata. For a truthful assessment it is necessary to take in all the components and all the activities the class participates in. For example, the firm backbone of the mass actions for civil rights in Birmingham and Montgomery has been the Black workers of Alabama.

Now let us examine the other school of thought: that the working class has ceased to exist as any "meaningful political factor" in American life. This conclusion would be wrong even if its proponents limited its application to the past and present. But to compound the error, they rule out any possibility of the working class ever playing any kind of a progressive or revolutionary role.

The arguments for this outlook are in fact nothing more than a warmed-up version of the old story that the working class has become fat, complacent, submissive and totally corrupt. The new version adds: "The working class has become a partner in the establishment," "It has become a guardian of the status quo," "It has become a conscious, active partner and a recipient of the spoils from U.S. overseas imperialist exploitation," etc., etc. How a class that is in such a sad condition has been able to contribute to progressive America — how it has been able to fight militantly for its rights, would be one of the miracles of our times!

Most of these contentions are based on a fraction of the truth. But the conclusions are set forth as if they were based on the whole truth. A conclusion drawn from a partial truth is always onesided. It limps, and if persisted in, the onesidedness increases until finally it turns into its very opposite. It becomes a totally wrong conclusion. In this case a discussion about the weaknesses of the working class has turned into an anti-workingclass position. A discussion about changes in the working class has turned into a discussion about its disappearance.

L ET US BRIEFLY TAKE A LOOK AT THESE PARTIAL TRUTHS. IN A fundamental sense the working class is a creation of capitalism. Because of its close relationship to the capitalist system of production, the working class is the same the world over. However, the speed and the level of its development, its class consciousness, how far it is along the path of realizing that a new economic and political order is necessary and its understanding and commitment that it must take the lead in that struggle — all this varies from country to country. The American working class is a creation of the United States capitalist system of production. Therefore, it must be studied, not in the abstract but within its natural surroundings of U.S. capitalism.

What are some of the specific factors that have influenced the course of U.S. capitalism as well as shaped the U.S. working class that has emerged in the process?

Capitalism in the USA has developed in the context of the most favorable circumstances that nature can provide. Ours is a country endowed with the greatest sources of raw materials, a land rich in soil with great areas where there is a perfect balance of moisture and sun, a country with tremendous water resources. This was a setting which truly could have been a land of abundance for all.

Because of the historic period of its emergence, the United States was for generations the recipient of the best skills, trades and professions of large sections of the world. U.S. capitalism exploited immigrant labor and pitted one national group against another in order to make ever greater profits. Thus, many factors contributed historically to the growth of capitalism in our country.

Capitalism was not responsible for the riches of nature. In fact capitalism in its greed has squandered the resources and ravaged the natural beauty of our land. The riches of nature truly belong to our people. Capitalism confiscated them and enriched itself at the expense of our people even as it was brutal in the exploitation and oppression of workers.

Capitalism waged the most scandalous, most criminal loot-ing of public wealth in the history of humankind. Within a few years the land area of the United States, with its tremendous natural riches was parcelled out, through schemes and swindles, to a few thieving families. This was the starting point for most of today's rich families. They are the inheritors of the loot from the most criminal robberies of all ages. The fact that the U.S. had no feudal past, as Europe did, eliminated many obstacles to rapid industrial expansion and creation of capitalist relations in production and trade. Unions were outlawed and persecuted as conspiracies.

At an early stage, capitalism benefitted from the war against Mexico. An imperialist era was launched with the war against Spain. Then the United States was spared the devastation of two world wars. While much of the world was bombed, burned and killed in the two world wars, the United States further enriched itself. The "arsenal of democracy" was in fact a lucrative military arms business. Taking advantage of these "favorable circumstances" when its allies and opponents were in ruins, U.S. capitalism moved in. It took over industries, sources of raw materials and markets throughout the world.

Thus, U.S. capitalism became the dominant imperialist power, with more overseas investments than the rest of the capitalist world put together.

All this has greatly enriched U.S. capitalism. It has given U.S. capitalism reserves that are not available to other capitalist countries. This has greatly enhanced U.S. capitalism's competitive position.

The economic gains won by our working class are not gifts from a rich, benevolent capitalist class. They are victories from long, sharp, hard-fought, militant class battles. U.S. capitalism has a record of brutality against the U.S. working class that no capitalism can match. The economic gains of American labor and the people are monuments to the tens of thousands of labor heroes, the thousands of martyrs who gave their lives in these struggles.

The riches of U.S. capitalism have in no way stopped Big Business from extracting the absolute maximum profits from the U.S. working class. As big as the overseas operations of

U.S. capitalism are, the main base of its exploitation — the main source of its fabulous profits — is the U.S. working class.

The USA has the highest rate of exploitation among the industrial capitalist countries of the world. Speedup on the production line is the most fearsome and the rate of industrial accidents in this country is the highest in comparison to the other industrial capitalist countries of the world. The U.S. has among the highest rates of unemployment in the world. The exhaustion of the total lifetime reserve ability to work is more rapid and devastating than anywhere in the world. The U.S. worker is a cog in the largest, most speeded-up, brutal, dehumanized industrial complex in the world.

The seatwarming philosophers should never forget that up to less than 30 years ago trade unions were illegal in the basic industries in all parts of the nation. Up to 25 years ago a union picket was fair game for a company gunman or a state trooper, without fear of arrest.

U.S. workers have had to fight for every concession. They are forced to be ever-vigilant and on guard. The pressure of the employer is ever present. As soon as the guard is down, the employers move in. It is only in this context that it is possible to discuss realistically the effect of secondary influences on class relations in the USA.

Imperialist exploitation has given U.S. capitalism reserves that it would not otherwise have. While the great bulk of these extra profits goes into the coffers of the big monopoly corporations, some of the crumbs trickle into the income of smaller businesses and into the paychecks of a small section of workers. It is difficult to judge exactly to what extent the additional reserves which U.S. capitalism has from its imperialist exploitation influence the nature of the concessions it is forced to give to the U.S. working class. However, it is one of the factors that influences these concessions.

This influence is not only in one direction. Imperialism forces down the wages and working conditions in its imperialist holdings and then uses this as a lever, as a threat over the heads of the workers in the domestic plants.

U.S. capitalism has used both its imperialist holdings and

the oppression of the Afro-American people as a source of superprofits and as a system to extract greater profits from the
working class in general. The threat of a runaway shop has become an effective instrument in the struggle against the working class.

To view the U.S. working class as a partner of monopoly
capital in its imperialist exploitation is a slander and a falsehood. The U.S. working class is a victim of the same monopoly
capital as are the workers of the U.S.-owned plants in other
lands.

This type of slander is not going to be helpful in getting the
U.S. working class to meet its historic responsibilities in fighting against imperialism. The people on the Left who spread
this slander are only placing additional obstacles in the path of
giving leadership to the working class.

SOME ON THE LEFT WANT TO BYPASS THE CONCEPT OF THE
class nature of capitalism by attempting to replace "working class" by the concept of "the poor." This also is a variation of the same theme. It is another way of saying the working class either "is no more" or "is not a political factor." Or it is
a way of saying the working class is not "poor." This variation
is based on some other misconceptions that being "poor" is all
that it takes to make one a revolutionary. From this premise
then follows the idea of "the worse, the better — the poorer,
the better." This then leads to the other side of the liquidation-
ist circle: "There is nothing you can do with the working class
because it is not poor enough; it is fat and complacent."

The truth is that most of the poor are a part of the working
class and most of the working class is poor. The unemployed
are the poorest section of the working class. They do not seek
solutions through private business ventures. They look for
class solutions, for jobs, unemployment insurance, etc. One
must not confuse the unemployed with the small number of
those who have become demoralized, the drifters. These people will never become the basis for mass struggles. These are
what Marx called the *lumpen* elements — who have given up

the fight for a better life, even as individuals.

It is true there are other "poor" besides the working class. There are small farmers, and even some small-business people who are very poor. However, this poverty does not necessarily lead them towards a revolutionary position. In fact, some tend to seek solutions by improving their economic status. They want to get more by improving their private business.

The very essence of capitalism is that it is a society of exploiters and the exploited. Class division results from one class exploiting another. The end result and the only purpose of this exploitation is private profit for the exploiters.

This exploitation — the source of all profits — takes place at the point of production. It is here that the working class produces more than it gets back in the form of wages. It is the difference between the added value this class produces and what it is paid back that is the source of all profits.

This is what capitalist production is all about. This is what has divided capitalist society into classes: the exploiters and the exploited, the haves and have-nots. This is the basis of the social volcano called the class struggle. The class struggle arises from this clash between the class interests of the working class and the capitalist class.

This basic class structure of capitalism has in no way changed. It is so in all capitalist countries. It remains so in the USA. It will remain so as long as capitalism exists. The two basic classes, the working class and the capitalist class, and the class struggle between them, are going to remain with us as long as we have capitalism.

The working class will continue to struggle for a bigger share of what it produces and the capitalist class will continue to do everything in its power to increase its already lion's share of what the working class produces. The economic struggle over a greater part of what is produced takes place in the form of speedup, lower wages, cuts in piece rates on the one hand, and labor's economic demands on the other. The new technology in the hands and control of the capitalist class has become an instrument in this struggle. It has given the exploiters an additional advantage. It has increased their profits while further separating the workers from their tools.

The struggle between the two dominant classes also sets the framework for all political activities in the country. There are other contradictions, other factors that influence the political picture, but the most fundamental and long-range influence is the struggle between the two main classes. The power and the organs of government, and most laws that are passed, are instruments in this struggle.

The "struggle for the minds of men" is in fact a reflection of the class struggle. This struggle is the most basic influence on all political, social, economic and philosophical trends. In fact, our dispute with the "liquidators" of the working class is a reflection of the class struggle.

Now let us go a little further into the nature of classes. A class is an economic community of people having in common their relationship to the system of production. The working class is such a unified class community. Workers have a common relationship to the capitalist economic structure. They are the producers, the exploited. They are therefore the source of all profits. They are a class because in common they are forced to make a livelihood by selling the only thing they possess: the power to produce, their labor power.

They are forced to submit themselves to be exploited by the capitalist class because they have no other possible way of making a living for themselves and their families. They make the equivalent value of a livelihood and then are forced to work additional hours from which the class of parasites gathers its profits. It is these additional hours that have produced all wealth: capital accumulated in the form of money, machinery, factory buildings, and including the new automated equipment that is replacing the working hands.

This also shows that error has its logic and development as much as truth does. The working class arises from exploitation. If the working class has disappeared, this could be possible only because exploitation has ceased. If exploitation has ceased, then the private appropriation of profits has disappeared. If the source of profits has disappeared, then profits are no more. If profits are a thing of the past, then capitalism must have tiptoed away, and for some "unexplained" reason we have "the rich and the poor." The reason we still have the rich and the poor is that poverty is too real for even the "liquidators" to deny!

H AS THE BASIC RELATIONSHIP OF THE WORKING CLASS TO capitalist production fundamentally changed? Is the class relationship of the present-day automated coal miner to such questions as production, profits, wages, and speedup in any basic way different from the class relationship of the old pick-and-shovel coal miners?

Have the questions of who is exploited and who gets the profits in any way changed? The working class is still exploited — except more so. The unpaid hours of workers' labor are still the source of profits — except even more so.

Whether they are operating automated equipment, or working only part-time, or unsuccessfully trying to sell their labor power, the basic class relationship of today's miners, steelworkers, autoworkers, and all other workers, remains the same as always. They are the exploited class. They are the source of all profits. Because they have this common relationship to the capitalist economic structure they have been and they remain the working class.

There are changes that take place within the ranks of the working class. These are important but they do not change the basic class status of workers. How dirty one's hands get while working or the color of one's shirt are not factors that determine class status. They are signs of one's trade or skill. New technology has brought about some very drastic changes of this nature.

Technological advances within capitalism have always had the dual effect of replacing working hands and speeding up the production processes for the remaining workers. Automation and cybernation have dramatically speeded up these processes. The dual effects of new technology can be seen from the following figures.

Output per worker-hour has gone up from 70.9 in 1947 to

105.3 in 1960 and 113.4 in 1962. At the same time, output for each dollar spent on plant equipment per year has gone up from 724 in 1947 to 854 in 1957 to 924 in 1962.

All this adds up to ever higher rates of exploitation, record-breaking profits for Big Business and an ever higher rate of the permanently unemployed. Big Business has taken the new technology and turned it into a bonanza for itself and a Frankenstein for the workers and the mass of the American people. Not one penny from either the new higher-per-worker output or the higher output from each capital dollar spent has been turned over to the people in the form of price reductions.

Unemployment was born with capitalism. It arises from the very nature of wage exploitation. But new technology has added a new quality to this problem. It has already created an army of young workers who have never even been permitted to join the periodical cycle of work and unemployment. These are young workers who graduate from being teenaged to permanently unemployment. What is worse, large sections of these youth never hope to enter the labor pool. They are considered as "economic untouchables," as "outcasts." For most, as things stand there is no hope for them to become wage earners. As long as the possibility of being hired remains closed, then even training programs and youth camps become only temporary relief, something to tide them over.

Temporary relief is helpful when the problem is temporary. Such measures are acceptable as relief during a period of an economic crisis. But today this permanent unemployment takes place at the very top of a boom period. What happens when the training periods are over and there are even fewer jobs available than when the training started?

Unemployed workers are a section of the working class whether or not they are successful in selling the one thing they have — their power to produce. This does not change their class status. They are victims of the same system of exploitation.

All attempts to view the unemployed as some kind of "non-class" or "*lumpen* elements" must be rejected. All attempts to place the interests of the unemployed as being in basic contradiction to the employed workers' interests must also be rejected as totally false. The common enemy of both is the system of capitalist exploitation.

Does this mean that all workers understand the unity of their self-interests? Of course not.

In fact with the new technology this has emerged as a most crucial question, namely, how the trade unions can become defenders of the whole class. The fact that workers do not understand this fully does not excuse people on the Left from not understanding it. One of the major objectives of capitalist propaganda is to create false divisions within the ranks of the working class. The attempt to blame one section of the working class for the conditions of others is as old a diversion as is capitalism itself.

There are also other changes that take place within the ranks of the working class. The ratio of the unemployed to those employed changes; the ratio between manual workers and those on automated equipment changes; and the individual personalities, of course, are changing. But the class remains as long as capitalism does. In fact, the numbers in the labor market keep growing. This is a fixed, built-in feature of the capitalist system.

It has always been a part of management's scheme to water down the consciousness of workers as to classes and the class struggle. In the shops this takes the form of paternalism: a system of titles, uniforms, bonuses, banquets, and, of course, stock-selling and profit sharing. All this is to create the illusion of their not being a part of the working class. With automation, management is trying to create the illusion of "technicians of automation" who belong to no class. These efforts do have their effects. But these effects are temporary. It is the effects of exploitation that have permanent influence on the class.

In today's level of economic activity, what fires the boilers of the class struggle is the natural desire of workers to get a greater share of the new level of productivity. The increase in output from each worker-hour and each capital dollar spent means the time a worker spends on producing the equivalent of his or her wages gets shorter, and the unpaid period of the workday spent producing for the exploiter gets longer. The rate of exploitation has continued to increase.

ONCE THE BASIC CLASS NATURE OF CAPITALISM AND THE place of the working class within it is firmly established, then it is possible to view the working class as a part of a much wider and a more complex social, political and economic framework. To understand capitalism is to understand its class structure. To understand class structure is to understand capitalism.

The laws of capitalism are such that they have set into motion processes of economic squeeze at different levels, but all moving downward. The center of the brute force squeezing all other layers is monopoly capitalism. The level toward which all the squeezed layers gravitate is the working class. This is a historic process governed by the inherent laws of capitalism. The tendency for other social strata to gravitate toward the working class when they are squeezed is not only because of a closer economic affinity. There is also an ideological and a political gravitation towards the working class.

These could be called economic, political and ideological gravitational fields. Marx called this the overall process of "proletarianization." He viewed this process in its broad scope, affecting different layers of the population. With the growth of monopolies this development has taken on a new quality. In one way or another all other sections of society have become victims and are being squeezed by monopoly capital. New technology in the hands of monopoly has become a very great factor as an instrument of squeezing.

Monopoly is squeezing the non-monopoly sections of capital. Small business is being squeezed by both monopoly and non-monopoly capital. The continuing process of mergers and the high rate of business failures are manifestations of the squeezing on the top economic layers of U.S. capitalism. As this pressure from the biggest monopolies continues, more of business begins to see its self-interest being served by a movement against monopoly power.

These pressures and reactions are within the capitalist class itself. The squeezing and the pressures continue. But from this point there is a new quality added when the squeezing crosses class lines. Then the squeezing takes on the form of exploitation. The levels affected by the pressures are closer to the working class. Because of this there is also a different quality to the political and ideological reactions.

In the USA the processes of "proletarianization" have been very drastic. In 1941 the farm population of the USA was 30 million. By 1962 it had declined to 14 million. And the squeezing is continuing.[3] What has happened to these millions pushed off the land? Some have entered the ranks of the working class as full-time workers, as part-time workers, or as unemployed workers. Some may have gone into business. But the trend is gravitation toward the working class. Some of those left on the land are able to stay there only because they also have become part-time members of the working class.

The processes of squeezing and exploitation are inherent laws of capitalism. These processes move society in a direction where increasingly it is more difficult and impossible to find solutions to economic and social problems within the framework of capitalism. In these most favorable circumstances U.S. capitalism can stay in business only because the government pumps in ever-increasing billions of dollars in public funds in the form of subsidies, grants, military orders, tax writeoffs, etc.

As this basic failure of capitalism becomes more obvious, intellectuals, students, professionals, scientists who are also victims of the squeeze, gravitate towards the class that is in the center of the oppression — the working class. These sections increasingly tend to identify their self-interests with the working class. Ever greater numbers of them become an integral part of the class struggle.

Those intellectuals who not only identify their own self-interests with the working class but understand the historic role assigned to this class gain a perspective and role in relation to the working class and the onward march of civilization. And some become outstanding workingclass leaders. That some intellectuals understand the role of the working class even before the masses of workers are conscious of their role as a class is not surprising. These intellectuals have arrived at such conclusions on the basis of a study of past experiences and theory. Their studies have led them to an understanding of the class nature of capitalism and the role of the working class.

A SPECIAL FEATURE OF PROFOUND HISTORICAL SIGNIFIcance to our working class and the future of our country is the role of Afro-Americans. U.S. capitalism has practiced a special, ugly and fiendish policy of exploitation and oppression against Black Americans. To its overall policy of class exploitation it has grafted a special system of slavery-like oppression, discrimination and segregation of Black people. To its class oppression it has added a brutal policy of the oppression of a people. This has been carried out through a systematic campaign of murder, lynchings, imprisonment; denial of all constitutional rights such as the right to vote; chauvinism, racism and bigotry.

Besides the enslavement of a people, this has given U.S. capitalism an additional weapon in its oppression and exploitation of the working class. U.S. capitalism has reaped profits both directly from the oppression of Afro-American people, and from its indirect effects on the exploitation of the working class.

This evil system has kept the southern half of our country in the status of an internal semi-colony with a lower standard of wages, hours and working conditions. Because of the system of terror the working class in the South remains largely unorganized, and Black people and the South as a whole have remained a source of extra profits for U.S. capitalism. This system has been an instrument for a policy of divide, rule, oppress and exploit all.

On a world scale there is a class relationship between the

forces building the new socialist world and the forces behind the countries newly liberated from colonialism. Between the newly liberated countries and the countries of socialism, as well as between the working class and people within the new independent nations, there is the historic unity of the working class and peoples who have been under colonial oppression. Here on a world scale we see the same process — the squeezing from the top monopoly-imperialist centers of capitalism and the different levels of gravitation towards the working class.

We are seeing this same process taking place in the USA. The motivating force for this process is in fact that the self-interests of Black people in the struggle against the policies of the oppression of a people and the self-interests of the working class in the struggle against class exploitation are interrelated and intertwined by life. What adds greatly to the vitality of this partnership is that these interrelated, parallel self-interests are also the self-interests of our people and nation. They merge as the self-interests of democracy, economic security and overall social progress.

The workingclass and Afro-American movements are natural allies. Neither can move forward without the other. The enemy is the same because the source of the oppression is the same. The issues of the struggle overlap. The people that make up the ranks of the two movements overlap.

The great majority of Black Americans are in the ranks of the U.S. working class. They are workers who feel double oppression. They are part of an oppressed people and also part of an exploited class.

Within the overall movement for social progress, these two components — the working class and the Afro-American people — are going to take on ever new meaning. Their coming together as a team in the struggle against monopoly capitalism is as inevitable as any can be. This is a lasting alliance. The alliance will grow in the struggle against racist discrimination and poverty. It will gather strength as it moves in the struggle against other evils of capitalism. This alliance will play a very important part in the struggle for a socialist America.

T HE QUESTION IS NOT WHAT THIS OR THAT WORKER, OR even the whole of the proletariat, at the moment considers as its aim. The question is what the working class is, and what consequent of being that, it will be compelled to do. — Engels.

The historic role of the working class is not a matter for some organization or group to decide. Its task flows from its relationship to the means of production and the inherent laws of capitalism. Economic relationships are not the only factors determining the behavior of classes. The human mind is capable of retaining and reflecting experiences not directly related to one's economic status.

But how one makes a livelihood, the relationship one has to the means of production, is the most basic factor in molding one's outlook. How one makes a living greatly determines how one thinks and reacts to events. The owners of industry have the ideology of an exploiter. Their ideas are rooted in the defense of their right to exploit other human beings. It is associated with the right to take for themselves what others have produced. All other thoughts are foreign to this slavemaster ideology. Human interests have no place in this outlook. It is the cold, inhuman, calculated ideology of a thief.

The starting point for a workingclass outlook is the reality of being on the outside — an alien in relation to owning, controlling or in any way determining anything about the tools with which he or she works. In relation to the machines, equipment and plants, he or she is a hired hand. This outlook is further molded by the knowledge that as a class they are the producers, but that the fruits of their social labor are snatched from them — a realization of being the producers of all wealth and the source of all profits.

This class outlook is further shaped by a constant knowledge on the part of workers that they are not getting a fair shake, that exploitation is unjust and has no moral justification whatsoever. The knowledge of being exploited by one's own countrymen gives further color to the outlook of the working class. This tends to give workingclass people a different sense of a nation. Workers are not satisfied with their lot.

The level of struggle is a reflection of how the workers view the possibilities of winning. However, this should never be interpreted as an endorsement of the system that exploits them.

These are some of the basic ingredients that mold a workingclass outlook. But there is more. The experience of struggling against exploitation itself becomes a part of the cumulative objective framework that molds a workingclass outlook.

The class of exploiters has political power. They have the governmental machinery, the armed forces, the police. They have control over the press, radio and television. The ideology of the capitalist class justifies the use of governmental authority in the interests of a few — even when such use is against the best interests of the people as a whole and of the nation. This is clearly seen in the defense of fascism by some bourgeois ideologists.

The working class under capitalism has no such instruments on its side. Workers are compelled to seek strength in their great numbers. Their only weapon in struggle is the unity of the many. Mass action and mass movement are concepts that grow from this realization. Disjointed action by individuals are not workingclass traits. Workers are compelled to seek strength in the great numbers of their class. There is no other section of the population that has such compelling reasons for acting in mass as is the case with the working class.

Through experience in struggle class instincts turn to a consciousness of being a class, a class with common relationship to capitalist production, a consciousness that they as a social group are the producers only to have the fruits of their labor stolen from them. These objective factors compel the working class toward a conclusion that all this can be changed. The working class is compelled and prepared by its position in capitalist society, by its experiences in struggle, to accept the outlook: "Yes, it is necessary to resist the exploiters, but what has to be done is to do away with the system that perpetuates the class of exploiters."

And so workingclass consciousness leads to socialist consciousness. There is no other class or section of the population that is compelled, is pushed to play such a role. This is why the working class is made — by capitalism — the leading class.

When workers fight for higher wages, even though their viewpoint may originally be that of fighting for a larger share of capitalism, the struggle leads to recognition that they are fighting for a bigger share of the product they have socially produced but which has been stolen from them.

A workingclass outlook about the nation and the world tends to be molded by two realities. One fact is that the exploiters — the people who steal the product workers socially produce, the people who show no regard for their interests, who lay them off without a second thought even after a lifetime of service, the people who speed up the production, the people against whom they have to fight daily — are their countrymen. Therefore, to the workers the nation is not one "happy family" but a nation of two classes with one dominant class: a small group that robs the nation of its natural riches and continues to steal the fruits of the masses' labor.

At the same time, the working class identifies its interest with that of the nation. It rejects the old profiteers' claim that "what is good for General Motors is good for America." Labor proclaims and history affirms the exact opposite. The fact is that the interests of labor are primary and serve the health and progress of the nation. Thus the working class gives a progressive human quality to patriotism. It protests and struggles against those who exploit patriotism and nationalism for narrow purposes of profit.

The other factor that influences the working class is its growing realization that workers in all capitalist countries are in the same boat. There is the sense of a bond and a community of interests with workers in all countries. The working class tends to see its self-interests served by the united strength of its class. That unity is strengthened by its bonds of internationalism as labor seeks the progress of the nation in a world of peace, a world free from exploitation.

At all times the working class is deeply concerned for the family and the individual. There is a humanism and high sense of purpose in the struggles of labor. Thus, in the workingclass outlook there is not the sharp contradiction between class interests and there is a sense of internationalism.

Each worker is a participant in the productive process which is social by its very nature. The products or goods produced under capitalism are not the results of an individual's efforts. This daily experience of producing socially the products of industry is also a process of molding. This is a factor in developing a social as well as a class conscious human being. This gives the working class a discipline, a basis for developing of a "new human being" who views his or her personal well-being in relation to, and as part of the advancement of, their fellow worker with whom they are engaged in the process of social production.

The economic and social position of the working class, more than any other section of the population, develops in it an outlook that is diametrically opposite to the "dog eat dog" concept of capitalism. That gives a different and more significant quality to the humanism of the working class.

The process of alienation that takes place under capitalism leads non-workingclass elements to helplessness and to shifts and swings as individuals. Such helplessness and frustration is nullified in the working class as the worker has a class to turn to and from which to gain strength. And this leads to struggle and collective effort.

The class struggle has a long history. It is constant. It has its ups and downs but it never disappears. Each battle is important, but it is also only a phase of a long struggle. This reality is reflected in the workingclass outlook on struggle. There is a sense of feeling: "We are going to be here after this battle is over." The realization that as a class, under capitalism, they have no place to go and that the class will remain also adds to the molding of a workingclass outlook. Other groups who "rebel" have a different outlook. They approach it as if to say, "I have tried other things. So now I'll give struggle a try."

The working class is compelled not to view the class struggle as a "try." It is life itself.

The Living Science

[From: "The Study and Development of Marxism-Leninism," Political Affairs, July, 1960 — abridged.]

THE UNITED STATES INFORMATION AGENCY IS AN OFFICIAL ARM OF the State Department. One of its many publications is a bimonthly magazine called *Problems of Communism*. In the March-April 1960 issue, there is an article entitled, "What Happened to Revisionism?" The author sets out to find the causes for the collapse of this development called "revisionism of Marxism." As he says, a few years ago it showed "great promise." And, "Those antagonistic to Marxism in any form saw in it primarily a disintegrative force which might divide and weaken the Communist movement everywhere." Because their hopes soared so high, their disappointment was so much the greater.

Thus this State Department writer laments, "Neither of these hopes obviously has been borne out by developments of the last three years." And what makes life really look dismal is that "revisionism has now ceased to be an effective force in political life."

But in order not to demoralize the opponents of Marxism completely, in the spirit of "Hello, mom, it was a good fight," the author says: "To point out that revisionism has ceased to be an effective force in Communist life, and probably will remain quiescent for some time to come, is not at all to minimize the importance of its past achievements. For all the brevity of its hour in the limelight — revisionism played a major role in the historic drama."

In the spirit of "where there is hope there is life," and so as not to sound completely negative lest the apologists for capitalism abandon the sinking ship, the article concludes on the following hopeful note: "Like the molten lava in a volcano which erupts, revisionism is always there and may spring to life when a confluence of certain essential factors occurs to release it." And it adds: "Its influence is in abeyance at present, but chances are that it will eventually arise once more and repeat the historic role it played in the years 1955-56."

Such is the past, present and future of the role of revisionism in the Communist movement as seen through the eyes of the spokespeople of capitalism. These expressions of high hopes and deep concern are in themselves a back-handed tribute to the science of Marxism-Leninism. The writer is not a confused individual with questions about some specific aspect of Marxism or its application, but one who considers the elimination of revisionism a serious defeat for his class, for capitalism.

These spokesmen for capitalism not only are concerned about this science of Marxism-Leninism — they are also bewildered. These doctors for a dying system cannot understand why it is that, even where objective conditions may foster revisionist thinking, the body of this workingclass thought, despite relapses, repels the poison they inject into it.

Their confusion is understandable, for their experience is with a dying system. Marxism-Leninism is the healthy, growing, vigorous science of the future, of advancement and progress. In the process of development and growth — the process of observing, testing and in turn changing the life that it studies — Marxism-Leninism corrects errors and wrong concepts, and so cleanses itself of alien ideas.

This process is continuous so long as two opposing classes are on the ideological battlefield. As long as there are such classes they will battle for the people's minds. Even after classes have left the scene of history as compact groups, it will take some time for the dust from the battle to settle down completely. And even after classes have disappeared altogether, the correction of errors and the advancement of Marxism-Leninism through criticism and self-criticism will continue.

WE ARE MEN AND WOMEN OF SCIENCE. WHEN A SCIENTIST becomes complacent and smugly rests on past studies, he or she ceases to be a scientist and becomes a sitting duck for all kinds of twisted notions that cannot meet the test of reality. Instead of a scientist one becomes an idle dreamer. Thoughts run wild with speculation and fancy. Because science is a matter of life and reality, a scientist must have his or her guy-lines secured to both life and reality. This is above all a necessity for a Marxist-Leninist.

In science one must be continuously studying and testing so as to guard against ideas that are alien, that would distort the meaning of the science.

Thus it would be nice to be able to accept assurances that "revisionism has ceased to exist." But we cannot accept such ideas from any quarter and certainly not from the enemy, because such assuring words could very well be the "conditioning injection" to prepare the body for the really crippling injection to come later.

We must never lose sight of the fact that in no country and at no time in history has a dying class spent so many resources on its ideological efforts as does the capitalist class of these United States. In money alone it runs into billions each year. This is most likely the single largest effort being exerted on any one thing in our land.

Wrong ideas or distortions never come with warning labels. As a matter of fact, humanity has never been able to develop a camouflage or smokescreen in any other field of endeavor that even comes close to the sugar-coating on the ideological pill put out by the apologists for capitalism. This is their masterpiece. As a matter of fact, as is the case in many fields of science, we can only see the symptoms and the effects and from this draw conclusions as to the cause.

Physicists study and draw conclusions about the nature and properties of sub-atomic particles not from direct observation — because one cannot directly see or feel such particles — but rather from such phenomena as the tracks these particles make in specially built chambers. In a way this is true in the field of ideology. The ideological influences to which one is subjected become discernible only as reactions to specific developments. The best testing chamber to study ideology is the class struggle, masses in motion.

The ideological pills are not only sugar-coated but the doses are so minute that the victim can never really know just when he or she started to be fertile soil for such poison, or when their ideological resistance has dropped to the proper level. The effects begin to appear, to one extent or another, as negativism, defeatism, accommodation to difficulties, dogmatism, also retreat to abstractions, sloganeering and phrasemongering. In short, they take the form in one way or another of giving up the fight, of course always covering up the retreat either with new theories that reject and revise Marxism or by mouthing "Left"-sounding slogans that have nothing to do with giving leadership to masses in motion and struggle.

The cause of such behavior is overestimation of the power of the opposition, arising mainly from seeing only the surface manifestations of apparent strength — from losing sight of the direction of history, or from permitting subjective attitudes to take hold of one's thoughts, and from seeing only the weaknesses of one's own class and people. If the ideas of the enemy class once get a foothold, and if they are not rejected, they finally take over completely.

Thus, at first Earl Browder became convinced that by gentle persuasion at least the more intelligent sections of the capitalist class could be brought around to see the errors of their ways. Now he has graduated. Now he sees more socialism in the United States than in the Soviet Union and more capitalism in the Soviet Union than in the United States.

As a rule, wrong ideas in the natural sciences have their source in lack of material — lack of known facts or difficulty in testing theories — and in drawing wrong conclusions or misinterpreting the facts at hand. In the main, such wrong concepts arise because of honest, mistaken interpretations. In the field of ideology the above is also true.

But there is one very important additional element one must take into account. Here, besides honest mistakes there is a continuous, calculated, insidious campaign of misinterpretation, of falsification, of perversion — all directed to confuse, to mislead, to cover up the truth and the facts. Revisionism is one of the old standbys used in this campaign. A class like the capitalist class that history has designated for early retirement needs falsehoods and lies to cover up its misdeeds. Marxism reflects in truth the forces that move forward; hence the constant efforts to distort and emasculate it.

A S IS THE CASE IN ALL FIELDS OF SCIENCE, THE STUDY OF Marxism is not a matter of studying or memorizing set phrases or formulas. The study and the development of this science, as well as the growth of one's own understanding, is itself a living, continuous process. It is the study of the laws of motion of social development.

As in all fields of science as well, the level not only of one's own understanding but of knowledge in general is relative, and there is much beyond what we already understand and know. If this were not so we would not need a science. All we would need is the "good book" with all the facts and formulas listed. In the field of science one never says: "Now I know it from beginning to end." This is true in part because there are continuous new developments to be studied: new experiences, new forces, new forms, new relationships.

It is also true in studying the past. One hears it very often said: "I had read this before, but somehow I missed such and such a thought." This is particularly so in the study of Marxism-Leninism, because one retains and understands theory if it makes sense based on one's own experience. One goes through new experiences in struggle and then goes back and rereads Lenin, Marx and Engels, and wonders how he or she had missed such wonderful and obvious ideas. To a student this should be a sign of progress. He or she now has a deeper understanding of theory and it is now obvious because it has been tested in life. It now becomes a part of one's experience, of one's ideology.

While knowledge is relative, there are things we do know. When the laws of nature or society are discovered and then they are tested against the realities, experience and reason permit us to accept them as truths. It is always valuable to know the process by which such truths were arrived at.

For example, in times now past the medical profession

thought that dampness was the cause of malaria. This conclusion was arrived at because malaria occurred mainly among people living around marshes and swamps. After digging deeper we now know that this was a surface observation — we know that the culprit is the germ and that the mosquito that flourishes around swamps is the carrier. This is now the accepted, tested truth. Marxism-Leninism embodies such truths and laws of human society. These include such laws as those governing the relationship and position of classes, the class struggle, the role of the state, and many other such tested truths.

There is no law that says you cannot become a steel manufacturer and so become a millionaire. As a matter of fact, Madison Avenue says this is quite possible in our free enterprise system.

But try it. It would take millions of dollars to start. No banker in his right mind would lend you such money. And if somehow you got over that hump, the big corporations now in the field hold all patent rights, they control the sources of raw material, they have all the marketing facilities. They have the big say in government so the tax policies, the tariff laws and other regulations favor them. In short, they have cornered the market. They have a monopoly in the field.

So the concept that everyone has a right to become a steel manufacturer turns into its opposite in short order. But to come to such a conclusion, one need not go through the attempt. From studies and testing, Marxist economics has drawn this conclusion which can be taken as one of the truisms of this stage of capitalism.

Of course, revisionism denies and tries to replace such truths. As is to be expected, this inevitably leads into ideological swamps and marshes. In times past, the yellow fever germ and the mosquito — the real culprits — got away with murder. As a result of theories of revisionism, it is the real culprit capitalism that gets away with murder. Are not such theories as "welfare state," "people's capitalism" and others like them found in the swamps of revisionism?

ARXISM-LENINISM DEVELOPS AND EQUIPS ITSELF TO deal with the manifold ramifications of theory through the process of finding and correcting errors and weaknesses. This is a law of scientific development. It is because of this understanding that men and women of science take such an impersonal and objective view about their own errors. We Marxists have something to learn here that is very important. To be wrong is not something to be ashamed of.

As in all science, in Marxism-Leninism there is the need for continuous study. There is a continuing flow of new experience. There is the need to dig deeper into the causes and the many-sidedness of all phenomena, a continuous process of observation and testing.

There is the need to fight against mechanical applications. Every so often in all fields of scientific development, mechanism has reared its ugly head. It seems people have a tendency to take the easy road out by taking truths and laws as formulas and mechanically trying to fit everything, for all time, into them. Life is motion, change. A study of it must be a continuous process. A development or a phenomenon is never an exact replica of some past development or phenomenon. Therefore, there cannot be a set of formulas from some past experience that can be applied mechanically to the new.

A true Marxist is one who not only knows the experience of the past, knows theory, understands the Marxist dialectical-historical method, but applies it to the specific situation as a good scientist should. The first prerequisite for such application is to know the specific: to be close to it, to understand it not superficially but in its many-sidedness, in its past, present and future; to know what caused it and what effects it will have; to know in what direction it is moving and how it is related to other surrounding specific phenomena.

To know the specific, to have a many-sided view — this is in itself a part of the process of study. Scientific study is not only continuous in the abstract but continuous in application.

Therefore we Marxists, as men and women of science,

must demand of ourselves that we work in such a way that we are in a continuous process of studying events as they unfold. Moreover, we must continuously strive to get a deeper grasp of the laws that underlie such events. We ourselves must be engaged in a continuous process of observing what is new, testing and applying our new knowledge and drawing ever deeper conclusions.

Marxism-Leninism enriches itself and draws from experience in all fields of life. It then becomes a guide to changing life, and in turn again draws from such new experience. Marxism-Leninism is not the viewpoint of a mere observer. It is not the outlook of a camera. It is not the outlook of a "know-it-all."

It is a world outlook and a methodology for action — the best that the human mind has brought forth.

It is a science that is firmly rooted in the materialist concept of reality. Its method and approach to such reality is that of dialectics. Just as in other areas of scientific study, Marxism has discovered, and has tested in practice, specific objective laws of social development: laws of social motion that explain the past and the present, and indicate clearly the direction of the future.

It is a guide to the most rounded, deepest understanding of life. It is the best guide to changing life. It is the only theory that clearly points the path to a higher form of civilization. It is a body of thought that is alive and growing, relying on tested laws where they apply, but in a living way.

Workingclass Intellectuals

[From: "Workingclass Intellectuals," Political Affairs, April 1977.]

THE PARTY HAS ALREADY ENTERED THE STRAIGHT ROAD OF LEADER-ship of the working masses by advancing "intellectuals" drawn from the ranks of the workers themselves. — V.I. Lenin.[4]

Many working people, especially in the capitalist world, go

through life in the belief that the world of ideas, of theory and science, is beyond their ability to understand. They believe theory and science have very little to do with their everyday lives or activities. They accept the idea that the world of ideas, the realm of thought, is for intellectuals and professionals.

That, of course, is how the ruling classes of all past and present exploitative societies have wanted it. They know that a class that thinks will not for long accept exploitation or slavery. In all past exploitative societies books and schools were for the ruling-class elite. These elites were "ordained" to do the thinking for the working people. Such concepts, of course, reflect reality in societies where there is a sharp division between physical and mental labor.

U.S. capitalism has always promoted the concept that thinking should be limited to the chosen few. The capitalist class fought against the establishment of the public education system. They lost the battle but never gave up. They have continued their attempts to limit the number of students and as much as possible to limit the scope of education only to satisfying industry's technological requirements.

Educational restrictions have always been aimed against workingclass youth. And there have always been special racist restrictions against Black, Puerto Rican, Chicano and other racially oppressed young people. The stubborn resistance to bilingual education is one current instance of this resistance.

After World War II, the government's education program for veterans opened the door to higher education to tens of millions of young working people. Now, however, it is attempting to close that door again. Today, state monopoly capitalism is continuing to enforce the policy limiting the scope of education for the working class.

But that is not the whole story. Because of the internal contradictions of capitalism, the advance of science and technology, and because of strong public demand, capitalism has not been able to keep the realms of thought, science and theory closed in the same way previous exploitative societies did. In this sense reality has changed. But many old notions and prejudices stubbornly resist the new reality.

This is an important question because a historic truth is being used by many to put over ideas that are not true, including the anti-workingclass concept that working people are not able to think. For many the reflection of past realities has become the basis for a timeless, anti-workingclass dogma.

One does not have to be a professional historian to realize that important changes have taken place which have their effects on the working class, such as the availability of mass public education and higher education, the higher rates of literacy in the industrialized countries and the mass publication of basic books. Even winning the eight-hour day has given workers more time for studying and thinking. The new level of mass communication, of science and technology has created new relationships between the broad masses and the world of theory and thought.

Many still hold to outdated and very narrow notions of what intellectuality is and who intellectuals are. Many cling to the old, elitist concept that only those who "think full-time" qualify. That, of course, conveniently disqualifies all who work with their hands.

Many intellectuals use the past reality to justify and sustain their prejudices that workers are not able to think. Even in some of the best circles this erroneous concept gives rise to attitudes of intellectual snobbishness or elitism. In many instances it gives rise to ideas that only people with professional training, or middle-class intellectuals, can or should lead workingclass organizations. In the U.S. this is one of the concepts that social democracy promotes in the trade union movement. It is a defense they use because most social democrats in the trade union movement have non-workingclass backgrounds.

This problem is not limited to the U.S., or to capitalist countries in general. There are reflections of this in the world Communist movement and it occasionally appears in Marxism-Leninist literature. However, it is necessary to state that, while on the surface the problem appears the same, in essence there is a difference.

In the non-capitalist world it is a leftover of old ideas. The following is a rather typical example of this kind of statement appearing in Marxist literature. As a rule it seems to appear without much thought. It is not defended, discussed or elaborated upon:

> It must be borne in mind that in an exploitative society, where there is an impassable gulf between mental and manual labor, the classes whose lot is manual labor are unable as a rule to advance ideologists from their own ranks. Their ideologists most often are members of other classes who have enough time and money to get an education, and at the same time are capable of understanding in what direction history is moving.

Such a formulation, while having an element of historical truth, leaves the door wide open to all kinds of misinterpretations. It certainly does not indicate that there are and have been changes in class relationships and in the role of classes in society.

When referring to the working class, phrases like "are unable," combined with the implication that other classes "are capable of understanding in what direction history is moving," are unacceptable. If the working class is not "able" to provide people "from its own ranks" who "are capable of understanding in what direction history is moving," then it is not "capable" of providing people who are "capable" of understanding Marxism-Leninism. However, life proves otherwise every day.

WITH THE ADVENT OF CAPITALISM THERE EMERGED A new class — the working class, which in many ways is unique and to which history has assigned the unique task of the final elimination of all classes, including itself. A class that is capable of carrying out such a monumental task is more than capable of making contributions in the field of thought.

Even in the last century when the educational gap between manual workers and intellectuals was much greater, the advantage in grasping complicated ideas was not always on the side of intellectuals. For example, as Engels noted in his Introduction to Marx's *Wage Labor and Capital:* "The uneducated workers, who can be easily made to grasp the most difficult economic analyses, excel our supercilious 'cultured' folk, for whom such ticklish problems remain insoluble for their whole life long."

The question of theory/science and its relationship to the working class must be dealt with in present-day terms. It can not be approached as a timeless cliche.

As the working class matures and develops and as it fulfills its historic assignment, two processes take place. The first is that the class struggle and the working class become increasingly greater influences in molding a new type of intellectual: an intellectual who, although not of workingclass background, is a workingclass partisan.

An outstanding example of this kind of intellectual is John Reed, a founder of our Party, who was described by Mike Gold in these words: "He identified himself so completely with the working class. He undertook every danger for the revolution. He forgot his Harvard education, his genius, his popularity, his gifted body and mind, so completely that no one else remembered them anymore. There was no gap between Jack Reed and the workers any longer."[5]

The second process is that the working class is increasingly producing new workingclass intellectuals from among its own ranks.

It must be kept in mind not to confuse the role of the intellectual with the role of a vanguard workingclass revolutionary party. The task of such a party was defined clearly by Lenin: "The task of the proletarian party is to introduce socialist consciousness into the spontaneous workingclass movement, to impart to it a conscious nature."

How well the Communist Party fulfills this task in a planned, organized way is a very basic measure of how it fulfills its vanguard role and of how well it helps to prepare the working class for more advanced struggles. This task is fulfilled by parties in which the cadre who come from workingclass backgrounds and those who come from non-workingclass backgrounds blend into one Communist, workingclass revolutionary/intellectual collective.

Therefore, the concept of introducing class and socialist consciousness "into the spontaneous workingclass movement" must not be interpreted to mean that this can be done only by intellectuals of non-workingclass origins and status.

There are many significant changes that must be taken into consideration when dealing with the question of intellectuals and the working class.

The birth and building of socialism in the world has added a new — a qualitatively new — element to this question, because the working class in socialist societies is the dominant influence, not only in everyday political affairs but also in the development of theory and science. As socialism does away with the differences between mental and physical activities, it is also removing the barriers which have prevented workers from making their full contribution in the field of thought and ideas.

In the socialist countries the working class is doing what Karl Marx and Frederick Engels said in *The Holy Family* it would be forced to do. The working class "cannot abolish the conditions of its own life without abolishing all the inhuman conditions of life of society today which is summed up in its own situation."

The effects of the changes in the socialist countries are felt worldwide. This is a very important new factor, a new influence on the development of intellectuals from the ranks of the working class. The example of the historic achievements of societies where the working class is the leading force acts as a source of confidence for workers, a stimulant to enter the area of ideas, of theory and of science.

The Communist parties have made unique and historic contributions to opening up the world of thought, the world of theory and science, to workers. The Communist parties are themselves schools for the development of intellectuals with a partisan class viewpoint.

As capitalism decays, the capitalist class becomes less and less the basis for the development of intellectuals with a healthy social consciousness, and even less so for intellectuals with a partisan workingclass consciousness. Life has shifted that historic responsibility to the working class.

A S WORKINGCLASS PARTIES, COMMUNIST PARTIES ARE A factor in helping the working class carry out that responsibility. However, the recent period has produced evidence that not all Communist parties or leaders of parties accept that responsibility. There are leaders of some Communist parties who have difficulty accepting the idea that life has forced the working class, because of its unique position in the economic structure, to become the most advanced revolutionary class in society. This is related to opportunistic ideas about the class struggle and the working class in general.

In essence, opportunism is a policy of making unprincipled concessions to the capitalist class. Opportunism is always related in one way or another to the class struggle, which is not surprising because that is the hub of the relationship between the two classes. That is where the capitalist class presses for concessions. Opportunists invariably soften their stand on the class struggle and from that point onward there is a line of retrogression.

To dilute the concept of the class struggle is to downgrade the role of the working class. From that point on the idea of socialism becomes a conversation piece; the role of the working class in the struggle for and building of socialism is diluted to nothingness. The concept of the dictatorship of the proletariat is dropped, not because the words can be misused but because the concept of workingclass rule is objectionable to the capitalist class and those influenced by it. And, as is the case with at least one Communist Party, the opportunistic decay has reached the point of dropping Marxism-Leninism. When a Party leadership regresses to that level, perhaps dropping the claim to Marxism-Leninism is simply a reflection of the truth.

The idea that the working class is not able to develop intellectuals from its own ranks is turned into a coverup for antiworkingclass concepts.

In some cases this weakness leads to situations where middle-class, professional intellectuals tend to take over and hog the leadership of Communist parties in capitalist countries. Often they use the words "class struggle" and "the working class" as cliches, but take no steps to make it possible for the workingclass cadre of these parties to be a factor in policy decisions.

Such leaders are not willing to accept the leading role of the working class in the field of thought or in their parties. They dilute the concept of class struggle. They downgrade the historic role of the working class. They eliminate the working class in the struggle for socialism and they do not think the working class is able to produce an intellectual.

The time has come to bury the idea that the working class is unable to think. In fact, Marxism-Leninism is a science so closely related to the rise of the workingclass movement that to eliminate the working class as a basic influence and participant in the further development of the science is like eliminating the heart in a living being.

The historic role of the working class was clearly placed by Marx and Engels: "Before the proletariat fights out its victories on the barricades and in the lines of battle, it gives notice of its impending rule with a series of intellectual victories."

Many errors in the history of our Party can be traced to periods when there was a lack of workingclass participation in the leadership of the Party. The history of the world Communist movement argues for greater participation of workers in the field of theory and science. It is time to drop concepts and cliches that do not correspond to the new realities of this period of history.

the plus factor

The Party
of the Working Class

The Communist Party, USA

[From: "The Communist Party: A Product of History," Political Affairs, September, 1978.]

THE TURN OF THE TWENTIETH CENTURY MARKED MORE THAN THE lapse of another hundred years. It was above all else the beginning of a stormy, explosive century of revolutionary change. History had prepared the soil, molded the forces and set the direction for historic changes. The changes and the events that have taken place since the turn of this century are truly monumental. But they are in keeping with Karl Marx's observation that humanity sets for itself only those tasks that it can fulfill.

In past centuries, wars ended in the redistribution of territory and markets between private enterprises. The results of the First World War were different because history had matured a new force, the working class, whose class interests were not served by wars of conquest.

Before the turn of the century the idea of taking political power had not yet become a serious mass concept in the ranks of the working class. Because of this, history gave rise to socialist-oriented parties that toyed with the ideas of workingclass political power. When the world moved towards the inevitable war to redivide the loot among imperialist powers these parties did not meet the test of time. History had prepared the soil for revolutionary changes and they were not revolutionary parties. They were parties only for reform. The explosive elements associated with the transition from a world of capitalism to a world of socialism were building up steam. Sooner or later something had to give way. History posed the question of workingclass political power for resolution.

The end product of the First World War was different because history had given birth to and raised to maturity the working class, and assigned it the task of leading the forces of transition from capitalism to socialism. So the new century brought forth the "ten days that shook the world."[1] The transition had begun. The working class in Russia, in alliance with other forces, took political power. They named their new state the Union of Soviet Socialist Republics.

With the turn of the century history had set into motion a worldwide revolutionary process in which the transition to socialism was the pivot. From the very beginning the class struggle and the workingclass forces in the capitalist countries became a primary force within this historic process.

An inevitable feature of the revolutionary process is the worldwide struggle against colonialism and for the liberation of all nations. On the waves of the three currents propelling the world revolutionary process — the advance of socialism, the class struggle in the developed capitalist countries and the struggle for independence of the developing countries — ride the fortunes of human progress. Because racism and chauvinism have been an ideological pillar in the oppression of nations, the struggle against racism and chauvinism emerged as an important factor in the revolutionary process. The struggles that accompany the process cut down many of the weeds of racism, but only the transition to socialism destroys its economic, political and ideological roots.

No revolutionary class in this epoch can come to power or fulfill its role in history without a political party that understands the historic tasks assigned it. So inevitably as the working class grew in size, as it cut its ideological wisdom teeth, it faced the tasks of organizing, of giving birth to political parties that would meet the test of leadership for the period of revolutionary transition.

There was also a need for a body of thought, a science that would probe and explain the laws, the inner workings and the forces involved in the transition. It is in this basic sense that the science called Marxism-Leninism and the workingclass revolutionary parties (most of which include the word "Communist" in their names) are products of history. They are a response to the unique tasks set for this period of revolutionary change.

The world revolutionary process and history in general have a definite progressive direction. But as is the case with all processes it does not move with the same speed or in the identical way in all the countries of the world. However, no country is exempt from the process itself.

Because of a number of objective factors, capitalism in the U.S. has had the benefit of favorable circumstances. This has been a factor influencing many developments, including the relatively slow growth and maturing of the workingclass movement. But the U.S. is not immune from the basic laws of capitalist development, including the laws of its general decay.

I N THE UNITED STATES THE NEW CENTURY GAVE RISE TO THE growth of mass production and giant corporations. This was accompanied by brutal exploitation: a 12-hour day, total disregard for the health of workers, child labor and inhuman speedup paced by the production belt line. It soon turned into the century of high corporate profits, escalating rates of exploitation, dehumanization and alienation. This gave rise to the organization and legalization of trade unions.

Objective developments continued to give rise to many different kinds of radical and socialist-oriented groups. Frustration led some of them to establish communes. They tried to get away from the evils of capitalism in isolated enclaves. They were crushed by their capitalist surroundings. This rebellion led some people into anarchist and syndicalist organizations.

They took their anger out on a one-to-one basis.

There were a number of socialist organizations which did not see socialism as a practical alternative for the United States. So for many it remained a beautiful idealistic dream.

These formations did not meet the challenges history was preparing. The struggles for the resolution of the problems the working class faced needed a different kind of political party. Of necessity it had to be a party that understood and accepted the task of working with and guiding the spontaneous mass movements that objective developments were giving rise to.

It had to be a party that accepted the class struggle as its primary point of reference, but also understood how it related to the problems and struggles of all sections of the people. It had to be a party that would be in the very forefront of all the struggles for reforms, but would reject reformism as a way of political life. It had to be a party that understood that the struggle against racism was a special task for a workingclass party, but that it also had to be a part of all struggles, especially struggles related to the class struggle. It had to be a party that took a principled stand against imperialism and accepted as its acid test the struggle against U.S. imperialism.

It had to be a party that understood the dialectical relationship between fighting for a better life under capitalism and the advocacy of and struggle for the transition to socialism. It had to be a party that did not opportunistically succumb to the ideological pressures of Big Business, a party that saw slander of the Soviet Union and other socialist countries as basically a slander of the working class and of socialism in general.

It had to be a party that understood and accepted the science of Marxism-Leninism and that continued to develop it as a guide and a methodology for its work. It had to be a party that was democratic, but with a structure through which it could come to policy and tactical conclusions.

In 1919, a group of men and women who had participated in most of the radical and Left organizations, who had studied the experiences of world revolutionary developments, got together and gave birth to just such a party.

The Communist Party, USA, and the men and women who

participated in its founding, were products of the same history, the same worldwide revolutionary process, that had given rise to workingclass revolutionary parties the world over. It is in this sense that the founding of the Communist Party, USA was a product of history and is the finest achievement of the U.S. working class.

The rise and fall of "Left" and "radical" sects has continued apace. Many of these groups attach themselves to such words as "Communist" and "Marxist-Leninist." But such groups come and go because they do not meet the test of history or reality. There is an opportunist streak that runs through them. They try to maneuver with and go around the main political and ideological attacks of the class enemy. They join with reaction by being anti-Communist. The special Trotskyite accommodation with anti-Communism is to say they are for socialism in general but to attack it wherever it is a reality. Anti-Sovietism is a special opportunistic hiding place for most of these groups.

Most of them maneuver with and accommodate to racism. The latest maneuver is to say: "The basic struggle against racism has been won." Therefore, they conclude that there is no need to ever raise the issue. For some these groups provide a place to express their individualistic, middle-class anger. Many are honest but misled. In many cases they are lost to the revolutionary movement.

These sects do not meet the test of history because they do not accept or understand the laws of capitalist development, the class struggle or the role of the working class. Their anti-Communism, anti-Sovietism and their playing with super-radical phrases make them an easy mark for penetration by the FBI and other enemy agents. Some of these groups are used by the FBI to disrupt broader mass movements.

T HE SCIENCE OF MARXISM-LENINISM PROVIDES THE COMMU-
nist Party with an understanding of the laws, the forces and the direction of this period of history. The Communist Party, USA grows and matures but it never gets old because it continues to reflect and work with the forces of a

changing reality. It makes contributions, takes part in and helps to guide the spontaneous movements which the changing objective developments give rise to.

The Communist Party can be proud of its decades of contributions. It has been a major factor in the building of our trade unions. It was the main force in the organization of the mass production unions. It was the spark plug in the struggles for Social Security, for unemployment insurance. It has an uninterrupted record of struggle against racism since its founding. It has been a leading force in the struggle for equality of women. It has continued to provide the anti-imperialist content to all struggles for world peace. It has an honorable record in the struggles of family farmers. It has provided leadership in the struggle for democratic rights and against the ultra-Right and fascism. It survived the years of McCarthyite, anti-Communist hysteria.

The Communist Party has not only survived, but continues to influence events because it is a product of and is sustained by the working class and the people's struggles in the U.S. The objective developments gave it life and they sustain it. The need for it grows, and because of this the Communist Party grows. There are serious unsolved problems, but there has been more bread, more justice, more democratic and civil rights, better working conditions, higher wages, more housing, Social Security and unemployment insurance because of the contributions of the Communist Party.

The primary factor that influences everything in a capitalist society is the class struggle. On the world scene this factor is reflected in the contest between the two systems — capitalism and socialism. These forces of history do not permit any neutrality. Even political passivity becomes a factor on the scales between the two basic class forces. The Communist Party, USA accepts that challenge. It does not evade or capitulate; it carries out its responsibilities proudly and honorably.

The historic transition from capitalism to socialism has basically changed the world relationship of forces. World imperialism is no longer the unchallenged master. Because of this, many new avenues and possibilities along which the transition can proceed have opened up. Wars of conquest are not now inevitable. New paths to socialism have become possible. Colonialism can now be destroyed for all time. Human progress can take even bigger steps.

To make these possibilities a reality it is necessary to fight for the unity of the forces propelling the world revolutionary process. The struggle for world peace and peaceful coexistence must get top billing, the highest priority. The Communist Party, USA accepts this challenge.

The Communist Party is confident that because it is a product of the rising forces of history it will continue to make history.

Fighting Big Business Ideas

[From: "Improve the Marxist-Leninist Content and Methods in Party Activity," report to conference on industrial concentration of the Communist Party in Ohio, 1949—abridged.]

IN ITS PLANS TO ENSLAVE THE WORLD, WALL STREET IS GIVING high priority to beheading the American working class by seeking to destroy the Communist Party. As a result of a careful and methodical study of the experiences of the late "anti-Communist" Axis in setting up fascist governments along parallel lines, a plan emerged for the United States. This master plan has three distinct parts.

The first step calls for an attack on the Marxist-Leninist ideological fiber of the Communist Party. In these calculations, great reliance was placed on the wishful thought that Browder's revisionism had created favorable conditions for this phase of the attack and that a concentrated campaign would quickly disperse the Communist Party into small factions and groups.

For more than three years we have witnessed this full-scale offensive. With unlimited funds at its disposal, the capitalist class has mustered all its resources for this campaign. This ideological barrage has consumed and still does consume the greater part of the time on the radio and space in newspapers and books, the tons of magazines, church sermons, after-dinner speeches, and movie footage. The United States Government Printing Office has issued millions of pieces of literature as its share in this fabulous political-ideological hysteria campaign. It is a campaign waged by the world's most powerful capitalist class, a class which is, nonetheless, suffering from an inferiority complex.

The second part of this anti-Communist crusade called for the isolation of the vanguard Party from its "mother earth," — the people in general, and the working class in particular. The central weapon for achieving this is discrediting our Party, labeling the Communists as "agents of a foreign power." This label is designed to destroy the effectiveness of the Party by repeating the same hollow charge about every activity: that the Communists "are not really interested" in the problems of the American people but are carrying on their activities only because they fit the "interest of a foreign power."

The final section of the plan calls for direct attacks: indictments, arrests, deportations, jailings on technicalities, physical assaults, and other forms of force and violence. These methods are geared to accompany the attempts through courts and the United States Congress to illegalize the work of and membership in the Communist Party. The very latest edition is the attempt to illegalize the Communist Party by actions of state legislatures.

A new twist in this war of ideology is the attempt to convince the Communist Party itself that it is dying and dispersing. The *U.S. News & World Report* says that our Party is "declining;" the Hearst papers proclaim that the Party is "disintegrating;" and Earl Browder announces that the Party is "friendless, isolated, and lies in ruins." As "proof" of the isolation of the Communist Party from the working class these gentry point to the betrayal of a Curran, and a Budenz, of a Browder.[2]

Thus the very developments that are testimony to our ideological unity and strength — the rejection of the very individuals and their politics that would have brought about the isolation of the Party — are here given as "proof" of that isolation. The strength and influence of a Communist Party cannot be measured by its relations with some top officials in the trade unions. A workingclass party's strength can be measured only by its ability to lead in struggle and to reflect correctly the needs and desires of the masses in a given situation.

The struggles are sharpening. Wall Street is intensifying its plans for world conquest and its attacks on the Communist Party. But a number of facts clearly stand out. The timetable originally set has been thrown off schedule. Ever-greater numbers of Americans are seeing the attack as part of a pattern of emerging American fascism. Growing sections of the population are identifying their interests with the defense of the Communists.

Our Party is rebuffing the attacks, and, in doing so, is strengthening itself in the process. The Marxist-Leninist ideological fiber of the Party is today at its best. The ranks of the Party are solid. The Party has strengthened its ties with the people. Communists have won back the honorable position of being the best, most militant and most capable leaders in the struggles of the people. The Party's spirit, discipline, and work reflects utmost confidence in its ability to fight back, and in its policies, its program and leadership. The fighting morale and spirit of the Communist Party are high.

In any warfare, the advance units are under the most concentrated fire. The profit-mad capitalist class, in its drive to enslave the world, fully realizes that it must attempt to destroy these advance units — the Communist Party — and simultaneously direct its fire against the frontline forces, the working class. Therefore, the class enemy is systematically trying to disperse, demoralize and win over part of the leadership of the labor movement.

While fully understanding that the drive toward war and fascism affects and involves the great majority of the American people, Communists must fully see and understand the specific, decisive role played by the working class in this struggle.

The Communist Parties of France, Italy, Czechoslovakia

and other important countries are large and have millions of followers among all sections of the population because above all else they speak for and lead the working class of their respective countries. We know the historic and objective facts that account for the different level of development in our own country. Among other things, this uneven political maturing of the working class reflects the uneven development of capitalism itself. However, we would make a great error were we to hide our weaknesses behind these objective developments.

A S AN EXAMPLE, LET US TAKE THE COMMUNIST PARTY IN Ohio. It is a Party of steelworkers, coal miners, machinists, autoworkers, rubber and electrical workers, and workers in other basic industries. This places heavy responsibilities on our Party. Among these responsibilities is the necessity to be doubly alert and vigilant against any weaknesses of our own making or influences of the enemy in this very decisive sector. We must learn to be as vigilant against and uncompromising with weaknesses as we are jubilant about our successes.

With this in mind, I want to discuss a few of the signs of weaknesses that have made their appearance in the work of the Party in Ohio. Since the Emergency Convention when Browderism was defeated, opportunism has not appeared in our Party as a rounded-out policy, a thesis, or a platform. But from this it does not follow that our Party is exempt and forever immune from this enemy class influence. In a class society, the ideological struggle is forever present. Since 1945 opportunism has not walked in full-grown through the front door; but it has sneaked in through the back door. It has made its appearance only as signs or manifestations. In most cases, the one who carries this germ of capitalist class ideology is unaware that he or she is doing so. The manifestations are usually covered up by rationalizations and "Left" phrases, or by silence.

In the struggle against these manifestations of right opportunism, generalizations on the question are not enough and by themselves are not very effective. It is possible for one to be guilty of right-opportunistic practices in one's own work and still go along with the most vigorous condemnation of opportunism in general, or as it appears in the work of others or of other Communist Parties. Therefore, these manifestations must be fought concretely, in the surroundings they appear in.

In his report to the Fourteenth National Convention of the Communist Party our Labor Secretary, Comrade John Williamson,[3] affirmed that "the outstanding feature of the present situation is the readiness of the workers to struggle if issues are made clear and proper leadership is given." This report was adopted and accepted as a part of the convention's estimate of the present situation. The test as to the real understanding of, and agreement with, this estimate, or for that matter with any policy, is in the application.

Let's examine some manifestations of right opportunism.

We had a few comrades who said: "Yes, the above estimation and the policies flowing from it are correct, generally speaking, but in my shop or industry we have a different situation. In my shop the workers are more backward, and what is generally correct does not at this time apply to them." Some held: "It is generally correct, but I come from a small shop and you know we can't start on these small shops while the big monopolies go free."

Then there were those from the big shops who said: "True, this is a big shop. But it is only one in a monopoly chain, and therefore you cannot win a struggle in only one shop out of a big chain." Then there is the tune pitched in another key: "Right now production is high. Workers are working overtime and making good money. Therefore this is not the time to initiate struggles." Six months later, this comrade stated: "Now production is going down. Therefore now is not the time to initiate any struggles. The bosses don't care if the workers strike." Or: "We must wait until the other unions start the struggle."

Then we have the comrade who argues: "The Party is correct in raising sharply the struggle to smash discrimination against Black workers in industry. But in my shop the situation is different. The workers are backward. There are many Southerners . . . " etc., etc. Here we have two concurrent streams of bourgeois ideology: opportunism in general, and white chauvinism. They are very closely related and are very often to be found flowing together.

These rationalizations, obviously, are a coverup for right opportunism. When put together and added up, they signify the rejection of the estimate and policy of the Party. It is true that we must take note of special circumstances, of special characteristics in a shop or in a local, but only to take special steps to overcome existing obstacles. "Special conditions" must never be allowed to become the cover for right opportunism, for the rejection of the Party's policies in practice.

Now let us look at the advanced worker who has fallen into a rut and has become the "annual contract negotiator" and "a year-round grievance processor." He or she helps to negotiate a contract once a year, and then "processes," or files grievances and argues about them the rest of the year. Some grievances are settled, the majority are not. He or she spends a lot of time "holding down" things, "keeping everything quiet," "keeping the *status quo*." In most such cases this worker has fallen for the class collaborationist idea that a "clever" trade union leader can "negotiate" a victory without a struggle by the workers.

The capitalist class has very methodically cultivated and elevated into prominence the "clever" negotiator type as the "respectable" trade union leader. To the workers, such a trade union leader begins to look like an "impartial" arbitrator, and not as their leader in struggles. He or she very quickly loses the respect and confidence of the workers who elevated this fellow worker to office.

This specific manifestation of opportunism is usually covered up by the rationalization that "our contract or grievance procedure makes action of any kind almost impossible." Such thinking might sound convincing but it does not correspond to the facts. It is actually a self-imposed prison. The management will always argue that a labor-management contract is a "truce" in the class struggle. But while doing so, they continue to speed up production and cut piece rates to increase profits. For a union leader to accept this class collaborationist idea in any form is a betrayal of the working class.

The "clever" negotiator notion flows from the basic illusion that the capitalist class is, or that certain members of that class are fair, reasonable and "intelligent," and therefore can be won over or convinced by "clever" arguments. All remnants of this dangerous illusion must be systematically and consciously destroyed.

The same general weakness also shows up in a tendency to think in terms of placing demands and organizing struggles around issues that the employer would consider "reasonable" demands that will not create too much "hardship," and issues that can easily be "agreed to" without a struggle. This reflects the ideology of the beggar. It results in being satisfied and grateful for crumbs thrown to the working class. It is part of the ideology of the capitalist class, which holds that for some reason or other the capitalist class is the rightful master of the means of production and resources, and therefore the workers should be satisfied and grateful for any concessions. Even the slightest tendency to think along these lines leads to policies of class collaboration in practice.

The basic, simple truth — that the capitalist class will compromise or negotiate only if it sees mass action or the solid organization and ideological conviction that can make such action possible — must be the foundation of a class struggle trade union policy.

A younger brother to the above weakness is the tendency toward reliance on spontaneity. Here there is no theoretical opposition to the idea of struggle, but before leadership is given, according to this view, one must wait until some "spontaneous action" takes place. Such "spontaneous" struggles often do not materialize, or else they are usually unsuccessful because of lack of preparation and because they are very often provoked by the employers at a time most unfavorable for the workers.

A vanguard Party cannot rely on spontaneity as the basis for its activity and leadership. Lenin once stated that a vanguard Party must boldly project issues and demands which the workers "only dare whisper about to their closest friends." A leader must initiate and project the issues, organize the struggle, find the proper form for each stage in the struggle, and encourage and build enthusiasm and confidence of victory in the struggle. He or she must systematically destroy the enemy's ideological arguments, expose the weaknesses of the enemy and help the workers draw significant lessons from their battle.

A vanguard Party must at all times dig for, unearth and expose all the hidden forms of exploitation, and not merely lead struggles that flare up spontaneously. If elements of reliance on spontaneity are permitted to go unchallenged, they will develop and grow into full-scale rejection of the policy of class struggle.

I N *WHAT IS TO BE DONE?* LENIN STATES THAT A MARXIST PARTY is a union of the workingclass movement and socialism. The mastery of this thesis, as a guide for the everyday activity of the Party, is a challenge and a fundamental requirement for all organizations of the Party.

A Communist party, or a member of the party, doesn't give life to this fundamental Marxist thesis by adding a slogan "for socialism" at the end of a speech or leaflet; this "union" is not made by publishing literature about socialism in the abstract. And of course this "union" is not made by the reasoning that "socialism isn't on the order of the day in America" and so we can leave it out of our present-day activities and wait for history to place it on the order of the day in some distant future. The first is an error flowing from a lack of Marxist understanding; the second is a rejection of the struggle for socialism. The result of both is the same — no struggle for socialism.

The fundamental Marxist thesis that the Party is the union of the workingclass movement and socialism must be the content, the very essence of our leadership of every struggle at all times. This means giving a Marxist content to all struggles for partial demands and reforms. It means making the connection between the present struggles and the future, the part with the whole. This idea is not something new. The Party has stated it before. But without periodic reemphasis, additions and continuous struggle for improvement in application, a policy becomes musty, left on the shelf and forgotten or used only for abstract lectures on a Sunday.

Let us take the issue of speedup and see how this problem appears to different elements in the leadership of the trade union movement.

The approach of the Right-wing, class collaborationist leaders derives from their slogan: "The more you produce the more you have." In practice such trade union leaders often sit on "joint committees" to devise new means by which to speed up production. To them speedup is not an issue, but a "joint responsibility of labor and management."

To the reformist, Keynesian type of trade union leaders, the essence of this issue is summed up in their slogans: "A fair day's work for a fair day's pay" — "A guarantee for a reasonable profit." This is also a class collaborationist policy, but these trade union leaders are obliged to give lip service against speedup, and when forced may even go along with some actions.

To a Marxist, the approach and content flows from the profound truth that all speedup, in all its multitude of forms, only increases the workers' rate of exploitation and results in a greater profit for the capitalists.

The "high production" and "fair day's pay for a fair day's work" notions are as old as the capitalist system itself. These slogans are becoming worn out from use in the coverup of their of their highway robbery that is capitalism. Almost a hundred years ago Frederick Engels exposed this slogan as follows: "Labor is, besides the earth, the only source of wealth. . . . The produce of the labor of those who do work gets unavoidably accumulated in the hands of those who do not work, and becomes in their hands the most powerful means to enslave the very men who produced it."

American capitalism, like capitalism everywhere, has used these slogans to disguise the fact that it expropriates — grabs — the total product produced by the working class and returns to the workers in the form of wages just enough for a bare existence, and often less.

There cannot be, and there is not, anything "fair" about the system of capitalism. This is why, if the workers are really to benefit from greater production (without speedup), the whole system of exploitation and profits must be done away with and replaced by a more advanced system — socialism.

This theoretical understanding offers a guide to an effective program of action. The need at all times is for organized actions against speedup. The exact form and character of these struggles must depend on the concrete circumstances and relationship of forces.

During such activities all the workers participating must be taught that speedup is going to result only in more profits at their own expense. By the use of highly skilled "time study" men, the exploiters have been squeezing more out of the workers every minute, hour and day. One of the immediate results is that in an industry such as auto, the Wall Street barons have squeezed every bit of energy out of the workers in ten years' less time than in most other industries, and so the autoworker's span of working life is ten years shorter.

The workers must be shown that it is not only the immediate boss who is involved, but rather that speedup is part of the whole system of exploitation and profits. The content of the struggle must be of such a nature that all workers will see that only a constant and united struggle can slow down this frenzied drive for profits. At the same time, the content of our leadership must guarantee that more and more sections of the workers will draw the conclusion that only a basic change, the scrapping of the system, will end this insanity forever.

LET US SEE HOW THE STRUGGLE FOR EQUAL RIGHTS FOR Black workers in general, and for upgrading specifically, is approached by the different elements in the trade union leadership. Among the Right wing, some work openly for a policy of discrimination. Others pay lip service to equal rights and upgrading or even vote for motions along these lines; but the "hitch" is that in most basic industries there cannot be any general upgrading or advancement until discrimination is done away with in the largely all-white skilled departments, in the trade schools and in the apprenticeship programs.

The Marxist understanding of this fundamental question flows from the truth that "labor in the white skin can never be free so long as labor in the black skin is branded." The purpose of the system of segregation and discrimination is to divide the working class in order to continue the system of exploitation. From the understanding that the ideology and practices of white chauvinism are powerful weapons of the capitalist class designed to perpetuate this system, from the understanding of the relationship of this chauvinistic offensive to the liberation battles of the Afro-American people — from this theoretical understanding flows a program of action:

1. To organize action at all times against every and all forms of discrimination.

2. To maintain a continuous, systematic campaign exposing the way in which white chauvinism serves as a weapon of the ruling class in propping up its profit system by means of the strategy of divide-and-rule.

3. To show the need for unity of Black and white workers in all struggles.

4. To conduct the campaign with such content that all workers taking part in the struggle will see the need forcefully to reject the policies and practices of discrimination and to see the need for class unity and solidarity. The content must be such as to enable the workers to draw the conclusion that a system that must resort to lynchings, frameups, and other barbaric forms of terror, that resorts to such hideous, divisive measures to poison the minds of the people in order to perpetuate its rule, must be destroyed and a new, more advanced system — socialism — built in its place.

As indicated in the foregoing examples, the unity of the workingclass movement and socialist consciousness must be made the content and essence of every struggle. When workers take part in a fight, they become more receptive to learning what are the deeper issues, the "big politics" behind the conditions they face and fight against. And it is especially in the midst of such a struggle that Communists have the opportunity to explain the basic policies of class struggle as they appear under the spotlight of Marxist-Leninist science.

The Marxist-Leninist thesis of the Party being the "union" of the workingclass movement and socialism is a source of limitless fighting morale and enthusiasm. Without this understanding one very easily slips out of the ranks of the fighters for socialism and into the ranks of the "negotiators."

To the extent that Party organizations strive to give a Marxist content to their every activity, to that extent they are active, vigorous, enthusiastic, growing organizations. To the extent that the content is reformist, mechanical or non-Marxist in general, the organizations lack enthusiasm, perspective and consistency in their activities. The content of our leadership must help all workers draw the general conclusions about classes and class struggle, about the need to fight for socialism.

A Party that relaxes or stops even for a moment in its struggles to improve its activities and understanding of Marxism-Leninism is a Party that has taken the first step backward, toward defeat. Our Communist Party, USA has advanced because we have struggled against all manifestations of alien, non-workingclass ideologies. We will continue to advance because we will continue to struggle against all such ideas.

Adding the "Plus"

[From: "Trade Union Work — Plus! The Communist Essence," speech to Communist Party conference on trade union work; additional remarks from speech to the People's Daily World *staff; 1986 — slightly abridged.]*

THERE IS A BIG DIFFERENCE BETWEEN GOOD TRADE UNION WORK and Communist trade union work. Communist trade union work means good trade union work *plus*. When a Communist does good trade union work without the "plus" it is opportunism; as good as the work may be, without the *plus* it is opportunism. Without the *plus* it will go nowhere — it is a path to nowhere and nothing. We have to understand this, once and for all. This is true whether a Communist is working full time as a union organizer or working in a shop.

Our new Trade Union Program is correct. Our assessment of the new framework of struggle is correct. Our ideas on raising the level of political development in the trade union movement are correct. But we must still work out how to raise the Party's work in this new framework, how to apply it.

For example, the Hormel strike.[4] Are Hormel workers more class conscious now than they were six months ago when the strike began? They are angry at Hormel. But are they angry at the capitalist system after six months? Do they question the system after six months on the picket lines? What have we done, specifically, to raise the consciousness of Hormel workers? Picketing the bank will not do it.

We have to ask this question about all strikes, all struggles. I think if we do we will find weaknesses.

What develops class consciousness is a very important question. It does not develop automatically or spontaneously. There has to be an injection and only our Party can do this. Class consciousness develops by explanations of how the system works, what exploitation is, labor as a source of value, explanations of class struggle and socialism, etc.

Of course we are interested in winning struggles. But we are interested in the "plus." There is no contradiction. On the contrary, the *plus* makes a stronger, better organized, better understood strike. The *plus* is a plus even for the strike and should not be seen as being in contradiction to it.

When a strike begins, do we ask ourselves: How can it help workers to develop class consciousness? What can we do to help this process? Too often we don't think in these terms.

I want to take this opportunity to correct a wrong concept that has been with us for a long time. It comes from a misuse of an unclear formulation by Lenin:

We have said that there could not have been social-democratic (socialist) consciousness among the workers. It would have to be brought to them from without. The history of all countries shows that the working class, exclusively by its own effort, is able to develop only trade union consciousness, i.e., the conviction that it is necessary to combine in unions, fight the employers and strive to compel the government to pass necessary labor legislation, etc.

The misuse is "it would have to be brought to them from without." Outside of what? This has been interpreted to mean that class consciousness and socialist consciousness must be brought to the workers by the professionals — middle class intellectuals.

What Lenin obviously meant is that such ideas must be brought to the working class by a workingclass political party that combines workers and intellectuals, outside of the trade union movement not from outside the class. The workingclass political party is inside the class.

This became clear when he said:

I speak of the organization of revolutionaries, meaning revolutionary social democrats. In view of this common characteristic of the members of such an organization, all distinctions as between workers and intellectuals, not to speak of distinctions of trade and profession, in both categories, must be effaced.

It was also clear later when he said that in Party committees there should be eight workers to one intellectual.

What Lenin meant is that such ideas must be brought to the working class by a workingclass political party outside the trade union movement: therefore, not outside the class, because the workingclass political party is within the class. When Lenin said, "I speak of the organization of revolutionaries, meaning social democrats," he meant that in view of the common character of members of such an organization all distinctions between workers and intellectuals must be eliminated.

Lenin went further into this question about how the Party looks upon class struggle as a revolutionary movement. After the upsurge of 1905, Lenin said the ratio should be two intellectuals to 100 workers.

W E HAVE TO EXAMINE ALL LEVELS OF WORK IN TODAY'S new framework of struggle. Very closely related to Party building is the organization of Left forms. The political concepts and ideas are closer between the Party and the Left than with the overall trade union movement.

The development of the Left in this new situation is uneven. The Left has become a mass development on economic questions. The increase in the number and militancy of strikes indicate this. The Left is a growing sector around the issues of Central America and South Africa. The resolution on Central America passed at the 16th AFL-CIO Convention last year was mainly pushed by broad Left forces, which gives an indication of the growth of the Left.

The Left sector is growing within the movements for political independence. The Left is growing in the struggle for equality. There are many indications of this, including the approach to affirmative action and seniority. There is a Left among women workers, youth, etc.

So besides overall Left formations it is necessary to help organize Left forms in the specific sectors rather than just overall general Left formations. We will move faster if we organize Left forms in these specific areas.

It is not quite true, but almost, that it is very difficult to build the Party without building Left forms. I want to leave this door open. Clearly, without Left forms we will not build very fast.

Generally, in this period, the danger is sectarianism. It is almost natural. When things move, you either have to move with them or you are lagging behind. The whole idea of a new framework means things are moving and we have to move with them — find new and bold tactics and initiatives. This is necessary at this moment. I think we must make a revolutionary change.

We are far behind on the question of Party building because the objective developments are increasingly preparing the soil for it, but the objective soil will not by itself build the

Party. Farmers are now preparing for planting, but without the seeds nothing will grow. So it is with Party building. The question is: How can we build the Party as a part of these new developments?

If your trade union work does not result in Party building, you are doing poor trade union work. It is dialectical. Communists cannot do poor Party work *and* good trade union work. These are tied together. What you do to prepare workers for a strike should also prepare workers for the Party. There should be no contradiction.

If you have to be reminded, or even if you have to remind yourself, about the need to build the Party, or if it is a once-in-a-while in your thoughts, you are not going to build the Party. If it is not a part of your life, you will not recruit. Party building consciousness must be a factor in everything we do, almost spontaneously, like a conditioned reflex. It must become a part of our lifestyle. It is not that way with most of us. It is a once-in-a-while thought. If we have to say, "The Central Committee said we have to build the Party!" we probably will not do it.

What do we gain from good trade union work without the *plus*? A momentary credit. It actually turns into a negative to do good trade union work without the *plus*, because you win results without the workers learning what it was all about. It turns into an illusion for workers. Not knowing what you are really fighting for, or about, turns into a negative because it builds illusions. It is not even neutral, but negative.

For example: recently I met with an old timer, a fine comrade. He was a full-time trade union official for 50 years, who always accepted the line of the Party, always paid dues — never behind — and always made contributions. He always attended state committee meetings. He was a member of a district trade union commission. But he never recruited anyone. So now he is retiring. How do we assess his work? What has he contributed to class consciousness, to socialist revolution?

It is a negative assessment. It is a wasted political life — at least. It is very sad because he believes in socialism and the Party, but he leaves nothing. That is trade unionism without the *plus*. It adds up to nothing. We have to think about this now, before we retire. Maybe this comrade will change, but it is a little too late.

We must examine our work from such a viewpoint. It is not easy. But it is not impossible and certainly not difficult if you eliminate opportunism. It is an excuse to say that it is too difficult to add the *plus*. We have the means of doing it.

THERE HAS BEEN A TREMENDOUS EXPLOSION OF SHOP PApers. This is a very positive development. But we must examine the content and see if comrades are achieving the *plus*. Also, we have to examine the content of our writing, our speeches.

Will workers join our Party because they see Communists as good trade unionists? A few will if they know a trade unionist is a Communist. Will they stay in the Party if they remain on a trade union level? No. They will come in, but they will leave.

Will workers join the Party because of our position on racism — both Afro-American and white workers? Yes. Will they remain based on this one issue? No. Most will not.

Some will join because of our position on peace. But if they remain on this level they will not stay in the Party. Pacifism is not a solid basis for remaining in the Party.

Will workers develop class consciousness during a strike? Some, but not too many. The Hormel workers are angry at Hormel, but this is not class consciousness.

Will workers who are not class conscious join the Party? Of course, and we should recruit them, but then we must help them develop class consciousness as soon as they join. The challenge is not only to build the Party, but to build Communists. This can mainly be done on the club level.

Do we have problems with comrades who become full-time trade union leaders? Yes. This is an old weakness. In fact, I resigned as a full-time trade union organizer mainly because of this and because of the unlimited expense account. When these comrades leave the Party orbit they almost always move to the Right. In the trade union they move to the Right, but in their rhetoric they become more Left. They move Right and talk Left. They become extra critical of the Party from the Left, while they are moving to the Right.

We have had cases where comrades were moving in a right-opportunist direction in the trade union movement and in the Party they were moving to the sectarian left — defending Stalin in the Party. Their lifestyles changed. They were going to more cocktail parties and fewer Party meetings.

What is the "plus?" It is explaining issues in a way that goes beyond reforms. It is making the connection between issues, using the *People's Daily World*, using shop papers.

How to deal with ideological questions — the mind is not a blank slate. One cannot write anything one wants on it. One must argue to make room for good ideas. One must argue against bad and wrong ideas and then present good substitute ideas. If you only present new ones without getting rid of the wrong ideas, the new ones won't stick.

For example, on class collaboration, you have to undo the ideas of class collaboration in order to replace them with ideas of class struggle trade unionism. You have to undo racist ideas and, in place, argue for equality and affirmative action. To develop class consciousness you have to clear out the ideas of class collaboration. That is why this is not a spontaneous process. Therefore, we have to think about how to do this.

T HERE IS AN EXCITEMENT EVEN AMONG NON-PARTY TRADE unionists about the launching of the *People's Daily World* on May 1 of this year. Of course, the fact that the paper is Marxist-Leninist, Communist, makes it even better, more exciting. We need a revolutionary change in our approach to our new paper. There cannot be a Communist who is not involved with the paper. This should become the "Year of No Excuses."

A most basic of all basics is an understanding of what kind of paper the *People's Daily World* will be.[5] Do we all agree that, in its basic essence, the *PDW* is the voice of the Communist Party, USA? If not, we must discuss it for as long as it takes to reach a consensus that the basic nature of the paper is that it is the voice of the CPUSA.

The fundamental character of the new paper is that the *People's Daily World* not only expresses but fights for the strategic, tactical, ideological and political line as well as the policies of the Communist Party. There is a difference between giving lip service to this and fighting for it everyday in every way.

We cannot accept a situation in which the Political Bureau fights for a line and its paper does not. There must be no differences in this structure.

The *PDW* fights for united front policies, but it is not a paper of the united front. The *PDW* fights for reforms, but it is not a reformist, rather a revolutionary, newspaper. It fights for Left unity, but it is not a united Left paper — it is not a voice of Left unity. The *PDW* fights for coalitions and alliances, but it is not a paper of the coalitions or alliances. The *PDW* fights resolutely for militant trade unionism, but it is not a trade union paper.

Do we fully understand that it is precisely because the *People's Daily World* is the voice of the Communist Party that it is the best fighter for the united front, for Left unity, for reforms, for coalitions and alliances, for class unity? More than others, we must understand this question fully and be able to reflect it in the pages of the paper.

Do we understand fully and believe that the source of the clout and influence of the *PDW* is its relationship to the Party, to the science of Marxism-Leninism? That this is the source of its strength, its clarity and its power? Do we understand and agree that the main point of reference for all that we write and print is the class struggle? This should be emphasized because we have had weaknesses on this point.

Our political and ideological reflexes must be conditioned by our clear and resolute partisanship for the working class. This should be automatic — the starting point and conclusion in all articles. Our political reflexes must be conditioned for this. And it is not enough to accept these basics. The acceptance and commitment must be based on understanding the questions of the class struggle.

There are some who are influenced by the liberal argument

that to be partisan to the working class, to Marxism-Leninism, is to be non-objective, prejudiced and onesided. This leads to the idea that the paper must express both sides. This concept is not openly expressed but comes through in hesitation, hedging, omission, etc.

The reality is that the class struggle is the most objective view of capitalism. From the viewpoint of the direction of history, from the standpoint of justice, fairness, morality and human progress, partisanship to the working class is placing oneself on the right side of objectivity. Therefore there should be no hesitations about being partisan to our class.

There are also some who are still influenced by the slander that to be a Communist, to be known as the voice of the Communist Party, is sectarian. To be influenced by this is to be ignorant of the changes in objective developments, in mass patterns of thought, and to reject the new framework of struggle. The ideas of the Party are not narrow, but in fact are the most broad and inclusive of the thinking of the great majority.

Our Party's policies are rooted in and are influential with the peace majority, the anti-fascist majority, the working class in struggles arising from the structural crisis, the broad anti-racist majority, the farmers in their struggles against the farm crisis, etc.

While the majority of Americans do not accept socialism as a practical solution, they are very interested in the subject today. Thus, to speak about socialism does not isolate us. When I am a guest on radio and television talk shows today there is no hesitation, by the hosts or listeners, to ask about socialism. In fact, 40 percent of all the questions concern socialism. Of the 40 percent, 80 percent are positive and only 20 percent nasty. This is my measuring rod for thought patterns.

However, I do not think we yet handle the subject of socialism well — not only in the *PDW*, but the Party in general. We have to find ways to talk about it more popularly and boldly. The great majority of questions reflect curiosity about how socialism will work in the U.S. People are beginning to accept the idea that socialism may be the solution to our problems in the United States.

Our decision to form the *People's Daily World* is historically right on target, because of these changes in the objective picture. To be the voice of the Party is to be non-sectarian.

Our Party is on the right path, moving in the right direction, and we have been for some time. There are no major weaknesses or deviations. We are more united than ever. We can look forward to a great future for our Party.

Industrial Concentration and the Changing Class Struggle

[Written for this book, July, 1987]

WITHIN EACH OF THE TWO OPPOSING CLASSES — THE CLASS OF capital and the class of labor — there is a special sector of unique importance which influences the class and the class struggle.

In the capitalist class this special sector is monopoly. Over a hundred years ago, Karl Marx foresaw the path capitalism would follow. He said the private corporations would behave like fish; the bigger ones would keep devouring the smaller ones and finally only the very big corporations left would be left. Life has proven Marx to be right. In most areas of production we now have the big monopoly corporations: in auto, steel, electrical, etc.

The monopoly corporations have great economic and political power, and not only over the workers in their plants. The majority of American people are victims of the monopolies' economic and political oppression.

The huge monopoly corporations control prices; they are the core of the drive to bust unions; they pay very little or no taxes, leaving the rest of us to take up the burden; they drive small businesses into bankruptcy and farmers off their land;

they exert a dominating influence on our government, pressuring it always to move in an anti-workingclass, racist and militarist direction.

It is therefore in the vital interests of the American people to organize coalitions against the monopolies, and in the interests of the working class to be in the center of these anti-monopoly coalitions. Such coalitions do not replace workingclass organizations, like unions, nor do they replace the class struggle. Rather the working class needs to take the lead in establishing these coalitions. Thus they become an important part of the class struggle itself.

The working class and trade unions must always look for allies whose interests coincide with their own. It is in the interests of the Afro-American community and all racially and nationally oppressed people, poor farmers, small-business people, professionals, students and intellectuals to join with the trade unions in the struggle against the domination of the megacorporations.

In the United States we have a great tradition of fighting the monopolies. The movement that fought to pass antitrust laws in the early part of this century, for example, was an anti-monopoly movement. With the further development of the huge monopoly conglomerates, anti-monopoly movements have become inevitable.

As long as such anti-monopoly coalitions remain under the influence of labor, they provide a broader base of support for workingclass movements. The movements against monopoly and people's anti-monopoly sentiments also give the struggle for democracy and the struggle against racism a broader mass base. Anti-monopoly coalitions are playing an increasingly important role in the electoral arena.

A living example of this growing anti-monopoly alliance came on April 25th, 1987, in the massive demonstration against U.S. policies in Central America and Southern Africa. Labor played a central part in organizing and coming out for the event, and this gave the action a qualitatively higher level of unity and strength.

MASS PRODUCTION WORKERS ARE TO THE WORKING class what monopoly is to the capitalist class. They are the sector of special importance for the working class and for the class struggle as a whole. Of course this does not mean other sections of the working class are unimportant — to the contrary.

Mass production workers are of special importance because they most easily see the class nature of their exploitation. Because of their relationship to the objective conditions of class exploitation they tend to be more militant, more conscious of themselves as a class and more ready to put an end to this dead-end economic system.

Objective conditions and the direct nature of their exploitation make it easier for industrial workers to understand that their collective labor is the source of corporate profits. It is easier for them to understand that Big Business is the enemy. Mass production workers have the least room for illusions or options. Their anti-monopoly sentiment is a response to the daily corporate drive for maximum profits.

Because they work collectively they develop an attitude of "we're all in the same boat," as opposed to the dog-eat-dog mentality inherent to the class of monopoly capital. They gain a sense of their own strength, a realization that they can keep an industry going or they can stop it, an understanding that in the unity of their numbers there is great power.

Basic industrial workers, and workers in mass production industries in general, are the most advanced. They lead the way in strike struggles, in the kinds of demands they present. Industrial workers have always forged new paths of struggle like mass picketing, sitdown strikes, etc. Their victories advance the interests of the class as a whole.

Monopoly capitalism is capitalism in the raw. Profit-making and greed are the only motivating factors for the monopoly corporations. In the struggle against the power of the monopolies, the anti-human nature of capitalism becomes exposed. The dead-end nature of monopoly capitalism forces its victims to think in terms of looking for an alternative system. In that searching process, workers are coming more and more to the logical conclusion that the basic industries should be turned into public property.

Mass production workers can most easily see that the way to put an end to the injustice of a system where a few get rich by exploiting the many is for the workers to take over the industries, to get rid of corporate profits and run the industries for the good of the people. Socialism is the logical solution to the problems that cannot be solved under capitalism.

Because of these characteristics of industrial workers, Communists have long held to a policy of concentrating efforts on aiding and building the movements of industrial workers, and in this process winning workers to become revolutionaries and join the Communist Party. This is what we call our policy of industrial concentration.

New developments in the U.S. economy are having an effect on the working class and therefore on our industrial concentration policy.

The structural crisis and the rise of high technology microchip industries has resulted in some dislocations, relocations and destruction of the basic industrial structure — and this has had its impact on the working class.

The structural crisis has been carving a path of havoc and devastation —destroying industries, turning industrial cities into ghost towns, creating dust bowls and rust bowls, closing thousands of industrial plants, leaving millions homeless and hungry.

Besides closing basic industrial plants, the new technology makes it much more possible to disperse manufacturing facilities by moving them into non-industrial, non-union areas of the country. The result is a decline and deterioration of the old industrial centers and a dispersal of the basic industrial sector of the working class.

There is also a worldwide trend for U.S.-based transnational corporations to move labor-intensive facilities to areas of the world where they can exploit the most low-wage, non-union workforces; where the corporations are not compelled to provide health and safety conditions, unemployment benefits, economic or social security, and where they often pay no taxes.

Thus, fewer manufacturing facilities in the U.S. are in the production process and are increasingly becoming only the assembly and distribution points for imported parts. The overall tendency is for U.S. industry to stagnate or decline and the decline is sharpest in labor-intensive industries.

The working class is changing. But it is not — as the capitalists and their ideologues would have us believe — disappearing or even declining. In fact, it is expanding in some of the new mass production, high technology industries.

None of the changes in the profile of the working class diminishes the role of the industrial core. For one thing, steelworkers, whether working or unemployed, are still steelworkers. This is true for all workers — we must not allow the ruling class to redefine unemployed workers out of the workforce itself.

Also, it is necessary to keep perspective and not allow the anti-labor naysayers to distort the truth. Even according to official statistics, there are still at least 22 million mass production workers in our country. They are hardly "disappearing!"

But further, and more importantly, the question of the central role of mass production workers is not only a question of numbers. It is a question of what position these workers occupy in the machinery of monopoly capitalism. The drive shaft of a motor may be small compared to the gears connected to it — but it provides the motive force that causes the machine to work. So it is with the machinery of the people's movements: the mass movements that have industrial workers at the core go forward with the greatest force and the greatest unity of purpose.

EACH OF THESE SPECIAL SECTORS — MONOPOLY AND INDUStrial workers — meet in the arena of the class struggle. The monopoly sector of the capitalist class is the most anti-workingclass; the industrial sector of the working class is the most anti-monopoly. This is the basis for the Communist

Party's policy of building anti-monopoly coalitions.

Thus there is no contradiction between our policy of concentrating on the industrial working class and building anti-monopoly coalitions. In fact, the two complement each other.

There is also no contradiction between the building of anti-monopoly coalitions and our advocating socialism, just as there are no contradictions between the struggle for reforms and the struggle for socialism. The struggle for reforms does not necessarily lead to reformism; only when pursued in a reformist way.

If the struggle for reforms takes place outside of the class struggle and is based on policies of class collaboration, it will inevitably become a policy of reformism. This then presents a dead-end situation. If anti-monopoly struggles are conducted in isolation from the class struggle, they will turn simply into a plea to the fabled goodwill of the monopoly corporations.

Anti-monopoly movements do not call for the abolition of the capitalist system, but objectively they are anti-capitalist because they weaken the position and power of the capitalist class and give broad-based support to the issues and struggles of the working class. The movements against monopoly are not in and of themselves for socialism. But objectively they clear the path toward socialism.

Today there are voices announcing that the idea of the centrality of industrial workers in U.S. capitalist society is out of date. These are echoes of the voices that have been proclaiming the disappearance of the class struggle for as long as capitalism has been on the scene.

But truth is not determined by wishful thinking or slick propaganda. The truth is that the class struggle is changing, as it always has; the working class is changing; and so policies of industrial concentration need to change. But just as the class struggle and the working class are not disappearing, neither is the policy of industrial concentration. The policy needs to adapt to changes in the structure of the U.S. working class because mass production workers remain the central force in today's growing, all-people's challenge to monopoly capitalism.

no power greater

Workingclass
Unity

Black-White Unity
and the Working Class

[From: "The Afro-American/Labor Community," Political Affairs, February, 1965—slightly abridged.]

THE AFRO-AMERICAN/LABOR ALLIANCE HAS BEEN THE FOUNDA-tion on which the forward direction of American life has rested for a long time, although this has not always been obvious because its influence has been indirect and without organizational forms.

This is an alliance of the oppressed and the exploited. It is an alliance based on mutual self-interests and the oneness of the enemy. It has deep roots in our history. At each critical turning point it has tended to close ranks and its influence has grown. Within the overall framework of these long-term and short-range mutual self-interests there have been and continue to be areas of contradiction. These contradictions create problems but they have not in any way changed the basic essence of the alliance or its role in our history.

The 20 million Afro-American citizens[1] are an oppressed people, subjected to a system of segregation and discrimination which has its historic roots in the plantation system of slavery. U.S. capitalism has adopted this special system to divide the working class and the people, to cut down the resistance to its oppression and exploitation. Jim Crow[2] is an instrument for extracting maximum profits from Black and white workers.

As is the case with colonialism on the world scene, ending the system of Jim Crow has emerged as the most crucial domestic question for the United States. Its time has arrived and it cannot be long postponed. All class groups are forced to take a stand on it, for it is not only the future of the millions of Afro-Americans that is involved. The future of the entire country rides on how this question is solved. This includes our democratic institutions, our educational system, the pattern of our economy, the future of organized labor, and so on.

The force that will largely determine the nature of the solution is the Afro-American/workingclass community. While Afro-Americans are all victims of special oppression, there is a growing class differentiation among them. In this, Black workers, who are part of both the U.S. working class and the oppressed Afro-American people, are of cardinal importance.

The destruction of the evil system of discrimination and segregation — directed against Black citizens but used to divide all the victims of monopoly capital — has emerged as an absolute condition for progress. The mass movement that now fights for its elimination has therefore emerged as the generative force that sparks the struggle for progress on all fronts.

All societies with class divisions inevitably produce one class whose self-interest propels it to become the leader and the center of gravity for all forces of progress. In our times, life has assigned this responsibility to the working class. On its broad shoulders rests the advance of civilization.

The opposite side of this historical coin is that simultaneously there also arises a class that embodies all that is reactionary and backward. In modern times, the sewer that carries all this refuse and dirt and sickness is the class of capital.

One class leads in the struggle for progress, the other creates obstacles to it. One is constructive, the other is destructive of all human values. One propels social advance, the other attempts to turn the wheels of history back. One class covers its resistance to progress with an ideology of cynicism and demagogy, and with an appeal to prejudice and backwardness. The other inscribes on its ideological banners all concepts that guide and support humanity in its rise to a higher form of civilization.

In each country the rise of these class forces is a distinct historical process. With time each of the classes increasingly takes on its specific role and nature, and this process continues until it leads to a qualitative shift which completely discards the reactionary class and the system that gave rise to it.

This class framework is as valid and real in determining the course of affairs in the United States as it is everywhere else in the world. With all its weaknesses our working class in the United States has fulfilled its historical responsibilities and is continuing to do so. The fact that it has not fully taken on what history demands of it, or that it has not carried the struggle to its final conclusion, does not in any way disqualify it as the most advanced element of our society.

It is only on the basis of this objective class relationship that one can give leadership in the struggles to end all evils of capitalism. The attempt to deal with social or economic problems on any other basis will lead to blind alleys. The very heart of capitalist propaganda is the denial of the class nature of capitalism and the role of the working class. The influence of such ideas penetrates even into the ranks of the progressive movement.

Only an understanding of the class forces and their role in society makes it possible for one to understand the phenomena of alliances, coalitions and united front formations in struggle. These are relationships built around parallel and mutual self-interests, which can and do cut across class lines. Because of its objectively designated role in history, the working class attracts all sectors of the population whose self-interests are served by a progressive direction in life. In some cases these self-interests run along parallel lines for only brief periods. Coalitions in such cases are of brief duration and are usually around very specific issues. But this does not in any way minimize their importance. The history of human progress is in fact a history of the rise and fall of coalitions and alliances based on parallel mutual self-interests.

There are also coalitions that are based upon long-range mutual self-interest. Such coalitions run the course of whole historic epochs.

With these things in mind, I want to deal with the historic role and nature of the Afro-American/labor alliance in the United States. This is a very distinctive kind of alliance, one that runs the course of epochs. Without an understanding of this central phenomenon of our society one cannot fully understand the American scene.

In a sense the Afro-American/labor coalescence is more than an alliance or a united front formation. It is a political and economic community, an overlapping, interlinked unit. As the consciousness of this grows in its ranks, this community will become the power that will determine the direction of events in our country.

On a world scale, the working class is emerging as that class on whose shoulders the future of civilization rests. Because the working class is the leading element in the world socialist, anti-imperialist, peace community, it is now the decisive force determining the course of world events. Hence the elements in the community are more than allies of one another; they are parts of one historical revolutionary process, part of one progressive community, of an interlinked unit. And one can understand the nature and role of this community only if one understands the nature and role of the working class.

A DISTINCTIVE FEATURE OF THE HISTORIC FORMATION OF the U.S. working class has been the molding of a class composed of Black and white workers, a class of many national backgrounds. This fact has always provided U.S. capitalism with a special ideological weapon in its efforts to create divisions and dissensions: the weapon of prejudice. Nevertheless within capitalist society there is nothing so inevitable, so absolute as the emergence, growth and political maturing of the working class. The development of class consciousness, class unity and class struggle are all rooted in the very process of exploitation. To deny the rise and the historic role of the working class is to deny the very class nature of capitalism.

And so, in spite of the obstacle created by the system of discrimination — the practice of keeping Black workers out of some industries altogether and confining them to the hardest, lowest-paying jobs in others — and in spite of the constant infusion of the poison of white chauvinism as an inseparable component of capitalist ideology, a united, integrated working class is taking shape and assuming its designated historic place. Indeed, the process of forming an integrated working class of Black and white workers as the basis of the Afro-American/labor community has paved the way for an integrated nation in which all of our people will live in equality.

The historic path to a united, integrated working class has been marked by many obstacles and many setbacks. Such a process is slow because it is fundamentally a process of development of a class ideology and class outlook. Ideology is the result of experience built upon experience. For long periods most white workers could not see their overall class interests because of the heavy fog of chauvinism and prejudice. The fog has slowly dissipated, though much of it still remains.

With the lifting of the fog, the process of unification takes place through a series of qualitative leaps. The unionization of the basic mass production industries remains a landmark as one of these qualitative leaps. It went a long way toward destroying the ideology behind craft trade unionism: hiding the workingclass nature of society. The craft union ideology was an instrument that long divided Black and white workers.

The CIO and especially the Left-led unions made historic contributions to this development. Their formation firmly established the concept that all workers, Black and white, of all trades and professions, belong to united industrial unions and locals.

A graphic illustration of both processes — the formation of an integrated, united working class and the development and rise of the Afro-American/labor community — was the Conference to Organize the Negro Steel Workers into the New Steelworkers Union, held in Pittsburgh, Pennsylvania in 1937. This was a conference representing all sectors of the Afro-American people and their organizations, meeting with the leaders of the newly emerging steel union. This participation was a clear indication of how the leaders of the Afro-American people's organizations understood both the role of a united, integrated working class in defense of its own class interests and that of the Afro-American/labor community in the struggle against Jim Crow. This conference was an important step in the development of both of these processes.

The process of integration and unification of the working class is continuing. Black workers have become a part of the most militant and most union-conscious sector of the U.S. working class. This process and the growth of class consciousness in the ranks of the working class are parts of the same development. Class consciousness is the most formidable antidote to the poison of chauvinism and prejudice.

The process of class integration has made its clearest advances wherever the need for class unity has been most obvious. Thus each economic struggle has been a classroom for integration and unity. In such struggles, class and individual self-interests rise to the surface, and the evil, divisive purpose of chauvinism becomes more obvious and therefore more easily exposed.

The influence of the rising integrated, united working class on the struggles of today is not always fully appreciated because this influence is not always direct or dramatic. But as the fog lifts, as workers get a new qualitative sense of their class position, they will increasingly have a greater influence on the character of all mass currents and movements.

The methods of mass struggle today already show the influences of workingclass experience. The sit-ins, boycotts, picket lines, mass demonstrations, combining economic struggle with political action, and the tactic of alliances and united front relations are all variations of methods originally developed in the fires of the class struggle. And the leaders and spokespeople of religious and social organizations take a more forthright stand for civil rights where they sense the influence of members of the working class in their organizations and communities.

The vote for the 1964 Civil Rights Act was a barometer of how elected officials assess the mood of the people in general. But above all it was an assessment of the mood of the Afro-American/labor community in the big industrial centers. Workers are most often not the spokespeople or the leaders of reform movements. But invariably it is the Afro-American/labor community that is the mass base of all of them.

Therefore, to appreciate fully the present role and influence of this community one has to study its grassroots base and the details of relations and forces that never appear in headlines or are not immediately evident. But it is from this base that all movements get their staying power and their militance. Movements that do not have the support of this mass base are usually very short-lived.

RACIST DISCRIMINATION AND UNORGANIZED SHOPS ARE closely related twin evils in the South. They are, in fact, two faces of one policy designed for one purpose: maximum profits for Big Business and the landowners. The net result of this policy is a "Southern differential" of lower wages, longer hours, mass poverty, mass misery.

The brutal oppression of Black Americans, combined with an open policy of violence against unions and progressive organizations — this is the strategy of Big Business for keeping the South a sort of semicolonial preserve for extreme exploitation, high profits, cheap labor, runaway shops and disfranchised people ruled by a racist, fascist-like gang through terror and murder. Big Business wants this kind of South not only because of the immediate profits it yields but because it is a bulwark of reaction throughout the nation. The ultra-Right Goldwater's attempt to use the South as a base in his bid for power strikingly illustrates the point.

The heart of the forces that will break this stranglehold of reaction on the South is the Afro-American/labor community. Toward this end it is necessary to find the link that brings together the drives to end Jim Crow and to abolish non-union shops. The trade unions will have to understand that they will never conquer the one evil by ignoring its inseparable twin.

Jim Crow is anti-union; anti-union policies are instruments in perpetuating Jim Crow. These are the two sides of the coin. The struggle against the common enemy in the South demands a new level of unity and integration of the working class and a new quality in the relations within the Afro-American/labor community. This is the central challenge facing the leaders and the rank and file of this community nationally.

The history of the American people is full of examples of how the objective forces in our society have pressed toward the formation of both the Afro-American/labor community and an integrated, united working class. Because these early efforts did not result in the full-blown product, or because there were numerous setbacks, is no reason to call them failures. Nor are these grounds for rejecting the idea that these things are in the process of development. Each of the experiences in our history has added something to this development. And each new development has in turn made the objective conditions more ripe and has thereby slowly increased the pressure of the objective screws of history.

In the last century the Knights of Labor[3] constituted the first real attempt to organize a national workingclass union. They were outlawed and condemned. But even these early class formations had in them the seeds of the unified, integrated class of Black and white workers. The objective forces were just beginning to turn the screws. In the South, Black workers led the heroic efforts to organize unions under the conditions then existing.

In 1885 these efforts were recorded as follows: "They are now everywhere joining the Knights of Labor. Do not discriminate against them. They are considered amongst their most faithful members." At about the same time a union leader reported from Richmond, Virginia: "The Negro workers are with us heart and soul and have organized seven assemblies (locals) in this city and are in Manchester with large memberships."

Trade unionism in the South today can be most meaningful if it rests on large industrial union locals of an integrated working class, which have put an end to the practices of discrimination in their shops and have outlawed racist discrimination by union contract and union constitution. This relationship can then become the basis for an Afro-American/labor community that can determine the direction of union affairs in the South. It was during the Civil War that the Afro-American/labor community left its first indelible mark on our history. The post-Civil War period is evidence of the fact that it did not take long for the capitalist class to realize the potential danger to its selfish aims which the development of such a community presented. It quickly let loose a campaign of murder and terror.

The capitalist class allied itself with the forces against the slave-based South only for as long as its narrow self-interests were served, and not for one minute longer. Ethical, moral or humanitarian considerations were not factors that motivated them. As long as the capitalist class of the North profited from slavery, it supported the slave society of the South. The ships owned by New England capital sailed to Africa loaded with rum, and there exchanged the rum for slaves whom they carried to the Southern states to be sold at the slave market. In turn they bought molasses from the slave markets and returned to New England where the molasses was turned into rum and the cycle started all over again.

Only later, when the slave system became an obstacle to the expansion of its profit-making empires, did the capitalist class give its support to the struggle against the slave society of the South. This was a very brief period, because capitalism was interested in doing away only with those features of slavery that were adverse to its self-interests. In fact it adopted as its own those features of slavery that aided its drive for profits. This is the background for the present system of segregation and discrimination, of white chauvinism and terror practiced against Afro-Americans.

The relationship of the working class to the issues and

forces involved in the Civil War was quite different. For example, how different the course of our history might have been if the working class of England had not stopped the English government from entering into armed struggle against the North when the outcome of the Civil War was hanging in the balance. The working class was the only force that opposed the armed attack. It put up a historic battle. Because of this, Abraham Lincoln regarded the attitude of the English working class towards Afro-American slavery as "an instance of sublime Christian heroism which has not been surpassed in any age or in any country."[4]

It is true that the working class was motivated by its own long-range self-interests. But these were also the self-interests of human society as a whole in its struggle forward.

In 1830 Thomas Wentworth Higginson, a New Englander, wrote: "The anti-slavery movement was not strongest among the more educated classes, but was predominantly a people's movement based on the simplest human instincts and far stronger for a time in the factories and the shoe shops than in the pulpits or colleges."[5] One of the first political parties to declare in its platform the need to abolish slavery was a newly-formed political party of labor.

The Civil War period also has rich lessons on the nature of alliances based on parallel self-interests. The victorious alliance against slavery finally included the slaves, the workers and the frontier farmers, as well as sections of the capitalist class, and the clergy and professional people, mainly in the Northern states. Though these were allied against slavery, the contradictions between the classes in the alliance did not disappear. The advanced sections of the working class fought to include and combine the struggle against wage slavery with the struggle against chattel slavery. The capitalist class fought against all concepts of classes and class struggle within capitalism. Most of the popular leaders for the abolition of slavery took a position favorable to the struggles of the working class. These were swallows heralding the future course of development of the Afro-American/labor community.

But not all of the anti-slavery forces could see the relationship of the rising working class and its aims to the struggle against the slave system. Even such a militant fighter against slavery as William Lloyd Garrison argued:

> An attempt has been made — it is still in the making — we regret to say, with considerable success — to inflame the minds of our working class against the more opulent. . . .

And further:

> There is a prevalent opinion that wealth and aristocracy are indissolubly allied; and the poor and vulgar are taught to consider the opulent as their natural enemies. Those who circulate this pernicious doctrine are the worst enemies of the people.[6]

These differences in the alliance created stresses and strains, but the objective screws pressed the alliance against slavery. The precursors of the Afro-American/labor community of today were even present in the actions of the beginnings of an organized labor movement in the South. Motivated by self-interest, as early as 1831 organized white mechanics petitioned the Legislature of Virginia to abolish the competition of slave mechanics. They complained that "the wealthy owners of slave mechanics were in the habit of underbidding them in contracts."[7] Their protest meetings were brutally smashed.

Not all of early labor understood the urgency, from the standpoint of their own self-interest, of the need to end the slave system. Some argued that an end to their "wage slavery" would then force an end to the slave system in the South. But then as now the special oppression of Afro-Americans constituted a roadblock to progress. Then as now it was in the self-interests of all exploited and oppressed to join together in an alliance to put an end to racist discrimination.

T HUS, THE AFRO-AMERICAN/LABOR POLITICAL AND ECOnomic community is a specific U.S. historical development. It has roots in history, and is fed by present-day objective factors. In the very center of this community is the developing united, integrated Black and white working class, ever more conscious of its class nature and its assigned role in our present and future history.

It is important to understand the nature of this community and the role of the working class in it because all future progress basically emanates from this source. It is important because all who try — for whatever reason — to create divisions in this community are acting to disperse and to dissipate the main driving forces of progress. What we are called upon to do is to find the issues, the organizational forms, the understanding that will help the objective conditions further unite this community.

Women and the Working Class

[From: "Class Approach to Women's Liberation," speech to Communist Party conference on work among women, 1970 — slightly abridged.]

LIFE IS PRESSING ALL FORCES TO TAKE A NEW LOOK AND TO MAKE a new appraisal of the role women are playing in the struggles for social progress.

Women are a most crucial force in the overall mass upsurge in the country. They are playing an increasingly leading role in the various movements and struggles, especially in the fight for peace. But beyond this there is an upsurge of struggle for the equality of women.

This is a many-sided movement, based on many issues. There are, for example, movements around specific shop economic issues, struggles for child-care centers, against the high cost of living and around welfare issues. There are also growing movements around the general problems arising from the special oppression and inequality women encounter.

I am sure you agree with me that the problems in the struggle for the equality of women are not just "women's problems." In fact, this is not a question of freeing women alone. The struggle for women's equality is an essential prerequisite and feature of the struggle for the liberation of human society as a whole. It is a struggle that is in the self-interests and is the responsibility of all who fight for social progress.

Most of my remarks will deal with the Marxist framework for an examination of these movements. I especially want to deal with the relationship between the struggle for the equality of women and the class struggle as the most fundamental of all questions.

T HE SPECIFIC FORMS OF OPPRESSION AND PRACTICES OF inequality — based on race, minority status or sex — have always been and remain today basically rooted in those social systems motivated solely by the exploitation of the many for the profit of a few: that is, social systems of one class exploiting another. There are additional forms of inequality in the overall system of class exploitation. They are special forms through which to extract superprofits. Therefore, the struggles against these specific and special forms of oppression and exploitation must of necessity be a feature of, and closely related to, the overall struggle against the class systems of exploitation and oppression.

It follows from this that the special forms of oppression and exploitation cannot be fully eliminated until the overall struggle against the system of class exploitation is victorious. In one form or another these will hang on until the system is destroyed, root and branch. Not theory but life creates the unbreakable relationship between the two. Any attempt to deal with the struggle for women's equality as a thing in itself, separated from the overall struggle, is self-defeating. It becomes a classless dead-end.

This is a fundamental question. It determines the direction the movement should take. It determines the nature of the alliance, of the allies, of the programs.

For us Communists this is the very cornerstone of the entire struggle because it rests on the relationship between the fight for the equality of women and the class struggle, the tie-in between the forces of the struggle for women's equality and the working class. It makes the necessary connection between these special struggles and the destruction of the system that breeds all forms of exploitation. It relates the final victory in these struggles with the establishment of a social system that outlaws class exploitation and with it the special forms of discrimination and oppression based on sex, race and minority status.

We believe that the basic form and content of oppressive systems is class exploitation. History is basically a history of struggle against such systems. Thus the main form and content of the history of struggle for social progress is the class struggle.

Under capitalism the working class is the product and the direct victim of this exploitation. As a class it is compelled to become the main force to end all forms of exploitation and oppression. It is this fundamental analysis of social forces that dictates the need for a class approach to all struggles — including the struggles against the special forms of inequality and oppression. This is a guiding principle for us. This is the only way to assess capitalist reality.

The class approach does not in any sense argue against the need for special emphasis, special programs and special forms of struggle against the special forms of oppression and exploitation. It argues for a correct relationship — the only winning one — between the two areas of struggle. This is the only path to victory in the special struggles because it is the only way the victims of special oppression can gain the support of the victims of class exploitation. It is the only way they can draw on the strength of the class forces fighting capitalism.

I do not think that the full story of the nature of the alliance between the suffrage movement and the working class — especially its revolutionary sector — has been written. Workingclass support for women's voting rights was the most crucial factor in that struggle.

The self-interest relationship between the two arenas of struggle is a two-way street. The task of Marxists is to make this clear. We must expose and reject all concepts that tend to separate the forces of struggle for women's equality from the working class. It is self-evident why the spokespeople for the exploiting class build walls, real as well as imaginary, between them. We must tear down those walls.

This basic class approach does not rule out other important factors and influences. The instruments of oppression are many. They are direct and indirect. They are both physical and ideological. Without the ideological weapon of racism, chauvinism and nationalism, the social systems based on class exploitation would have long since been discarded. They are the opium of the people. They are the ideological weapon for divide and rule. They are more potent than religion has ever been.

In this sense, the ideological concept of male supremacy is an instrument of the system for the special oppression and exploitation of women. This special oppression is economic, it is political, and it is social. Practices of inequality in home and family life reflect the social system in which we live. It is a live factor in most families and homes and is based on the customs and habits developed and nurtured by concepts of male supremacy.

The potency of this drug can be measured in men who will give their lives in the struggle against all other forms of oppression but themselves practice, maintain and defend concepts of the inequality of women on the basis of the backward ideology of male supremacy — an ideology springing from the very essence of slavery, feudalism and capitalism.

Struggle against these backward concepts is related to struggle against the roots from which they spring. I think this is true even in progressive families, where ideological concepts carry a bigger stick than in non-political families.

The explosive birth of the new society will eliminate the system of production for private profit. It will outlaw all practices of discrimination and oppression. But it will not end with its birth the ideological influence of the theory of the inferiority of women. The new human being will not arrive with the explosion. People will not shed the old ideological influences at the portals of the new society. Many of the ideological hangups will hang on for some time. Concepts and practices of male supremacy, as capitalist leftovers, still appear even in the countries of socialism. As is the case with all ideological leftovers, even here they will not disappear without a persistent ideological struggle.

With the above framework in mind, let us now bring into sharper focus the struggle for women's equality.

There is a great, new interest in the role of women as fighters for social progress because they are a decisive new force in today's mass rebellions. They are the most consistent contingent of the struggle against U.S. imperialist aggressions. Black women are writing a heroic page in the struggle for Afro-American equality. Women are giving a new dimension to the struggle of the Puerto Rican people. The same is true of Chicana women. From positions of experience and strength they are making a most important, unique contribution to all struggles. In a new way, and in greater numbers than ever before, women are a powerful force on the picket lines, in demonstrations, as well as in the mass movements against high prices, high taxes and high rents.

But I think the shift is even more fundamental. Both in number and in quality women are playing a distinctive role in this present turning point of history. The contribution of women as a revolutionary force in the transition from capitalism to socialism is qualitatively on a different level than at other historic turning points. Of course this is not to say that women have not contributed in past periods, including the past historic struggles in our country.

I think we must see the historic nature of the new qualitative shift in the role of women today. This new role of women can be dramatically seen in Vietnam and in the socialist countries. Women are also playing a new role in the national liberation movements throughout the world.

This new role is related to the nature of the present historic turning point, a turning point that is putting an end to all forms of exploitation, including the special forms based on race or sex. The historic process that has elevated women to the position of being greater molders of history than in the past will escalate further and make a new qualitative leap as life moves to the stages of socialism and communism. Because of this, there is a new qualitative significance to the struggle for women's equality.

Forms of oppression are universal. But the exploiters of each country give their systems of slavery certain national traits. There are also specific conditions in each country that affect the forms of struggle.

I THINK THERE ARE FOUR DISTINCT FEATURES OF THE SCENE IN the United States that have their effects on all struggles. They are reflected in the women's struggle for equality. The foremost of these features is the class composition of the female segment of our population.

American women are the most workingclass of any in the capitalist world. This is true in regard to the number of women at the point of production and in regard to the numbers who are wives and mothers in workingclass families. They are 37 percent of the workforce now in 1970 and the numbers increase every year.[8]

This class composition of American women has a profound influence on the working class. This must therefore be the starting point in the development of the struggle for women's equality.

Women working in industry are no longer merely a wartime phenomenon. They are not only in the light industries. While it is true that 80 percent of the workers in the apparel industry and 46 percent in textile are women, the technological revolution has added an important new dimension to the role of women in industry. It has increased the numbers of women employed in the basic industries. They are 36 percent of the workers in the manufacture of scientific and engineering instruments; they are 28 percent of the workers in the ammunition and ordnance industry. New technology is a factor in adding new dimensions to the policies of discrimination and inequality. Women are being made a factor in the frenzied corporate drive for even higher rates of exploitation through automation.

This higher rate of exploitation is related to a policy of dispersal of automated plants. Corporations have built many new automated plants away from the workingclass industrial centers. This is taking place both in the North and South. The Tennessee Valley Authority[9] has just reported that during the last three years almost 90 percent of the new industrial jobs resulting from building new plants in the seven TVA states have been created in rural areas away from the five big industrial centers in those states. A great percentage of these new workers are women — a much higher percentage than in the old plants.

These new runaway, automated plants, with the new workers mostly unorganized, are used by the monopolies to set low rates for the jobs of all workers in all plants. This increases the rate of exploitation. It is not surprising that this is one of the big issues in the current General Electric strike. This strike is the most important front of struggle for women's equality today. Like most of the newer factories this plant has a high percentage of women. Skilled women workers with over 12 years of seniority employed in the automated processes are paid less than the janitors who are men.

Why corporations foster and hang onto policies of discrimination against women workers is clear from the following. Women workers produce as much as men but they receive 24 percent less in wages than men for the same work. And if the comparison is made with the wages of Black women workers who receive 25 percent less than white women, then it is clear that the rate of exploitation here is more than double that of men workers. This is a source of superprofits. These increases in the rate of exploitation have all been greatly intensified by the new technology.

It is clear that class struggles against the effects of automation involve in a very special way the struggle against corporate policies of squeezing out extra profit through discrimination and higher rates of exploitation of women workers. The GE strike is a precedent-setting struggle in many ways. Most important is the effect it will have on women workers, their wages and working conditions.

It is also clear that many of the new unorganized workers are women. Therefore the problem of organizing the unorganized is closely related to getting the leadership of the trade unions to see the new importance of standing at the head of the struggle against discrimination based on sex.

Women are demanding a new role in the leadership of the unions. Based on other experiences, it is clear that women workers are becoming an important factor in the rank-and-file movements. There is no reason why women workers should not organize themselves into women's caucuses in shops and local unions. Such caucuses can join forces with other rank-and-file movements. This will add greatly to their power.

As the class confrontation sharpens, the working class is faced with many new problems. Most crucial of these is the struggle on the political front. The working class is forced to break new ground in establishing forms of independent political action. Such political action cannot be limited to shop talk or local union activities. It must be rooted in the workingclass neighborhoods. It must involve workers' families. From this it is clear that women are a key factor in labor's struggle for political independence.

Both the women who work in industry and workingclass wives and mothers are directly involved in this crucial phase of the class struggle. In a sense, women become the important links between the class struggle in the shops and the class struggle in the political and electoral arena. Labor cannot successfully develop political independence without the involvement of this 51 percent of the population.

From all this it follows that the struggle for equality of women in the U.S. is closely tied to the key developments of the class struggle. This is where its main allies are, this is where its main cadre must come from. It must reflect the issue of day care centers in general, but above all it must react to the problem as it is faced by workingclass mothers. It must reflect the general struggles against high prices, taxes and rents, but special attention must be given to how these issues affect workingclass families.

This special class emphasis is correct for all capitalist countries. But because of the unique class composition of the women in the United States, it is a crucial necessity for us.

We Marxists fight for the dominance of a workingclass ideology. In all struggles and movements we push for a workingclass approach. We must do this in the movement for women's equality. Our emphasis is on the working class because that's where it's at, that's where the meaningful action is.

A SECOND FEATURE AFFECTING ALL STRUGGLES IN THE U.S. is the role and nature of the struggle for Afro-American equality. The relationship between the forces of class struggle and the forces of struggle for Afro-American equality is a central, unique question in our country. A correct understanding of this fact is of decisive importance in the struggle against capitalism. This understanding is also necessary for a correct approach to all other areas of struggle, including the struggle for women's equality. The importance of the movement for Afro-American equality is further heightened when one takes into consideration that some 40 million of our citizens are victims of one or another form of racial oppression. It is further emphasized by the fact that the great majority of Black Americans — including the majority of Black women — are workers, class brothers and sisters in the workingclass family.

In all this, the crucible of life has placed Black women in a special relationship to all struggles for social progress. Of all workingclass women, the Black woman worker is the most exploited. Of all women who suffer inequalities and indignities, Black women are victims many times over. More than anyone else they are the prisoners of the ghettos. Therefore a movement for women's equality that is not related to the specific problems faced by Black women will go exactly nowhere.

If the need for day care centers is important for workingclass mothers, it is critical for women in the ghettos.

Because of all these factors, the women's movement has a special responsibility in the struggle for Black-white unity. In this, the white women have a special responsibility in the fight against the influence of racism. Black and white unity in the struggle for women's equality can have a very special influence on the struggle against racism as a whole.

In the struggles of recent years, Black women have written many a heroic page. They have made and are making a unique contribution in the area of Afro-American equality in the class struggle and in the general fight for women's equality. The tasks of relating women's equality to the struggle for Afro-American equality, to the special problems faced by Black women and to the working class as a whole — these cannot be separated. The elements of self-interest in all these struggles parallel, overlap and fuse.

The third special factor that gives the women's movement in the United States a unique quality is the fact that we live in the very center of world imperialism. The fact that U.S. imperialism has more imperialist holdings and that U.S. corporations exploit more human beings than any other country at any time in history must affect our struggles at home. Our mass movements cannot escape the ugly fact that U.S. imperialism is the criminal murderer of millions of women and children. We cannot close our eyes to the slaughter of defenseless women and children by U.S. troops in the My Lai hamlet.[10]

The struggle for women's equality must be uniquely tied to the struggle against U.S imperialism. We have not yet defeated U.S. imperialism but we can be proud of the massive struggle against it. More than to any other sector of our people, the credit must go to the women of America, especially young women. They have been the most consistent, militant force in the battle.

The fourth special factor is the high level of the development of U.S. monopoly capitalism — of state monopoly capitalism.

Women are the victims of the monopolies as workers, housewives, professionals, farmers and small-business people. Class exploitation and special oppression are now basically policies dictated by monopoly capitalism. The councils of the corporations, of the military industrial complex, are all staffed by men. I know it is not the goal of progressive women to sit in these councils, but these set the stage for the special problems women face. For these are the councils of the exploiters.

Women face the forces of monopoly on all levels of life: in the factory, in the supermarket, in the tax offices and in the actions of the rent gougers. Therefore the struggle for the equality of women must be related to and be a part of the anti-monopoly struggle and movement.

The new policies of forcing the unemployed off the welfare rolls into employment on a starvation level creates critical problems, especially for mothers who, in many families, are the only breadwinners. In the industrial centers, mothers who are on the rolls for Aid to Families with Dependent Children —and especially Black mothers — are forced to take some of the worst, dirtiest and lowest-paid jobs in industry. These are jobs workers accept only in an emergency. When these women leave such jobs they are refused aid of any kind.

Finally let me say that we Communists also have a unique responsibility in this struggle. It is we who must give the trade union movement, the movement for Afro-American equality, the youth and peace movements, and in a general way the male section of the population, a Marxist understanding and appreciation of the struggle for women's equality. This understanding is an essential ingredient of victory over capitalism.

Workers of
the World

revolutionary force

The Working Class In Our Era

World Workingclass Unity

[From: "The Struggle Against Imperialism — The Common Task of the Communists and All Revolutionary Forces," paper written after the 1969 International Meeting of Communist and Workers' parties — abridged.]

THE TRANSITION FROM CAPITALISM TO SOCIALISM IS A MANY-sided process. It is political, it is ideological, it is military, and it is economic. There are moments of explosion. There are periods of evolutionary development. There are violent transfers of class power and there are some not so violent transitions.

This transition from capitalism to socialism and communism is life's way of resolving the main contradiction of our times: the contradiction expressed in the class struggle and the world revolutionary process, giving birth on a world scale to the two social systems of socialism and capitalism. Only the class contradiction gives rise to this process. Only the transition to socialism will remove this contradiction, the main obstacle to human progress.

It is the anti-capitalist and anti-imperialist forces which now determine the overall course of human events. The process of transition from capitalism to socialism has resulted in over one-third of the world's people building their lives within socialist societies. It has resulted in national independence for most of the world's countries and peoples. It has given rise to powerful workingclass revolutionary movements in all corners of the world. It has resulted in capitalism being repeatedly defeated.

The greatest battle of our times, that is determining the course of all human events, is the historic contest now going on between the two world systems, capitalism and socialism. In this conflict the struggle for people's minds is crucial.

It is my firm conviction that capitalism is now losing this most important aspect of the battle. In the world today it is difficult to find an open, unashamed defender of capitalism, and there are no defenders of U.S. capitalism anywhere. The big debate throughout the world is about what kind of socialism is desirable, not about whether or not socialism is desirable. Capitalism is on the defensive and ideas for the advancement of human society come more and more from the socialist sector of the world.

The competition between the two world systems in the fields of industry, technology and science is now entering a new stage. Socialism has now overcome the handicap of the industrial and technological backwardness that it inherited from the past. From this point on it will compete with capitalism from the broad, modern industrial base that it has achieved. Consequently, the ground rules of the competition between the two systems have changed. Up to this point the score was measured by maximum productive capacity.

New technology is making overcapacity or at least sufficient capacity increasingly a permanent feature of society. Thus the question of how much a system can produce is turning into a moot question. Instead, what is going to emerge as the central point of the competition is what a social system does with this unlimited industrial capacity.

From our own experience we already know what the new technology has brought society under capitalism. It has aggravated the employment problem for unskilled and semiskilled workers. Automation has created a new permanent army of unemployed, sharply curtailed employment possibilities of youth generally and closed the door to employment of Black, Puerto Rican and Mexican-American youth.

As machines replace people in production, the hours of work should be correspondingly reduced for all. This is exactly what is being done in the socialist countries and it is in these countries, therefore, that automation is considered a great blessing for all. In the capitalist economy, however, it is something to be feared by workers. As the machine replaces people in production it reduces wages and consequently purchasing power. This creates the dilemma of too much capacity and not enough consumption. A distinction between the two world systems is that capitalism is developing increasingly towards overcapacity and underconsumption and thus towards an ever greater polarization of poverty and affluence, while socialism is developing towards increasing capacity geared to abundance for all.

Ever since the emergence of the world's first socialist state the concept "socialism" has been causing people to ask many questions. The nature of these questions changes constantly and this change reveals a shift in the attitude of millions of people. Fifty years ago the question often put was: "How soon will the Bolshevik experiment collapse?" Thirty years ago it was: "Will socialism work?" By ten years ago the question had become: "How well does socialism work?" Now, more and more, the question asked is: "How come it works so well?" And there is a companion question: "How come it works better than capitalism?" I think this question will become ever louder and more demanding of answers.

The answer, of course, is no mystery to Marxists. Irreconcilable contradictions are the undoing of any social system, and capitalism is built around such contradictions. When the 70 million Americans who do not have the means to buy even the minimum of subsistence read about surpluses of food and clothing, for them the contradictions of capitalism are a stark reality.

For years, peace forces in the United States have been demanding spending for welfare not warfare. But they could show little success. The bulk of the trade union movement stood aside from this struggle, or was misled by the monopoly-inspired slogan of "guns and butter."

Now this is changing. Everybody can see by now that the swollen military budget is an instrument for swelling profits and a prime cause of all the crises affecting our people, from the crisis of the cities to the debt crisis and the crisis of taxes. Important sections of the trade union movement are demanding a real cut in military spending, together with a real increase in spending for the social needs of the working people.

This is beginning to give the trade union struggles a new direction. The struggles around these issues are entering a more meaningful phase because the working class is becoming increasingly involved. On these issues there is much in common between the interests of shop workers and those of professionals, white-collar people, farmers and small-business people.

THE KEY TO VICTORY ON THESE FRONTS IS THE COALITION OF these forces, with the working class in the lead. That is what the idea of anti-monopoly coalition is all about. The experience of many Communist parties shows that the idea of the democratic anti-monopoly struggle is central in defining their strategic aims.

The choice of the anti-monopoly concept as the basis of our strategy is not an arbitrary one. It is dictated by our Marxist understanding of the basic character of present-day capitalist society. Those who wish to reject it reject also, whether they like it or not, the Marxist concept of the capitalist social structure.

A classical feature of revisionism is its rejection of the concept of the dictatorship of the proletariat. The line runs as follows: "We accept such fundamental Marxist-Leninist concepts as the class struggle, but we believe the idea of the proletarian dictatorship must be discarded as being no longer valid." But scientific theory is not a mere collection of propositions from which one can choose as one selects food items in a cafeteria. It is a logically interconnected body, a chain of propositions in which one emerges as the necessary conclusion from another. Thus the idea of workingclass political rule as the necessary basis of socialism flows inevitably from the Marxist concept of the class struggle. One cannot be discarded without discarding the other.

By the same token, the concept of the anti-monopoly movement and alliance emerges as a necessary consequence of the basic features of the monopoly stage of capitalism and especially of the dominance of state monopoly capitalism, which marks the capitalist social structure today. The rise of monopoly and state monopoly capitalism gives birth to a new contradiction: that between monopoly and the people, growing out of and superimposed on the basic class conflict. And this leads inevitably to the anti-monopoly character of all democratic struggles today and hence to the concept of an anti-monopoly movement, intertwined with the struggle for workingclass political power.

Those who would reject the anti-monopoly concept proceed from two lines of argument. The first of these downgrades and discards the democratic struggle, and calls for a "pure" revolutionary strategy — an "anti-capitalist" or "anti-imperialist" strategy. It pits these "revolutionary" strategies against the allegedly "non-revolutionary" anti-monopoly strategy. It is adherence to such a "non-revolutionary" strategy, say these upholders of "pure" revolution, that makes the Party itself a conservative, no longer revolutionary organization. They refuse to see the interrelationship of the democratic anti-monopoly struggle and the revolutionary struggle for socialism.

Views of this kind distort the attitude of Communists toward the democratic movement. "Theoreticians" of this brand maintain that Communists call for postponing the struggle for socialism until the democratic struggles are won. But this is sheer nonsense. The fact is that the development of the anti-monopoly coalition as a political force is impossible without the development of a powerful Left, without simultaneously advancing the class consciousness of the workers and building a socialist-conscious contingent within their ranks. The very process of radicalization is the necessary foundation for developing the anti-monopoly movement.

The fight for socialism thus develops within the heart of the democratic struggles. The two are inseparable. The task before us is that of mastering the art of making socialism a real, living issue within the context of the democratic struggles. As Lenin often pointed out, there is no such thing as a "pure" revolution. He ridiculed the idea that "one army lines up in one place and says, 'We are for socialism,' and another, somewhere else says, 'We are for imperialism,' and that will be a social revolution!"[1]

The result of looking for "purity" is in fact the abandonment of the democratic struggle against the monopolies, into which growing masses of people are being drawn. Without our participation, without our being in the very forefront of the democratic struggle, the fight for socialism inevitably degenerates into mere propagandizing and preaching and into building narrow, sterile sects. The placing of the democratic struggle as in contradiction to the struggle for socialism can only lead in one direction: towards the bog of ultra-Leftism and Trotskyism.

The second line of opposition sees only the existence of individual democratic struggles and rejects any idea of their integrated, anti-monopoly character.

The anti-monopoly concept has been a matter of long debate in the world Communist movement. Certain left-sectarian elements have been against it. In their attacks on the fraternal Communist Parties of France, Italy, the USA and other countries, they underscored the attitude of the Communists towards the anti-monopoly struggle. Most of the opposition to the anti-monopoly idea is based on an overall rejection of the fundamental Marxist concept of intermediate and strategic goals.

The idea of intermediate goals is that we walk with, talk with and fight unitedly with the masses for an objective that we have to reach anyway before we reach our goal of socialism. We do so with people who are not now ready to start the march for socialism. In fact most of them are convinced that they will part company with us when the halfway goals are reached.

But the inner logic of struggle is such that we can put forward the end goal and carry the masses along with us. Whenever possible we should have Left contingents, but as a part of the march. We should have a Party contingent, but as a part of the march — far enough in front to lead the way, close enough to the masses so as to be able to talk and walk with them. We can be close enough only if we can say: We are with you in our united efforts to reach our common goals. This is a fact of life and the only way to the end goal of socialism.

Why an anti-monopoly concept? Why not anti-something else? Because, in our opinion, it provides the best possible way of drawing to our side the masses fighting monopoly oppression but who do not yet see that this oppression is part and parcel of the capitalist system.

The very development of monopoly capitalism demonstrates that our concept is correct. The top financial-industrial dynasties of the United States are fiercely fighting among themselves for control and domination of the nation. There is no other capitalist country in the world where the anti-monopoly struggle has as deep a meaning as in the USA, and nowhere else has it reached such a level of development. The essence of the nature and aims of state monopoly capitalism should be explained to the masses with the United States as the example.

Lenin urged Marxists to study the specific conditions in each country in order to determine the path and direction of the struggle, in order to achieve the revolutionary objective. No Marxist views the path of winning the majority of the working class for socialism as a path without zigzags and turns, without victories and defeats, without advances and retreats. Nor does the path always remain the same. Should conditions change, the path may require revision.

During World War I, for example, the path indicated by the Russian Bolsheviks was that of turning the imperialist war into civil war through the struggle against one's own capitalist government. In the thirties, with the rising threat of fascism and a new world war, Communists fought to establish a broad popular front to prevent the outbreak of war and halt the advance of fascism.

So today the rise of state monopoly capitalism — the fusion of the power of the financial oligarchy with the power of the state to maximize monopoly profits by robbing the overwhelming majority of the population — confronts Marxists with the necessity of finding the forms through which to unite all who feel the brunt of monopoly domination. Under these conditions the economic, political and social interests of the working class necessarily coincide with the interests of other strata of the population, providing the basis for bringing into being a democratic alliance in the struggle against monopoly power.

AS IS STRESSED BY THE 1969 INTERNATIONAL MEETING OF Communist and Workers' Parties: "The desire of the working masses to effect a radical change in the economic and social system based on the exploitation of man is growing ever stronger. The big battles of the working class in a number of capitalist countries are undermining the power of the monopolies, intensifying the instability and contradictions of capitalist society. These struggles foreshadow new class battles which could lead to fundamental social change, socialist revolution, and the establishment of the power of the working class in alliance with other segments of the working people."

Today the question of proletarian internationalism plays an exceptionally vital role and becomes one of the key problems of the development of the world Communist and workingclass movement.

In regard to the relations between the socialist states, the view is that it is necessary to combine the principle of national sovereignty with the defense of the common interests against imperialism and with mutual economic assistance. The same is essential for the relations between Communist and Workers' parties. The national and international responsibilities of each Communist Party are indivisible. Communists are both patriots and internationalists. They reject both national narrow-mindedness and the negation or underestimation of national interests.

The fraternal socialist countries are united by a common ideology, a common socioeconomic structure and common goals — the building of socialism and communism. They are not divided by antagonistic interests of ruling classes, as are capitalist states. When divergences exist it is possible, given the spirit of socialist internationalism, to solve them through comradely discussion and voluntary fraternal cooperation.

Unity of the Marxist-Leninist Parties against imperialism, the common enemy of socialism and the world revolutionary forces, is imperative. As Lenin wrote, "Capital is an international force. To vanquish it, an international workers' alliance, an international workers' brotherhood is needed. We are opposed to national enmity and discord, to national exclusiveness. We are internationalists."[2]

New Problems of Capitalism: Fighting the Transnationals

[From: "The Working Class and the Import-Export Crisis," Political Affairs, August, 1985 — slightly abridged.]

TO THE MONOPOLY CORPORATIONS AND THE BANKS, IMPORTS and exports are all the same: a source of huge superprofits. They have it made, coming and going. On the other side of the class line, for workers and the people of the industrial capitalist countries, it also doesn't make any difference whether goods are imported or exported. Both ways, they get it in the neck, coming and going.

Internationalization of production, the new level of technology, finance capital that knows no national boundaries, crisscrossing of investments between countries, development of worldwide industrial and financial conglomerates — all have added a new dimension to the class struggle. And this new dimension has created new contradictions and new problems for the working class in capitalist countries.

The working class of each capitalist country confronts the challenge of their own country's ruling class, of monopoly capital. However, now the workers are increasingly forced to deal with the maneuvers and machinations of monopoly corporations that operate as worldwide syndicates, syndicates that have no boundaries except maximum profits.

This is a process of internationalization of class exploitation. The new world relationships, these global syndicates of monopoly corporations banded together, have given impetus to the further development and increased role of state monopoly capitalism in each capitalist country.

In this new situation, the state acts as an umpire for the monopoly syndicates. In each country, the state clears the legal and diplomatic path for the crisscrossing of production and financing. The state gets laws passed and regulations issued that help to maximize corporate profits from these new global relationships. Thus, the state in each of these countries has become an important factor in manipulating taxes, import and export laws, investment regulations, etc. — to the singular advantage of the monopoly corporations and international syndicates.

Because of the role of governments and their corporate relationships, struggles must, of necessity, include forms of political and legislative action.

THE NEW U.S.-JAPAN SYNDICATE DEVELOPMENT IS UNPRECEdented and is a perfect example of these new relationships. This worldwide syndicate operates like a conspiracy against the working class in both countries. It also operates like a syndicate conspiracy in Third World countries, as well as other capitalist countries.

This development presents some new, difficult and complex problems for the working class and trade union movements in the industrial capitalist countries. Therefore, we think this calls for a new look, a new approach and new tactics.

Each monopoly in the syndicate works to keep the workers of its home country divided. All promote empty, chauvinistic nationalism. They play on the contradictions that are inherent in the self-interests of the working class in each country. How to meet this new challenge of the capitalist world's monopoly syndicates is a most important question.

Because the U.S. is the chief culprit, the working class and trade union movement in this country have a special responsibility to help find solutions in the interests of the working class of all the capitalist countries and to help organize the fightback against this new assault on the international working class.

To start with, we are convinced the world trade union movements must reject any idea of joining or cooperating with the syndicates of their own countries. Rather we believe the starting point must be implementing tactics that will have the effect of cutting back the superprofits of the syndicates.

There are many ideas and possible solutions the trade union movements of the world can work together on. We would like to put on the table, for consideration, some of our thinking.

First, because of the role of governments and their corporate relationships, we think that trade union struggles, of necessity, must include forms of political and legislative action:

• Legislation that would equalize syndicate wages and working conditions in the affected capitalist countries;

• Legislation to prohibit banks from making capital investments in the same industry in more than one country — for instance, a bank could not invest in the steel industry in the United States and also in another country;

• Legislation barring the closing of industrial plants if the purpose is to move production to another area;

• Legislation that prohibits investment or transfer of industries to countries where official policy is the destruction of trade unions, such as Chile and South Africa;

• Demands for the shutdown of existing syndicate industrial facilities in countries like South Africa and Chile;

• Organization of negotiations on a syndicatewide basis: one worldwide syndicate, one contract.

In the U.S. trade union movement there is a need for new

approaches and tactics because the U.S. working class is facing an import-export crisis for the first time in its history. Therefore, the U.S. trade unions should begin now to work on basic positions, on ideas and solutions, in advance of those joint efforts with movements in other countries which can be organized.

Here again we would like to put some ideas on the table for consideration.

A STARTING POINT MUST BE TO ADOPT THE APPROACH THAT unions are dealing with corporations and with a class that do not care one whit about workers of any country, a ruthless ruling class that is not one bit concerned about national interests, about patriotism or what is good for the country if it in any way interferes with the drive for maximum corporate profits.

We think the basic approach must rest on the fact that there are millions of unemployed, homeless and hungry who are the direct victims of the import-export crisis.

Another premise must be that the culprits, the direct cause of the crisis, are the criminal monopoly corporations who are willing to sacrifice livelihoods and lives and devastate industries and whole regions to achieve their profit-seeking goals.

Another starting point must be the understanding that most of the foreign imports are not foreign at all. Many of the imported goods come from production facilities which are partially or wholly owned by U.S. corporations and banks.

1. The U.S. trade union movement should, therefore, call on Congress to ban all government-sponsored funding, including by the International Monetary Fund, for the purpose of paying debts owed to U.S. banks by foreign governments or corporations.

2. Because of problems the import-export crisis creates, now is the time to raise the demand for a six-hour day with no cut in pay.

3. The trade union movement should call on the U.S. president and Congress to implement the United Nations New In-

ternational Economic Order, which calls for special assistance to developing countries to overcome their underdevelopment and low standards of living. This includes many-sided assistance to these countries to help them develop nationally-owned industries, enabling them to make reforms or carry out social revolutions in order to provide decent wages and get fair prices for their products.

This means canceling the huge debts imposed on these countries by the imperialist banks which have made hundreds of billions of dollars in profits out of super-high interest rates and currency speculation. This policy would lead, among other things, to an increase in U.S. imports of nationally-owned products made in these countries.

4. The trade union movement should call on Congress to pass legislation to tax superprofits from foreign investments.

5. The trade union movement should call on Congress for legislation to require that for every one dollar a bank or corporation invests abroad, it must designate five dollars for domestic, job-creating projects.

6. The trade union movement should call on Congress to prohibit export of production capital that creates unemployment in the United States.

7. The trade union movement should demand an end to anti-Communist, colonialist embargoes and boycotts, specifically those against Cuba, Vietnam, North Korea, as well the 90 percent trade restriction on the Soviet Union and most other socialist countries.

8. The trade union movement should demand removal of all U.S. troops from foreign bases where they are in every case deployed to protect the interests of monopoly capital.

9. The trade union movement should call for the nationalization of U.S. banks and the money-lending insurance octopus, and for slashing interest rates. Banks should be placed under socialized control and management.

10. The trade union movement should advocate the nationalization of international trade and for it to be controlled by democratically elected government agencies who will run the nationalized banks and regulate international trade.

11. The trade union movement should demand that in the conduct of foreign trade, workers, through their unions and other organizations, should have major and direct representation in negotiating trade agreements, including the power to control prices on products under trade agreements.

12. The trade union movement should demand an end to the international trade in weapons and war production, which creates fewer jobs than non-military production.

13. The trade union movement should call on Congress to change the law on dumping: instead of placing restrictions on imports because of government funding of production, place restrictions because of low wages and slave-labor working conditions in capitalist countries.

14. The trade union movement should convene an international conference of trade unions and workers' political and other organizations to adopt international policies on trade, equalizing wage levels and other conditions in capitalist countries, ending apartheid and neocolonialism, and increasing employment by creating jobs in all capitalist countries.

Goals should include:

• Raising real wages in developing countries to the levels prevailing in the advanced capitalist countries;

• Formulating and enforcing a full-employment program in all capitalist countries;

• Enforcing affirmative action programs in the U.S. and other capitalist countries;

• Taking joint action against colonialism and neocolonialism, with complete economic and political isolation of apartheid South Africa.

COMBINED INTERNATIONAL STRUGGLES, MOVEMENTS AND tactics should be agreed upon to achieve these goals. This would reverse the current direction. Because of the internationalization and crisscrossing of production, the workers and trade unions in the multinational conglomerates should consider not only identical contracts but also united, simultaneous strikes. The unions should consider joint international funds and resources for organizing the unorganized. These considerations are necessary because there is no other way to react effectively to the syndicates' strikebreaking tactic: when workers strike a plant in the syndicate, management simply uses another syndicate facility to continue production.

To develop these new worldwide union relationships, unions should establish syndicatewide contact committees. These committees should arrange for exchanges of translated materials, including union papers and videotapes. There should be exchanges of union study groups and delegates to each others' conventions.

The national unions in each country should set up special departments and provide necessary personnel and resources to deal with and coordinate workingclass struggles on a syndicatewide basis. There should be world conferences of shop stewards as well as international conferences of members of congresses and parliaments who are on the workers' side.

Such an approach by the U.S. trade unions in adopting initial positions and tactics, both nationally and internationally, is the only process which will begin to solve the import-export crisis for the working class of the advanced capitalist countries. This has become a critical question for the U.S. working class; it must be seen as a crisis that is now one of the most important issues before the working class and trade unions.

It should be noted here that in the socialist countries and under the socialist system, no such problem can arise. The root of such a crisis — the drive for maximum profits by private corporations — is eliminated forever.

In its place is established a system whereby all production facilities are publicly owned and operated, all trade is conducted centrally in the interests of the working class and people, and all trade agreements are developed on the basis of mutual benefit, equality and international cooperation.

The approach and general framework for action laid out here is, we think, the only one that can mount a winning challenge against the transnational monopoly corporations, the new worldwide syndicates and the state monopoly governments that support and protect them.

Class Struggle
Is the Frame of Reference

*[From: "Class Struggle is the Frame of Reference," speech to conference of
the Institute of the World Workingclass Movement, 1986 — abridged.]*

IT IS ONLY NATURAL THAT ALL OF US ARE INFLUENCED BY AND
tend to reflect on world developments each from our own
national frames of reference. There is nothing wrong with that.
However, by itself such a national frame of reference is often
limited and can lead to an indistinct, undefined and even distorted view of the world. Such a frame of reference also tends
to lead to a kind of national nearsightedness, a political myo-
pia.

An open, honest exchange of experiences and assessments,
and even the expression of differences, will broaden, deepen
and round out all of our perceptions. Thus, with the class
struggle in the United States as the frame of reference and, to
the extent possible, without nearsightedness, I want to deal
with some of the new and developing questions which are all
in one way or another having their impact on the class struggle
in the United States and in the capitalist world.

There are overall, general factors that cast their shadow on
developments in the United States and the world. U.S. imperialism has never given up on the realization of its obsessive
dream of an "American Century," a century of projected U.S.
economic, political, military and financial world domination.
The timetable and tactics have changed, but not the ultimate
goal. The ultimate aim of the Reagan Doctrine is to turn back
the clock of history, to undo all the anti-imperialist and socialist
victories of the postwar period.

The U.S. imperialists' dream of an "American Century"
has taken on new meaning and magnitude with the frantic
drive to build weapons of first-strike nuclear superiority and
the nuclearization of outer space. They clearly see the Soviet
Union as the main obstacle to their drive for world domination.
This nuclear brinkmanship has taken on a new dimension with
the designs for Star Wars weaponry for world domination from

outer space — the extension of the nuclear arms race into space.

Added to the potentially catastrophic consequences of nuclear weapons, the astronomical cost is also beginning to cast its own shadow, affecting all U.S. economic developments. For instance, according to the Labor Research Association, the U.S. federal government debt is now over two trillion dollars. The interest payments to the banks take 15 percent of the annual budget. And the debt grows at the rate of $238 billion per year. Related to the cost is the fact that the negative U.S. trade balance now runs $230 billion per year.

In addition to the 85 percent of the American people who are now against nuclear and Star Wars programs, many on Wall Street are also raising questions not only about the aims but whether the policy is, in their Wall Street lexicon, "cost effective" — whether the cost is getting out of control.

Production of military goods has now become the biggest of all U.S. Big Businesses. The Pentagon signs 15 million corporate military contracts per year for the production of military goods.

Although over 30,000 corporations are involved in war production, the hog's share goes to a handful of a new kind of corporation — the military monopoly corporation. The out-of-control military budgets have given rise to this new sector of monopoly capital.

The new, billion-dollar military monopoly corporations are among the biggest of all the megamonopolies. Seventy-five percent or more of the production and profits of Boeing, Lockheed, General Dynamics and others come from Pentagon war contracts. They add a new dimension to the military monopoly complex.

These are the thieving, corrupt core of the military monopoly complex, the political shock troops for funding the trillion-dollar Star Wars projects. They employ most of the nuclear maniacs, including scientists, politicians and propagandists.

These military monopolies are the political and financial support base for ultra-Right and fascist movements. They know very well that if the nuclear arms race comes to an end, their sector of the military monopoly complex will collapse. For them, Star Wars projects are the means of survival. For this section of monopoly capital, military orders serve as a prop and a form of economic pump priming, an economic lifeline.

THE REAGAN DOCTRINE IS GLOBAL PILLAGE BY BANKS. FInancial imperialism has become the newest and biggest form of plunder of the developing countries, which are treated as neocolonies by U.S. banks and the U.S. government. One hundred billions dollars per year is squeezed out of the developing countries to pay just the interest on the trillion-dollar debt, half of which is paid by Latin American countries.

In ten years this debt has multiplied five times, and the interest burden has multiplied ten times. The original loans have thus been collected many times over through the interest payments. This squeeze play has a paralyzing impact on the economies of the developing countries.

This imperialist extortion and plunder has reached a new level. Most of the banks are now refusing to make loans on any basis. Therefore the demand for a total cancellation of both the principal and the interest payments emerged as the only realistic end to this imperialist extortion. On this demand, the U.S. working class and the peoples of the developing countries can mount a united campaign.

Also because of the growing transnational character of production, a finance capitalist class that recognizes no national boundaries, the ability of the multinational corporations to use their production facilities in one country against the workers in other countries, the ability of the multinationals to manipulate tariffs, taxes, prices and interest rates as well as wages and working conditions in the capitalist sector — because of all this there are new and difficult problems for the working class of all capitalist countries.

The most striking feature of the present moment is that the capitalist world has lapsed into an era of crises, of stagnation and decline. It is unusually volatile and unstable. Most of the tremors are centered in the United States. The backdrop for the myriad of crises is of course the general crisis of decaying world capitalism, which continues to gnaw at the foundations of the corporate system.

It is characteristic of the era of crises that in the United States the last economic cycle never fully reached its boom phase and the economy is now in the first stages of a new cyclical crisis. Back-to-back cyclical crises are becoming a "common feature."

For the past ten years, the structural crisis — which is the dislocation, relocation and destruction of the basic industrial structure — has been carving a path of havoc and devastation. It has destroyed industries, turned industrial cities into ghost towns, closed thousands of industrial plants, left millions homeless and hungry. The structural crisis has added a new dimension to the process of impoverishment of the working class.

Because of the structural crisis and automation, as well as the arrival of robots and microchips, the jobs profile of the workforce has shifted. Manufacturing industries now employ five million fewer workers than wholesale and retail trade. And while new technology is creeping into the labor-intensive basic industries, still 60 percent of the workforce in these industries are in blue-collar jobs.

THE WORKING CLASS IS CHANGING. BUT IT IS NOT DISAPEAR-ing or declining. In the last five years, the U.S. working class has grown by 10 million. However, it is estimated that 75 percent of the U.S. workforce are now in the service, communications and other clerical, white-collar industries.

In the last ten-year period, the United States has dropped from being the world's biggest and technologically the most advanced steel producer to one of the more backward, and is in the process of closing the last of the basic steel-producing facilities. Just ten years ago, the United States was the world's most technologically advanced and biggest producer of automobiles. Today no automobiles are completely U.S. manufactured.

Besides closing basic industrial facilities, new technology

makes it possible to disperse manufacturing facilities, moving them into non-industrial, non-union sectors of the country. The result is a decline and deterioration of the industrial centers and a dispersal of the basic workingclass centers.

As we know, the trend is also for transnational corporations to move labor-intensive production facilities to areas of the world with the most exploitable, low-wage workforce, where corporations are not forced to provide health or safety protection, unemployment benefits, economic or social security. In most cases they are areas where these corporations do not pay taxes. Thus, fewer manufacturing facilities in the United States are in the production process and are increasingly becoming only the assembly and distribution points for imported parts.

In the era of crises, the overall tendency is for industry to stagnate or decline. The decline is sharpest in labor-intensive industries. Lenin was right when he surmised, "The tendency toward stagnation and decay, inherent in monopoly, continues to operate in individual branches of industry in individual countries."

To a large extent this is the result of a "capital investment strike" by monopoly capital, a refusal to make capital investments in new technology to modernize basic, mass employment industries, but instead to transfer production to lower-cost, higher-profit areas of the world.

Another feature of the era of crises is the unprecedented growth in the number of long-term and permanently unemployed in the United States. Even during the upside of the economic cycle the rate of unemployment stays above ten percent.[3]

Because of the new technology, what is also new is that the number of long-term unemployed has continued to increase even in the boom phase of the economic cycle. Fifty percent of the unemployed are victims of plant closings and structural decay, with no hope of ever getting a job.

In the United States today there are 20 million unemployed. In addition to the permanently unemployed, 25 percent of the total workforce is now "on call" — called when needed for a few days at the lowest wage. This is a new and growing trend. These on-call workers receive no unemployment benefits, health insurance or Social Security, no pensions, life insurance, vacation pay, sick leave or prospects for full-time work.

There is a displacement of workers by robots and automation. And there is not enough growth in the industries producing automated equipment, or in the high tech industries, to provide employment for more than a fraction of the workers displaced by new methods. The section of the displaced millions who do find jobs in the service and communications industry are usually paid below the legal minimum wage, which means about a 60 percent cut in wages. This group is part of the 35 million Americans who live below the official poverty level. This describes graphically what is called downward mobility into poverty.

All this has created a situation in which U.S. monopoly capital and the Reagan Administration have been able to take the offensive in an unprecedented anti-workingclass, anti-union, racist drive. This has forced the working class and the trade unions to retreat in many cases, to make concessions and fight defensive battles.

This has been the trend of the last few years. However, that period is coming to an end. More and more of the struggles and strikes take on an offensive character. In the last six months alone almost one million workers have participated in militant strike struggles, some of which lasted for months.

It is true that after World War II, during the period of U.S. capitalist and imperialist expansion, the working class won important victories. But today U.S. capitalism is back on the old capitalist track, which Marx correctly projected would have the tendency of increasing "both relative and absolute impoverishment of the working class." Thus, in the past ten years real wages of the U.S. working class have declined over 16 percent while labor productivity has increased 65 percent.

All this is also related to Marx's concept of rising profits and the rising rate of surplus value. In the period of 1950 to 1985, the rate of surplus value rose from 150 percent to 300 percent. U.S. workers now work two hours to produce the value of their wages or labor power, and six hours for the 300 percent rate of surplus value that goes to the capitalists.

One of the characteristics of the era of crises is that in the period of decline and stagnation, corporate profits and the rate of surplus value continue to increase.

A number of features affecting the class struggle are unique to the United States. A new feature of the era of crises is the catastrophic farm crisis. U.S. farmers now owe the banks $260 billion. The interest on the loans each year is larger than the total farm income. Over 2,000 farmers go bankrupt every week and are forced off the land. High technology, the banks and the conglomerates are taking over agriculture.

Racism continues to be an instrument of superprofits. The income of Afro-American families is 40 percent below average family income. Sixty percent of younger Afro-Americans are unemployed. Thirty percent of all Spanish-speaking people in the U.S. live in poverty.

Another shift in the workforce profile is the fact that women now constitute half of the U.S. workforce. Fifty-five percent of all women with children work. The rate of exploitation of women is higher because their wages are 60 percent of male workers' wages. Sixty-one percent of those living below the poverty level are women.

T HE NEW OBJECTIVE FRAMEWORK IS GIVING RISE TO NEW modes of thinking in many areas. The structural crisis, new technology, robots, automation, the shift in the division of labor worldwide and the nuclear Sword of Damocles hanging ominously over humanity are all changing the objective battleground for the class struggle. The structural crisis not only destroys industries and jobs, but in the process destroys trade unions. The conglomerates and the transnational octopi have become protective bunkers for these corporate monsters.

Because of the new objective scene, the working class and the trade union movement are forced to take a new, hard look at their strategic and tactical approaches. The internationalization of production has on the one hand made it more difficult to strike a whole company, but on the other has made transnationals interdependent and thus more vulnerable. Both aspects call for closer international workingclass unity in action.

Also, under the new circumstances, it is not possible to conduct a corporationwide strike in our country alone. At the present moment in the United States, 45,000 steelworkers are locked out in a fierce life-and-death struggle against the largest of the steel corporations.[4] What makes this struggle so much more difficult is that USX Corporation is only part of a worldwide steel operation, which is only part of a huge conglomerate.

In the United States the new challenges are bringing about some significant changes in the class struggle and in the trade union movement. This new situation does not provide fertile soil for the old policies of class collaboration. Thus there is a shift to more militant policies of class struggle trade unionism.

It is necessary to differentiate between policies of class collaboration based on opportunism and situations in which the working class is forced to retreat and fight defensive struggles. In content, the defensive struggles are more anti-corporate and more militant.

The U.S. trade union movement has taken the lead in the struggle against the reactionary policies of Reaganism. It has become the strongest and best organized politically independent force in the electoral arena. It has become the most consistent anti-monopoly, anti-ultra-Right, anti-fascist and anti-racist force.

The U.S. trade union movement is an active contingent in the struggle against the U.S. imperialist policies of working with and supporting the reactionary, fascist, racist regimes in South Africa and Chile. It has a strong position against the U.S. policies of aggression in Nicaragua and El Salvador. Most of the largest U.S. trade unions have joined the movement to freeze all nuclear weapons production.

At its October, 1985 convention the AFL-CIO declared: "The AFL-CIO welcomes the resumption of the Geneva negotiations between the USSR and the U.S. and endorses the objective of a balanced reduction of nuclear arms within a system of verification guaranteeing collective security."

These shifts in workingclass thought patterns and trade union policies constitute the beginnings of a fundamental, spontaneous response to the new challenges. What are needed are new, creative tactics that motivate and activate the new mood and the new mode of thinking.

There is a growing understanding that the old tactics and solutions do not work in the present situation, that more basic and radical solutions are necessary. Concepts that are new for the United States, like public takeover, nationalization of industries and banks, are increasingly discussed on all levels of the trade union movement and considered as realistic solutions.

There is a new understanding of the need for class unity and thus the need to struggle against racism, which is an obstacle to such unity. There is a growing class oneness of our multiracial, multinational, male-female working class. There is a growing unity in action on the picket lines, shop floors, in mass demonstrations against apartheid and in the electoral arena. There is a new awareness of the need for labor to take the lead in building broader coalitions with other sectors and especially with people who are victims of racial and national oppression.

The new atmosphere of the class struggle accelerates the process of radicalization, of class self-confidence and, most important, the maturing of class consciousness. As the reality grows that options for basic solutions under capitalism are ever more limited, interest in socialism grows accordingly.

The new challenges give rise to new modes of thinking. The dead-end, crisis nature of capitalism forces workers to think about their living standards, not only in terms of wages, but also taxes, rents, inflation, imports and exports, the environment, toxic waste, tariffs, job security, unemployment benefits, social security and the role of the state.

The overall deterioration of the infrastructure of U.S. cities, all-pervasive corruption on all levels of government and in the corporate structure and society in general, crime and drugs which have become a national emergency, the crisis in education and the growing illiteracy rate — all add to a general decline in the overall quality of life for the working class in the United States.

But of course, what is influencing thought patterns more than anything else is the growing realization that we now work, sleep and play surrounded and threatened by nuclear weapons, which if triggered for any reason would set in motion a nuclear chain reaction a second after the launching of the first missile. A nuclear winter, bringing with it the end of all nature and human existence, would begin one second after the first explosion.

Thus in today's world the class struggle increasingly becomes involved in more than the struggles over economic issues or the production process. In the era of crises the monopoly capitalist drive for maximum profits comes more and more into conflict with national interests. This gives the class struggle a new dimension.

The role of the working class is expanding to include the issues of community and nation. The new mode of thinking moves in two parallel lines: faster maturing of class consciousness, and a growing concern with the broader issues of the people related to community and nation. Thus the working class moves to take its place in the front ranks of the struggle for human progress in general.

There can be unity in the struggle against the transnational corporate empires. There can be unity in the struggle to remove the Pershing and cruise missiles from Europe. There can be unity in the struggle to achieve a disarmament treaty and an end to the nuclear arms race.

The emergence of the new mode of thinking has become the centerpiece in the ideological struggle.

The truth is that the new objective developments, including the necessity to preserve the human race and nature from a nuclear end, has greatly enhanced the role and responsibility of the working class as the only truly revolutionary force.

It is more evident today than ever before that in order to emancipate itself, the working class must emancipate all of humanity.

the future works

Socialism
and the Working Class

Lenin and the U.S. Working Class

*[From the introduction to New Outlook Publishers' 1970 edition of V.I.
Lenin's Letter to American Workers.]*

LENIN'S *LETTER TO AMERICAN WORKERS*,[1] WRITTEN IN 1918, IS ONE
of history's most interesting and most unusual documents. It is
a letter written from the barricades of a successful revolution. It
is a letter written by a head of a workers' state to workers of
another land. It is a family letter, a letter of mutual confidence
between class brothers and sisters. It is not a letter in the form
of a Russian writing to Americans, but from one worker to another. It is an inspiring revolutionary message — a message
from a victorious class. With no bravado or boasting, it conveys
a deep sense of revolutionary confidence.

Lenin's letter is a report to U.S. workers on the nature of a
critical, historic moment in the world and on the criminal activities of U.S. imperialism.

Lenin wrote the letter at a most explosive turning point of
human history, at a moment when the first revolution establishing workingclass power had achieved its victory. It was a
moment of great victory but also a moment when the new so-

cialist republic faced a serious danger: the menace of a foreign imperialist invasion. U.S., British, French and Italian imperialism and 11 other capitalist states had started their counterrevolutionary military invasion against the Soviet Union.[2]

In this brief letter, in clear and concise terms, Lenin presents the essence of history's most meaningful turning point. And in an indirect way the letter draws a sharp focus on the nature, the thought patterns, the genius of the man who wrote it and who, more than any other, influenced and determined the nature of those explosive events. It was a moment of victory for the working class. And the course of events placed history's stamp of approval on the teachings of Lenin. Thus the letter, which was written during the most explosive days by the man who molded their course, has tremendous historic importance.

In this letter Lenin places the world's first workingclass revolution in its proper framework. In sharp, clean strokes he describes its significance, its class essence and the basic overall nature of this new workingclass state.

Lenin's letter was geared to influence U.S. workers. He masterfully used the reality of the new workingclass power in the Soviet Union to heighten the class consciousness of U.S. workers. He used the international significance of the victorious socialist revolution in his country to deepen the internationalism of U.S. workers. He used a clear characterization of the role of world imperialist powers, especially that of U.S. imperialism, in order to heighten the anti-imperialist consciousness of U.S. workers. He used the description of the first socialist state to heighten the socialist consciousness of workers in the United States.

The letter is a brilliant example of the class approach to all problems. It rests on Lenin's deep class partisanship. It breathes with a total sense of both immediate and long-range confidence in the working class in general, and a deep confidence in the working class of the United States in particular:

The American workers will not follow the bourgeoisie. They will be with us, for civil war against the bourgeoisie. The whole history of the world and of the American labor movement strengthens my conviction that this is so.

And further:

... Just at the present time the American revolutionary workers have to play an exceptionally important role as uncompromising enemies of American imperialism. . . .

Both on a short-term and long-term basis this confidence was well founded. The rising mass actions by U.S. workers in defense of the Soviet Republic and the rebellious actions by U.S. troops at the Archangel and Siberia fronts were important factors in forcing U.S. imperialism to give up its criminal aggression. The growing class consciousness, the rise of socialist consciousness, the birth of a revolutionary socialist movement in the United States in those days — all are witness to Lenin's deep insight and to the correctness of his confidence in the workers of the U.S. During the 1920s over one-third of the local unions of the American Federation of Labor (AFL) passed resolutions which called for recognition of the Soviet Union.

In the letter Lenin sought out the points of unity, the areas where the self-interests of our two peoples merged. In his unique fashion he tied the fibers of our revolutionary traditions to those of the new socialist revolution. He took the fibers from our revolutionary history, from our war for independence, from the civil war. He took fibers of sharp class warfare, the struggle against racism and slavery, the struggle for Afro-American equality. All these he tied to history's greatest event, the world's first socialist revolution.

Thus he injected a new current and life into the fibers that had carried the power of our historic revolutionary developments. He tapped the progressive wellsprings of our revolutionary traditions. "The American people," he wrote, "have a revolutionary tradition which has been adopted by the best representatives of the American proletariat. . . . "

He cut through the meaningless generalities, the petty-bourgeois fears and objections to revolution. He said:

... and so it will be in the eyes of world history, because, for the first time, not the minority, not the rich alone, not the educated alone, but the real people, the vast majority of the working people are themselves building a new life, are by their own experience solving the most difficult problems of socialist organization.

He blasted the "hypocrisy of formal equality." He rejected concepts of abstract classless "freedoms" and "democracy." For the world these were new concepts. They were revolutionary concepts.

THE SHARPEST EXPRESSION OF THE IRRECONCILABLE AND basic class contradiction of our times is the life-and-death opposition of world capitalism to workingclass state power. This is reflected in capitalist ideology, in its economic and diplomatic policies. It was expressed in the military attack by world imperialist powers on the new socialist state. It was expressed in the anti-Soviet economic blockade. It is today expressed in the never-diminishing anti-Soviet drive by U.S imperialism. For capitalism the birth of the first socialist state was the beginning of the end. The capitalists have always viewed it as a life-and-death struggle.

But this opposition is also expressed by other forces. Petty-bourgeois liberals and many classless radicals throughout the years of the Soviet Union have also had difficulty in accepting the concept of workingclass state power. They continue to hide their disdain behind general and abstract concepts of "democracy," of "individual rights" in opposition to workingclass rule. The class concept of workingclass rule is in essence a higher form of social consciousness. When a social structure serves the best interests of a class embracing the overwhelming majority, it serves the best interests of society.

In this historic period of revolutionary transition, the dictatorship of the proletariat, the rule of the majority class, correctly takes the interests of the working class as the yardstick for the best interests of society. A socialist revolution for the first time places the interests of the majority as primary.

This is the basis for the real democratic concepts embodied in the dictatorship of the proletariat. A revolution demands class priorities and class concepts. Lenin stated these openly and honestly. Without such class priorities the socialist revolution would have failed. Lenin placed all "rights" and "interests" squarely within the framework of the interests of the revolution:

> When it is a matter of overthrowing the bourgeoisie, only traitors or idiots can demand formal equality of rights for the bourgeoisie. "Freedom of assembly" for workers and peasants is not worth a farthing when the best buildings belong to the bourgeoisie. Our Soviets have confiscated all the good buildings in town and country from the rich and have transferred all of them to the workers and peasants for their unions and meetings. This is our freedom of assembly — for the working people! This is the meaning and content of our Soviet, our socialist constitution!

Lenin used the lessons of the U.S. war of liberation:

> In their arduous war for freedom, the American people also entered into "agreements" with some oppressors against others for the purpose of weakening the oppressors and strengthening those who were fighting in a revolutionary manner against oppression. . . .
> . . . I shall not hesitate one second to enter into a similar "agreement". . . . Such tactics will ease the task of the socialist revolution, will hasten it, will weaken the international bourgeoisie. . . .

Lenin was not writing about agreements in general. He was referring to the use of differences between imperialist powers. He emphasized that he would not hesitate to use differences when such a tactic would serve the best interests of the revolutionary movement.

This Leninist concept has remained a guiding principle of the Soviet Union in its relationships with and struggle against world imperialism. When in 1939 the U.S., France and Great Britain refused an alliance with the Soviet Union against the Rome-Berlin-Tokyo Axis and were maneuvering for a united world imperialist front against the Soviet Union, the Soviet Union used the contradictions between these powers, split their ranks, and defeated their conspiracy. This was the meaning of the Soviet-German non-aggression pact of 1939. The basis for such an action is clearly stated in Lenin's letter to American workers.

Life has fully sustained Lenin's confidence in the victory of the October Revolution. The Soviet Union has grown into a world power — into a workingclass state that in every way now stands toe-to-toe with the strongest of the capitalist states.

BESIDES THE *LETTER TO AMERICAN WORKERS,* THERE IS ONE other very interesting message Lenin wrote to the American people. President Wilson, for his own reasons, had sent a message to the "Russian people" in the form of a message to the Congress of Soviets. On March 13 or 14, 1918, Lenin wrote the following resolution in reply:

> The Congress expresses its gratitude to the American people, and primarily to the working and exploited classes of the United States of America, in connection with President Wilson's expression of his sympathy for the Russian people through the Congress of Soviets at a time when the Soviet Socialist Republic of Russia is passing through severe trials.
>
> The Russian Soviet Republic, having become a neutral country, takes advantage of the message received from President Wilson to express to all peoples that are perishing and suffering from the horrors of the imperialist war its profound sympathy and firm conviction that the happy time is not far away when the working people of all bourgeois countries will throw off the yoke of capital and establish the socialist system of society, the only system able to ensure a durable and just peace and also culture and well-being for all working people.[3]

The note was addressed to a president of a capitalist country but the message was clearly addressed to the workers — the people. Lenin in this message kept the class lines clear. It was a message in which the concept of peaceful coexistence between two state powers with different social systems is present, but there is not even a hint of class peace.

Through all these years the Soviet Union has been and remains the greatest source of strength, the strongest supporter, the most powerful bastion of the world revolutionary process. It is the protective umbrella for all of the developing socialist states and for the peoples and nations fighting for independence from world imperialism.

The Soviet Union on this 100th anniversary of Lenin's birth is without doubt the pivotal force in the world struggle for social progress and peace.

Lenin's remarkable *Letter to American Workers* introduces millions of Americans to the total writings of Lenin, whose *Collected Works* in English translation come to 45 volumes. The content of his writings, and of this brilliant document in particular, is fresh, meaningful and totally relevant to our struggles in the United States today. The revolutionary fibers are now energized by the massive upsurge of our people on many fronts. The struggle against U.S. imperialist aggression in Vietnam, the struggle for Afro-American equality and the sharp class struggles of our workers, fed by the brutal system of exploitation and racism, draw strength from the world revolutionary process.

Where Workers Have Power

[From: "Would You Believe . . . U.S. Workers Running the Economy? (What Every Worker Should Know About Trade Unions Under Socialism)," 1980 — slightly abridged.]

SHOULD A TRADE UNION LEADER SIT ON THE BOARD OF DIRECTORS of a large corporation? In itself this is not the most important question. The real, bottom-line question is: whose interests does this union leader serve? Who does he or she represent and fight for? Which side is he or she on: the workers' or the corporation's?

Life in our capitalist society does not permit one to serve both classes at the same time because the basic self-interest of the corporations is to make maximum profits, while the workers' basic self-interest is to make a decent standard of living. This puts the corporate board of directors and the trade union on opposite sides of the fence since both wages and profits come from the same pot. This makes it impossible to serve both employer and employee interests at the same time.

Since Douglas A. Fraser,[4] president of the United Automobile Workers, became a member of the Chrysler Corporation's Board of Directors, he has expressed some views that raise some serious questions.

Whenever capitalism nose-dives into one of its periodic economic crises the U.S. ruling class gears up its propaganda machine to divert the working class from a path that threatens its profits. The propaganda program they count on most is a fired-up cold war hysteria and a stepped-up anti-labor, anti-Communist, anti-socialist slander campaign.

Perhaps unwittingly, Douglas Fraser has become an accomplice in this smear campaign with his recent *New York Times* article, "At Togliatti, Gorky, There is No UAW." Like any other corporate board member and without a shred of evidence Fraser repeated the unconfirmed rumors that the autoworkers of the city of Gorky in the Soviet Union went on strike, "perhaps to protest food shortages."

Because of his new split personality — one as president of the UAW and the other as a member of Chrysler's Board of Directors — on the one hand he writes, "Seventy-thousand workers at the Togliatti auto plant struck for two days." And on the other hand he says that in the Soviet Union " . . . you don't strike; you don't even think about striking. . . . "

Trying to sound somewhat objective, Fraser begrudgingly admits that Soviet autoworkers "have won over the years social and medical gains that are good," but hastens to add, "when measured by the low Soviet standards." And repeating the old Chamber of Commerce propaganda, Fraser insults Soviet trade unions when he says, " . . . Theirs is . . . a company union."

By "company union" Fraser means that the trade unions in socialist countries are government controlled. In fact, just the reverse is true because it is the workers through their unions who are the biggest influence on the government. Workers are the majority on all governmental bodies. For instance, the president of the Soviet Union, Leonid I. Brezhnev, was a metalworker and Valeri Kuznetsov, the vice president, was an autoworker who, incidentally, worked for some time in a Detroit auto plant. It is unheard of for U.S. workers to attain such positions of power.

The basic truth is that it is only in a socialist society that trade unions acquire real political and economic power because they work, speak and act for the class in power — the working class. For example, in the Soviet Union management cannot cancel a labor contract without the agreement of the trade union organization. This is the law of the land. Management cannot fire a worker without the consent of the trade union. Trade union committees in every plant have absolute veto power over questions such as wages, piece rates, speedup, upgrading and plant safety. In most industries women can retire between 45 and 50 years of age and men between 50 and 55. And workers in socialist countries are not required to contribute to pension funds.

In true cold war fashion, Fraser sneers condescendingly at real workers' power: "What is their word?" he says. "Oh, 'paradise.' " Well, let us see what Fraser is sneering at.

I'm sure the workers who used to work at Dodge Main, Wisconsin Steel, Youngstown Sheet and Tube, Mahwah Ford and the more than 500 other industrial plants shut down during the last 12 months would consider guaranteed employment, which every Soviet worker enjoys, closer to "paradise" than the problems they face. The right to a job of one's own choosing is guaranteed by the Soviet Constitution. There has been no unemployment in the Soviet Union since 1930.

Squeezed by the costs of astronomical hospital, doctor, dental and medical insurance bills, U.S. workers would readily agree that the best of medical and dental care free of charge that every Soviet worker and their families enjoy gets closer to the goal of "paradise."

As the cost of educating their children keeps climbing out of reach for U.S. workers, they can see that the socialist system of free education up to college and advanced degrees is also closer to what Fraser calls "paradise."

Close to 40 percent of a U.S. worker's paycheck goes to pay taxes. It is now estimated that workers in the U.S. have to work from January 1 to May 15 just to pay their taxes for the year, while many large corporations pay no taxes, get tax writeoffs for depreciation and other tax subsidies and use all the tax loopholes to reduce their share of taxes — which, by the way, comes to about 15 percent of total taxes. In comparison the Soviet example is closer to "paradise."

BROTHER FRASER STATES THAT " . . . WE ENJOY FREE COLLECtive bargaining and have the right to withhold our labor if necessary to gain redress for our grievances," hinting that Soviet workers do not have such rights.

However, Fraser neglected to mention that the right to "gain redress" in the U.S. is severely hamstrung and restricted by legal strikebreaking injunctions, laws that make strikes illegal for public workers, union decertification, scabbing and a whole slew of anti-labor, anti-union laws and practices. The huge backlog of grievances on safety, working conditions, etc. in most U.S. plants, and the companies' resistance to settling them, is testimony to the uphill battle workers have to wage to "gain redress."

Any worker knows that if in the U.S. the corporations would settle grievances and grant wage increases fairly and willingly there would be no need to strike. If Soviet autoworkers were faced with "over 300,000 workers laid off" (50,000 workers have been laid off at Chrysler alone since Fraser joined Chrysler's Board of Directors), with a declining real wage, with plant shutdowns, runaways, whole communities being destroyed and ravaging inflation — they would indeed have good reason to strike.

If Soviet workers were confronted with a Chrysler Corporation bailed out with taxpayers' money[5] to the tune of a billion dollars, while Chrysler workers are living in debt and insecurity — they would certainly have good cause to "redress their grievances."

This simply isn't the socialist reality. These kinds of disasters do not and cannot happen to workers in socialist societies. In the socialist countries workers are their own bosses. They are the real economic and political power. There is no drive for maximum private profits, there are no privately-owned corporations, and no tax shelters inducing companies to close plants and move to more profitable locations leaving human devastation in their wake.

There are few strikes in the socialist countries not because the workers don't have the right to strike but because of the position of power workers enjoy. They have the power to settle grievances and disputes. No worker can be fired without consent of their trade union committee and unions have a right to fire bureaucratic or inefficient managers. Unions have the power to give wage increases and improve working conditions. And they do just that.

All grievances are settled on the spot. Because of the extensive economic and political power the working class and their trade unions enjoy under socialism they need not fear plants being closed down and workers laid off. The right to a job is a sacred right of every Soviet citizen. The trade unions have full control and a veto over all health and safety questions.

In the United States we are going through the seventh economic crisis since World War II. Such crises are a built-in feature of capitalism. There are no economic crises in a socialist society. This is because the relationship between wages, buying power and production is planned. As production goes up, wages go up. As a result there are no periods when the market gets glutted with unsold commodities.

Not only is there no unemployment in the USSR but there is full employment without racism or discriminatory practices. The nationalities which make up the USSR — over 100 — need never fear racism or discriminatory practices because such practices were outlawed 60 years ago. There is equal pay for equal work and equal opportunities for advancement regardless of race, religion, sex or geographical area. Acts of racism and discrimination are criminal offenses, punishable by law. Whatever inequality there was as a residue of the old feudal czarist and capitalist systems has been eliminated through a consistent program of affirmative action.

From his seat on Chrysler's Board with representatives of big banks and other stockholders, Brother Fraser cynically sneers at the USSR's "classless society" at the "workers' state" where, he says, " . . . You don't even think about striking." I suppose when one sits on the board of directors of a huge multinational corporation it is difficult to even comprehend a society without classes.

But socialism is just that. There are no private corporations, bankers or landlords who own the means of production and the land. Therefore the useless, unproductive, parasitic leisure class of stockholders and owners does not exist. When the workers at Chrysler, G.M. or U.S. Steel take over the plants and property, retire the present big stockholders and the corporate gang that continues to get rich from exploiting the workers — this will create a classless situation. In our society Big Business has always promoted the concept of U.S. society as classless. In fact, a recent issue of *Business Week* devoted the whole magazine to the advocacy of a so-called "reindustrialization" process in the U.S., opting for a new "social contract" by trying to reinvigorate the old notion of a partnership between labor and management: " . . . The two sides have too often behaved as if there were an unbridgeable gulf between worker and boss. It is almost as if they are trying to perpetuate a class-struggle notion in one of the least class conscious of nations. But a social contract in the U.S. can work only if labor and management see where their interests coincide and put the energy they employ as adversaries to solving mutual problems."[6]

What *Business Week* really has in mind is attempting to cure the incurable ills of U.S capitalism by convincing workers to make more sacrifices, to invest their tax money to save dying industries, to tolerate raging inflation, layoffs, plant closings, reduction in safety, health and working conditions, and intolerable speedup. This is the "collaborative relationship" *Busi-*

ness Week is advocating. This so-called "labor participation in management" is posed as a dimly veiled threat that if labor and management don't "get together" and eliminate "the adversary relationship" workers will lose more jobs than they are now losing.

Big Business wants a completely free hand. They want the complete cooperation of the unions and the government in their drive for maximum profits and they want to convince the workers and their unions that it is in their interests to cooperate. But the fact of life is that the only way corporations can maximize profits is by intensifying the exploitation of the workers through all means at their disposal. It is not in the interests of workers to cooperate in their own further exploitation. It is in their interests to fight back and take over when necessary to save their jobs and their lives. The right to a job, to decent wages and working conditions must be the demand of all workers.

In 1917, the working class of the Soviet Union decided they didn't need the owners who were getting richer while the people got poorer. In fact it was just this class of leeches that held back all social advances for working people. So the working people took over. And ever since then they have been running things. There is no need for "adversary relationships," for one class to constantly fight the other for their share of the wealth they produce.

Even Fraser, in the same *Business Week* issue, admits that "things have to get sufficiently bad before we address the problem, and may be we're reaching that point." But in socialist countries problems are dealt with before things get bad.

WHY DOES BIG BUSINESS PROMOTE A CAMPAIGN OF ANTI-Soviet slander, which Mr. Fraser takes part in? It is not because there is an inherent prejudice against Russians, Ukrainians, Georgians and the over 100 nationalities of the Soviet Union. Also they don't believe their own Big Lie about the "Soviet threat." And they certainly know "the Russians" aren't coming. Why then the shameless anti-Soviet Big

Lie campaign for over 60 years? For the very same reason the corporate executives are anti-union.

The trade unions, when under good, militant, class conscious leadership, are the workers' instrument, their weapon in the struggle for a better life. Socialism is a system that does away with the big private corporations and their profits. The people, led by workers, are the political power. For the workers of the Soviet Union, the soviets[7] are the instruments of their political and economic power.

U.S. Big Business is worried about socialism. They are especially worried in bad times such as these when the rapid decay of our socioeconomic system becomes particularly obvious to working people.

They are worried when U.S. workers begin to see that socialism works. They are worried because the workers may come to the conclusion that socialism is also the solution to all our problems in the USA. They may want to try it.

The discussion now taking place about the need for government takeover of closed plants is a step in the direction of realizing that workers can operate and manage plants without the owners and managers whose primary function is to extract maximum profits. Further, it is a recognition that the present managers are not able to keep these plants running and productive. The basic reason they can't is that their only motive for operating a plant is profit.

The debate on government takeover, the militant strikes and fightback send chills through Big Business circles and the result is an intensified anti-Communist campaign, focused on the most powerful, successful and influential socialist society, the Soviet Union. And their anxieties are indeed justified.

The growing anti-monopoly sentiment, the profound distrust and anger against the corporate ripoff of the people is an opening for socialist ideas, for the socialist alternative to capitalism. It becomes a threat to the very existence of the capitalist system. And the capitalist ruling class becomes frantic in its efforts to prevent the people from learning about real, existing socialism. There is also the big fear on the part of the U.S. top labor bureaucracy who are staunch supporters of the capitalist system, who are for a unionism that supports it, and who are partners in the conspiracy to keep American workers from seeing or hearing the truth of developed socialism and of the unions under socialism.

However, there is a validity to their worries and anxieties, because if the truth becomes widely known among U.S. workers the threat to the capitalist system itself increases immeasurably.

There is cause for capitalists' concern about a system where there are no private corporations and no private profit. Profits from all social production go into various funds for improving the well-being of workers, for public service of all kinds, for renewal, modernization and expansion of industry which in turn makes working easier and more productive, for health, safety and the overall enrichment of workers' lives, for housing, better health and child care, educational and recreational facilities, paid vacations, pensions, and housing. This, and much more, are where the profits go — which are higher under socialism than capitalism because there are no private owners or corporations to appropriate them.

Under socialism people come first and profits are made to serve them. And the trade unions are the workers' instrument which assures these policies and improvements are carried out. They have the power to speak and act in the workers' interest in making decisions about how the fruits of labor are to be invested, and the power to see that all decisions are implemented in the interest of advancing the overall quality of life of all the people.

How do the Soviet trade unions do this? And what is the relationship between the unions (the workers) and the management (the executives and managers of enterprises)?

Soviet trade unions have a membership of over 122 million, nearly twice the membership of all western European and U.S. unions combined. They have nearly 712,000 work location branches and 29 national industrial unions. There is a trade union committee in every plant, factory and enterprise. Every enterprise has a collective agreement between the union and management covering all workers: skilled and production workers, engineers, scientists and professionals.

Unions are the instrument by which control and implementation of all aspects of the socialist way of life are observed and developed. Collective bargaining covers, by law, everything related to wages, hours, working conditions, safety, sanitation, health, protection, conditions affecting women, youth, vacations and disputes. Unions watch over observance of the law, combat bureaucracy in management and educate millions of unionists on their rights and responsibilities.

In every industry in the USSR the objective is higher productivity, not to make higher profits for a private employer but for the good of the general public, the real owner and operator of all industries. In every industry, union representatives and management deal with production norms, conditions of work, etc., as set out under the conditions of the collective union agreement. Any disputes on such matters come before the management and the union committee. The disputed problem is not between the workers and an owner who seeks to hog a maximum of profit, but between workers and management, people who have a common interest as employees of a public enterprise. In all Soviet industries there is agreement between the union and management to do everything possible to provide the most humane conditions.

The influence of the working class is everywhere. Most of the officers of government, the Communist Party, the judges, etc. are former workers. Leonid Brezhnev, the president, is a former metalworker. By law in a socialist country, no one can get rich by exploiting others. In the United States the real owners of the plants do not live anywhere near the industries — in fact in most cases they have never seen the plant. In a socialist country the owners are the workers who work in them.

In the U.S. the reality is just the opposite. Every humane condition that workers win is the result of a fierce class struggle between the owners and managers who are on one side squeezing the profits from the labor of the worker, and workers who are trying to gain a decent wage and working conditions.

Socialism inherently brings with it a foreign policy of peace and peaceful coexistence for it is only in a world at peace that a socialist society can develop its full potential. In a socialist society both the profit motive and the class force that pushes for policies of war and war production are eliminated. And this means that socialist countries are not out to dominate or exploit other parts of the world or other countries because there is no class force that would profit from such a policy.

The drive of private corporations for maximum profits —no matter how or where they have to go to get them — is the root cause of policies of conquest, domination and military superiority to protect these interests. This is the very nature of private corporations, multinationals and conglomerates. That is why the inherent characteristic of socialist countries is the drive for peace and detente. And it is only under such conditions that a socialist society can thrive and advance.

If we did not have private corporations and their drive for profits, the foreign policy of our government would also be the opposite of what it is today — a policy of aggression and destabilization of regions and countries in order to gain or protect profit interests.

This policy is not in the interest of the workers and people of the United States. We do not gain from or need foreign plants, nor the domination of other lands. There are over 2,000 U.S. military bases throughout the world. The 30-ship armada in the Indian Ocean is in place to guard and protect the interests of the multinationals, to take back the oilfields of Iran — not for the benefit of the American people, but for the profits of Exxon and Shell. The military budget of hundreds of billions of dollars is not in the interest of the American people.

It is for the multinationals to protect their interests in foreign lands and to work toward halting the advance of the socialist countries and national liberation movements around the world, to keep the underdeveloped and developing countries from freeing themselves from the yoke of neocolonialism and U.S. imperialism.

IN ADDITION TO CONCEALING THE TRUTH ABOUT SOCIALISM, Big Business also wants to hide the source of their profits. They want to cover up the fact that there is only one element in the production process that produces more than its value or cost, and that is the labor power of workers. That is the source of all profits. The raw materials that go into making finished products change forms; for instance, the steel that goes into a car is still the same steel but in another form. By itself, the steel does not add new value.

The corporations' profits come from the only source possible, the exploitation of workers. Corporations pay their workers only enough to keep them and their families alive and able to work. Anything above this, such as a higher standard of living, the workers are forced to fight tooth and nail for. In other words, workers and their unions are forced to fight for some of the wealth that only they create.

Other methods used to extract superprofits are speedup, forced overtime and so-called productivity methods. The more productive workers are, the higher the profits of the corporations. Increases in productivity and advances in technology do not come back to the workers in better living conditions, they go into the profit pot of the bosses. Only in a socialist country does the increased productivity, the increase in wealth, come back to the workers and their families in the form of all kinds of benefits. This is the only place the wealth created can go: to advance the quality of life and pursue a foreign policy of peace and detente with all nations. There is no capitalist class to suck up the profits for itself.

So you see the Soviet workers and their trade unions don't need anyone to defend them. The fact is that slanderous concoctions and outright lies cannot hamper the building and advancement of socialism.

Why then the continuing and stepped-up campaign of slander, deprecation, mudslinging and belittling of socialist society? Because the lies are meant to discredit the idea of socialism. They are lies about socialism. Their purpose is to keep U.S. working people ignorant about the achievements of socialism. Their purpose is to make it possible for the big corporations to continue exploiting, to continue making their huge profits from the labor of U.S. workers.

In a socialist society, the full product of labor goes for the benefit of all the people. There are no Chrysler, Ford, General Motors and U.S. Steel stockholders and executives to siphon off the cream, because there are no corporate profits.

The struggle between capitalism and socialism on a world scale is but an extension of the struggle between the corporations and the workers on the domestic scene. It is the same struggle on a world scale that goes on between the workers and bosses, between the trade unions and the corporations. It is the same class struggle. To slander or lie about a socialist society is to slander and lie about a society in which workers are the dominant economic and political power.

It is understandable when the corporate executives, the large stockholders or their mass media slander a socialist country because they are defending a system that gives them all kinds of special class privileges and makes it possible for them to exploit and oppress the majority for their own enrichment. It is understandable why the *New York Times* prints articles that slander the Soviet Union. But it is a little more difficult to understand why Douglas Fraser, president of a trade union, would lend himself to what is basically an anti-workingclass propaganda campaign.

Are there weaknesses in the socialist countries? Do their leaders make mistakes? Of course there are and of course they do. An example is the recent strike in Poland. However, what the strike in Poland brought to the surface was not weaknesses in the socialist system but weaknesses in government and Party leadership.

The economic pressures began to build up because for the past period of time the government had spent huge sums of money in order to speed up the industrialization process. The intentions were good but the judgment was not. The situation in Poland finally reached a point where 96 percent of the income from exports went to pay interest on loans from both the capitalist and socialist world. Many of the industrial enterprises which cost huge sums of money were never completed and therefore were not producing products to pay for the building of such plants. It is also obvious that the government leadership and the management of the plants were not in close enough touch with the grassroots. And while the strikes in Poland will have many negative effects, including a necessary slowdown in the industrialization process, it will also have the positive result of correcting the existing weaknesses.

As a result of the situation in Poland, much is being said about whether workers in socialist societies have the right to strike. Their constitutions do not take up this question. But that is true also of the U.S. Constitution. However, there are dozens of specific laws in the United States that restrict the right to strike. The president of the U.S. has the power to issue strikebreaking injunctions. In most states it is illegal for transit workers, railroad workers, teachers and other public workers to strike. The steelworkers union and many others contain no-strike clauses in their contracts. There are no such laws or labor contracts in any socialist countries.

The strike in Poland was used by the capitalist countries to try to convince their workers that socialism doesn't work. The U.S. government and some trade union leaders have been applauding the Polish workers and the AFL-CIO International Affairs Department has pledged moral support and material support. Yet none of these leaders take note of the fact that the acts of Polish workers would be illegal under present U.S. labor laws. U.S. government employees are barred from striking by federal law. There are state and local laws which prohibit public employees from striking with harsh penalties for violations of these laws, as was the case in the New York transit strike under the anti-labor Taylor Law.[8] In other words, Polish workers have engaged in a successful struggle to win their demands and their counterparts in the U.S. would be subject to jail, fines and loss of union recognition for the very same acts.

It is time that U.S. labor leaders turned their attention to the rights of U.S. workers and stopped worrying about workers in socialist countries who already enjoy the right and power to "redress their grievances." There is much to be done to win labor reform in the U.S. and the AFL-CIO leadership might well start with a fight for legislation that would guarantee the right to strike to federal, state and local employees as well as all workers by limiting the power of the courts and the president to issue strikebreaking injunctions.

But the slander campaign is conducted not because Big Business is concerned about weaknesses, mistakes or the workers in socialist countries. The solicitous concern for the Polish workers is nothing but the height of capitalist hypocrisy. In fact, corporations and the mass media they control aren't concerned about workers' welfare anywhere, including in their own plants. Their wage rates are as low as possible, whatever they can get away with. They push speedup to the maximum. They cover up health hazards, fight safety and environmental regulations and resist all restrictions and regulations that would benefit workers. They close plants whenever it fits into their game plan of maximum profits. That's the nature of the beast.

A socialist society operates under the very opposite principles. What matters under socialism above all else is the welfare of the people, the workers.

Capitalism is bad enough today. But as time goes by the problems of the people will get worse as capitalism continues to slide deeper into crisis and decay. Capitalism, as a socioeconomic system, has served its historic purpose. But science, technology and life in general continue to develop. Because capitalism cannot basically change its nature it cannot serve the present, and especially the future, needs of society. The people of the U.S. will be forced to consider socialism as a solution.

The fact is that the world is moving toward socialism. It is an inevitable historic process; that is why it is important to know the truth about socialism. Mr. Fraser would better serve his membership if he would recognize this fact of life. No amount of threats, lies, slander campaigns or nuclear weapons can stop this worldwide revolutionary process.

An important aspect of the Big Business slander campaign is also directed against the Communist Party, USA. The CPUSA is the target of the anti-labor, anti-Communist campaign because it is a workingclass party that believes socialism is the solution to our problems. They slander Communists because they know that Communists who are trade unionists are part of the militant sector. They are aware that when workers join the CPUSA this adds new strength to the trade unions.

T HE BIGGEST, MOST DRAMATIC DIFFERENCE BETWEEN CAPI-talism and socialism is the fact that under capitalism a few rich stockholders own the industries. They are privately run solely for profits and for the benefit of the privileged few who don't work a day in their lives. Under socialism, the industries are owned socially, by the entire people, and the entire people are the genuine masters of their country. Production is motivated solely by the humanist objective to satisfy the steadily growing material and cultural requirements of all the people. Opposing class interests are eliminated forever.

Capitalism was an advance over slavery and feudalism. It was able to use the technology of its day. But now capitalism is increasingly out of step with modern times. The scientific and technological revolution is passing it by. The problems of today's world are too complex for a socioeconomic system that is at the mercy of individual corporations operating without concern for people or society.

Capitalism in the U.S. careens from one crisis to another because it is unplanned, chaotic and anarchistic. Its credo is each dog for himself and dog-eat-dog. The new advances in science and technology become entangled in its single-minded determination to milk all the benefits of production for private profits. New technology needs a socioeconomic system that can develop it, use it and distribute its benefits to society as a whole.

Socialism is uniquely designed to serve humanity and distribute its vast products to all people in society.

When capitalism acquires new technology, the corporations lay off workers, constantly adding to the vast army of permanently unemployed. Under socialism, when new machines take over from workers the workers are not thrown out on the streets. They either get new jobs or their hours of work are cut, assuring full employment for the whole population. Because of these policies there are no unemployed workers in the Soviet Union. Job security is a permanent feature of socialism.

Capitalism is a system of anarchy. As the process of the bigger corporations swallowing up the smaller ones accelerates they become even less concerned about human life and society. As capitalism develops into monopoly capitalism, the anarchy increases on an ever-bigger scale and the crises and disasters become more frequent and intense. The Chryslers and Lockheeds[9] are only the forerunners of things to come.

It is just these crises and disasters of capitalism that set the stage for socialism. Socialism is the realistic, common-sense solution to the critical problems people cannot find answers to under capitalism.

U.S. monopoly capital lies about socialism because it is in competition with the socialist system for the hearts and minds of our people. It is anti-labor, anti-Communist and anti-Soviet because it wants to continue to hold onto its special privileges and domination over people's lives.

Trade union leaders should view everything critically, including socialism. But because socialism is a workingclass society, it is not in their interests to take part in spreading lies and slander about socialism. When they do they are spreading lies and slander about workers, about a society in which workers, through their trade unions, are the dominant force. Socialism is workingclass power.

Worker's
Flashbacks

Worker's Flashbacks

[A selection of workingclass stories — all true — from the author's lifetime of experience.]

How I Became a Steelworker
and Gus Hall — Both by Accident

THE NATIONAL OFFICE OF THE YOUNG COMMUNIST LEAGUE HAD decided to send me from Minnesota to work in the coal fields, both as an organizer for the YCL and to help the coal miners' drive for union organization.

On the way to West Virginia we were to get together to discuss my work. I hitchhiked to Cleveland. On the same day there was a Party leadership meeting that included the leading comrades from Youngstown, Ohio. More than anyone else, Joe Dallet, a wonderful, enthusiastic comrade, who was later killed in Spain, convinced me to stop at Youngstown while awaiting further instructions from the National Office of the YCL. So I joined the comrades and went to Youngstown that night.

Before I knew it I became fully involved in the struggles of Youngstown, and they were everywhere — the unemployed, the youth, the Black community, steelworkers — everything was in motion. There were continuous demonstrations.

In a few weeks it became impossible to leave Youngstown.

So the national office of the YCL and the Party agreed I should stay there. That's how I landed, by accident, in Youngstown. It became clear that in order to organize steelworkers some of us had to get jobs in the steel industry. That was not an easy task; there wasn't too much hiring going on.

So some of us younger comrades went to an electric welding school at night. I had already had some training but didn't think I was a good enough welder to get a job.

However, I decided one morning to go to the steel plant and observe how the hiring was done so I would be prepared when I was ready. When I got there there were about 200 men lined up for jobs. Below the hill where they stood there was a long hourglass building where the men who did the hiring spent their days in luxury. I always picture them as butchers selecting their hogs for slaughter.

I joined the men on the hill and was there but a few minutes when one of the ones from the glass building pointed his finger at me and motioned me to come in. I knew that meant a job offer. Slowly I walked down the hill, making some quick decisions on the way: one, whether I was skilled enough, and more importantly, I knew that if I gave my real name, Arvo Gus Halberg, I would not last a day, because I had already run for the City Council of Youngstown on the Communist Party ticket. I made up my mind to try for the job and in desperation, just as I got to the glass building, I decided to cut both ends of my name and use what was left — Gus Hall. I was hired.

Next morning, when I entered the department I was assigned to, I realized immediately why I was hired so quickly. Everyone in the department weighed 200 lbs. or more. The job required lifting heavy pieces of steel so they were hiring only big strong men for that department.

Years later, in Leavenworth and other prisons, I thought about that job of mine. The job was to put together and weld the structure for rows of prison gates — those inside of prisons. During my spare time in prisons I always looked for the gates I had welded, but I never found any.

So I became a steelworker and an organizer for the steelworkers union. Before the union came into being I was fired twice from two different steel mills. But the activities I took part in were all as Gus Hall because I couldn't have two names — one in the mill, and the other as an organizer of the union. Then came the strikes and the name Gus Hall became widely known. So it became impossible to go back to my full name — Arvo Gus Halberg.

A few years later I decided to make Gus Hall my legal name. However, I didn't know it would cost anything. So when the judge asked for the $5 fee there was again a headline reading, "Halberg — now Hall — had funds for change." How did it get into the papers so quickly? Because of a one in a million shot. The clerk at the court was an old rat — a witness I think — in the Bridgman, Michigan case against our comrades. That's how Arvo Gus Halberg became Gus Hall the steelworker.

The Raid on the Armour Corporation

THE MASS DEMONSTRATIONS OF THE UNEMPLOYED WENT ON FOR years before they began to bring results. As the struggles developed, tactics became more militant. In Minneapolis we Communists led the mass struggles of the unemployed. In the later period, with 30,000 to 40,000 unemployed, we even took over and held the City Hall complex, which is a block wide, for almost a day.

This was already a tactic on a higher level. But in the very area where the demonstrations took place there was a huge central retail outlet owned by the Armour Packing Co. Real hunger was becoming more and more a critical problem for people. We decided to raise the tactics of struggle at that moment. This was before Roosevelt began to move in the New Deal direction. We decided to open the packing company building to the hungry who were in this big mass demonstration. The committee in charge was to lead the demonstration to the building and break away the big front windows in a way that would protect the workers from getting cut.

It was some sight; as if by plan workers took their places behind the counters to pass out food in a very orderly fashion. In my memory there are many vivid scenes from that particular moment. One worker whose arm seemed to be five feet long pushed it through rows of bologna and was passing the bologna out to the workers on the street.

There was a man walking away from the building taking bites out of a whole slab of bacon he had taken, talking to himself between bites, saying, "I'll be goddamned if I'm going to die of starvation." There were women, walking away from the plant with armfuls of food.

What impressed me was how these workers — who were not in on the plans — quickly organized the whole operation. The police stayed out of sight and the whole packing plant was cleaned out within a few minutes. The unemployed were hungry and there was the food in large quantities, owned by a huge corporation, and the workers felt perfectly justified in satisfying their gnawing hunger by taking from the fat cat corporations.

It was tactics like this that began to shake the foundation of the system and to strike fear into the hearts of Big Business. It was these militant tactics that brought about the change in tactics of the Roosevelt Administration.

Workers' Initiatives I
The Little Steel Strike in Warren

I HAVE NEVER STOPPED BEING AMAZED AT THE SELF-INITIATIVE OF workers during periods of struggle. It rises to the top in a way that is just unbelievable. This of course rises to its very highest level during revolutionary moments. And I, of course, have only seen it during strike struggles and the struggles of the unemployed — it gives one a sense of confidence of what workers will do during really serious revolutionary crises.

In 1937 the U.S. Steel Corporation, the biggest steel producer, decided to break class ranks and for the first time in the history of the industry recognized and signed a contract with a union. It became obvious then that the other steel corporations, led by Tom Girdler, the reactionary president of Republic Steel, would not deal with the union; there would have to be a strike in the rest of the steel industry, which was called Little Steel only because the biggest corporation, U.S. Steel, had already signed the contract.

Little Steel involved all the rest of the steel corporations. They were smaller than U.S. Steel, but they were not little. That's when Tom Girdler made his famous statement that "I would rather go to the farm to pick apples than to sign a union contract." Republic had two important plants in Warren and Niles, Ohio. The Warren plant was an especially key plant because it was at the time the only complete steel plant that Republic had. In other words, any kind of steel could be produced in that one plant.

The union leadership faced a dilemma. Everything pointed toward a strike. But these two key plants were not organized or ready for a strike.

The big factors holding back organization in the Warren plant was a company union — very common in those days — and the old organization of craft workers in the old class collaborationist Amalgamated Association of Iron, Steel & Tin Workers (AA). They refused to admit steelworkers into their ranks, but this craft union demanded jurisdiction over the whole steel plant. So it remained largely unorganized and the union had not come through, as was the case in many other areas.

When the union organizing drives were in trouble, the leadership of the Steelworkers Organizing Committee would ask one of the Communists to take over the task. This happened a number of times. So I was asked to take over the task of organizing and preparing the Warren and Niles plants of Republic Steel for a strike that was only weeks away.

It's interesting that later Phil Murray said publicly that the

Warren strike was the best organized labor strike he had ever seen in his life. It was the rank and file steelworkers that made it possible. It was their actions of self-initiatives that made the strike such a success.

When the strike was called in all the steel corporations except U.S. Steel the workers and the union in Warren and Niles were ready for the struggle. As we know, it was one of the most bitter struggles in Chicago, Youngstown, Cleveland, Pittsburgh, etc. It was really the last of the battles to break down the resistance of U.S. monopoly capital and their ability to operate non-union industries.

The basic industries had remained non-union industries. For Republic Steel, the Warren plant was the key plant. Because Warren had been a more conservative city, Republic went all out to defeat the strike. They prepared for war and this was especially true around the Warren plant. The plant was also situated in an area where it was difficult to place pickets everywhere. For miles along the back side of the plant was a large swamp and wooded area. The front of the plant faced the poor workingclass slum section of the city, with its streets running into the plant.

These became real problems along the way, as the strike progressed. And the corporations were out to use all these factors, including the swamp land in the back and the fact that so many streets ran right into the plant. They were out to use them to break the strike. One must keep in mind that this big corporation had made all its plans and the solid decision that this was one strike it was going to break — because if it did, the steel industry would remain unorganized.

The Republic Steel plant in Warren was big enough for landing planes. So Republic hired small planes filled with scabs and food from around the country. That's how they brought in strikebreakers. But Republic underestimated the determination and ingenuity of the workers. Here again, the initiative of the workers took hold. Many of them were deer hunters, so they got out their guns and placed themselves in the swamps waiting for the planes to come. They shot at the scab planes enough so that two of them crashed upon landing inside of the plant.

This brought Republic's scab flights to an end.

Later on, the Vietnamese people developed this tactic into a science; with the concentration of small rifle fire on fast planes they brought down many U.S. jets based on this tactic.

The workers who initiated this tactic at Republic years ago were mostly inexperienced new workers, and it was something to see how fast they grew militant and creative when the situation demanded it.

Once the strike had started, I left the strike committee meeting the evening of the third day — when we had discussed the problems of the back side of the plant, the streets, etc. I was going to discuss these questions with the pickets, with the workers. It was hardly dark, and when I reached the pickets I didn't believe what I saw. The back side looked like a scene from the First World War — a battlefield.

There were barbed wire fences and floodlights lighting the place up from one end to the other. The idea itself was unique enough. But when I asked where they got the money to buy the materials, the answer was just as unbelievable. These workers — the rank-and-file workers — had organized themselves in teams and they canvassed the local business people and got materials donated for free and set up this warlike scene with floodlights and barbed wire fences.

Later the streets running into the plant became a problem. The action of the steelworkers was direct and simple. They simply closed the streets off, and only those with a pass signed by me, as chairman of the strike committee, could come and go. There were a number of crises about these street closings, especially when the Mayor and the Chief of Police were forced to get a pass signed by a known Communist, strike committee chairman. The police chief especially was very vindictive and to his last day he said to many people of the press that in his mind John Dillinger was not enemy number one, Gus Hall was.

The same initiative was evident on the question of security. Republic Steel tried every possible provocation in order to bring in the National Guard. One day a rank-and-file worker brought in word that there was going to be an attempt to assassinate me. How he got all the details I'll never know. So the strike committee decided to give the information to the local police only a few hours before the time the attempt was to be made.

Strikers were also present when the police were there. And sure enough, a young man appeared with a rifle, a five-gallon can of gas, and a pile of rags soaked with gasoline. He was arrested. The case, however, was never brought to trial. Because the workers had information that it was an official of the Republic Steel Corporation who paid for the effort that failed, it was not brought to trial.

It was difficult to get strike headquarters in this conservative Little Steel town. But here again the initiative of workers came to the rescue. Some workers knew a small underworld character who owned a large, fully-equipped nightclub and gambling place. It was closed at the time but with plans to open soon. These workers also knew that the owner had a grudge against steel companies in general because when he was a boy a steel company fired his father. As a result we had the most elaborate, well-equipped strike headquarters in all of labor history, and it didn't cost us a penny.

These were actions by workers who lived in the traditional conservative Republic Party-controlled town, and who themselves had just joined the union. They were very new in the union. However, when the strike was over, because of the experiences many of the best of these workers joined the Communist Party, and many of them still remain in the Party.

Workers' Initiatives II
The Minneapolis Teamsters Strike

IN THE 1930s A TROTSKYITE CLIQUE GOT INTO THE LEADERSHIP OF the Teamsters local in Minneapolis. It was a period of great strikes, including the general strike in support of West coast longshoremen in San Francisco led by Harry Bridges. The

Teamsters in Minneapolis also struck. It turned into a bitter battle. The Trotskyites, instead of doing what the West Coast longshoremen did — appealing for support from all the workers and people — played footsie with the governor of the state of Minnesota who was out to break the strike with the use of the National Guard. So the strike began to peter out.

It would have been a lost strike if it were not for the activities and actions taken by the Communist Party. I was one of the comrades assigned to give leadership to the strike. The Mayor of Minneapolis had just deputized 15,000 thugs to break the picket line. Developments came to a showdown battle. The Trotskyites repudiated confrontation tactics, but it was the only way to win the strike and it was the only thing that did win it.

So it came about that thousands of strikers filled one street for blocks and the 15,000 deputies and the whole police force occupied the same street in the opposite direction. They faced each other with just a narrow street between them. It was difficult to bring about the confrontation under those circumstances.

The workers took up collections among themselves and sent teams to buy eggs. Farmers also donated to the strikers eggs, potatoes — anything that one could throw. At a signal, the workers showered the police and deputies with thousands of eggs. The police chief decided to move his forces a half block away. It was this that gave the strikers enough room to gain the necessary momentum for the attack. In a few minutes the battle was over, with the police on the run. The deputies who didn't get beat up were running all over town throwing away their badges. Even years later, in another strike, the county sheriff and police chief were not able to find anyone who would accept a badge for the purpose of strikebreaking in Minneapolis.

To this day the Trotskyites have never admitted that with their opportunistic maneuvering with the Governor they had all but lost the strike. It was our tactic of confrontation at a critical moment and the initiative of the workers that won the strike. Tactics of confrontation are not always correct, or not always necessary. They were correct in the Minneapolis situation.

Reino Tantella

REINO TANTELLA WAS UNIQUE AND OF A SPECIAL MOLD. MY FIRST full-time assignment in the Communist movement was as the YCL organizer on the iron-ore range in Minnesota. The Party and League had a joint office in an old storefront. This was in the days of the economic crisis. Our offices were downstairs and there was a house of prostitution upstairs. Sometimes during our meetings someone would be thrown down the stairs with a lot of tumult.

Hundreds of small farmers were members of the Party. But they had no money so they paid their dues and gave donations to the Party by giving eggs or potatoes. We had eggs piled to the ceiling in our office. We ate eggs day and night and made them in hundreds of ways. We organized egg-eating parties to turn the eggs into money. Such were some of the problems of the early Communist movement.

One day, a young man of about 17 years walked into our office. He had a nice smile. He was shy, but most serious. He said, "I'm Reino Tantella from Sax. I'm here to become a full-time revolutionary." It was obvious he was dead serious.

I told him "We really don't have money for many full-time organizers, as you can see from the pile of eggs in the corner there." "Oh," he said, "I'm not asking to be put on the payroll. My father, brother and I had a small farm back of a swamp in Sax, Minnesota. We sold it a few weeks ago and divided the money. So I will live on what I have until it's gone." That's how Reino became a full-time revolutionary.

Reino had a pleasant face, but I never heard him laugh. He never took part in idle chatter. In fact, he was a very quiet young fellow.

Reino became an organizer of farmers, because he had a farm background. One of the unexplainable things about Reino was the fact that most of the comrades, including myself, thought he was the dullest speaker ever to take the rostrum. But in a very short period Reino became the most popular speaker among farmers in northern Minnesota. He drew crowds of farmers like no other speaker.

I went with him to some of the meetings just to study what there was about his style that the farmers liked. But he had no style in speaking really. It was the *content* and Reino's own character. Because of his background he was one of them. The way that he placed questions made sense to the farmers. Reino led some of the biggest protest marches of farmers in that period of U.S. history. He recruited hundreds of farmers into the Party.

He died as he lived. He was one of the first to volunteer to fight fascism in Spain. There he also volunteered to fight a rearguard action to make a troop-retreat possible. Everyone knew there was very little chance for anyone to come out of such an action alive. Comrades who were there when the retreat started saw Reino sitting on a log whittling a stick, nonchalantly humming a tune. When comrades hesitated to leave, Reino very calmly said, "What are you waiting for? Your orders are to retreat." Reino died in that action.

One story demonstrates how totally involved and dedicated Reino was in the struggles and movements of the farmers.

Late one evening we were at a comrade's house who had gone to a farm meeting with Reino. About 11:00 p.m. Reino came in rather excited about the meeting. He told us about the big crowd, the militancy and how the farmers reacted. Finally, someone said, "Where's Jack?" Jack was the comrade whose house we were in. "Oh," Reino said, "A train hit us. Jack went to the hospital to have a wound taken care of."

The train wreck was a secondary matter to Reino. There are hundreds of such stories about Reino Tantella who came out of the swamp to become a full-time revolutionary. The name Reino Tantella still creates excitement and fond memories among farm families in northern Minnesota.

I never heard Reino even mention the word "theory."

Theory for him was not something just to talk about. But all his spare time he spent studying Marx, Engels and Lenin. Marxism-Leninism was a guide to action for Reino in his leadership of the farmers of northern Minnesota. As a matter of fact, Reino brought the books by Marx, Engels and Lenin in one of his suitcases when he came into the office. He had already studied Marxism-Leninism before he volunteered to become a full-time revolutionary.

Elizabeth's Family

IN MANY WAYS MY WIFE ELIZABETH'S FAMILY AND MINE WERE very similar, both workingclass families. Our families were refugees from hunger and poverty in Europe — Elizabeth's from Hungary and mine from Finland. Elizabeth's father worked in the Pennsylvania coal mines and my father in the Minnesota coal and iron ore mines. Both our parents were active in Left-radical activities most of their lives and were early supporters of socialism and the Soviet Union — the first workingclass state — and supporters of the Communist movement in the U.S.

The "Turner Farm," as Elizabeth's folks' place was called, had a distinguished record. In the 1930s and '40s when Communists were being arrested, they stayed in jail as a rule because there was no bail money. In Youngstown and Warren, Ohio, when Communists were arrested, the "Turner Farm" very often became the bail. I don't think there was a period when the farm was not put up as for bail for Communists.

After Elizabeth and I were married the similarities continued. I went to work in the steel industry and Elizabeth was one of the first women steelworkers. She played an important role as the secretary of a large steel local. As a matter of fact, the roots of the women's caucus movement in steel go back to those days. They were the days when women really had to hack through the resistance to their being in the union.

Family background had much to do with Elizabeth's political and personal makeup. I have never known a day when she has shown even the slightest lack of confidence in the working class of the U.S. and the world, in our Party or in the inevitable direction of history. She has been critical of tactics and personalities, but always within the context of total confidence in and commitment to the overall workingclass struggle for a better life and for socialism. Such a partner in life and struggle is a source of great strength.

Elizabeth had to raise both our children, Arvo and Barbara, alone during critical periods in their lives. When Barbara was a child, I was either in the Navy or in the county jails; when Arvo was a child I was in Leavenworth.

When Elizabeth and I decided to get married in 1935 we made plans to go to Erie Pennsylvania because there was no waiting period. Before we left the "Turner Farm," Elizabeth's mother asked, "Where are you going to get a witness?" When I said, "We'll pick up a hitchhiker," she smiled and said with a twinkle in her eye, "Be sure he or she is a citizen." That's the way she approached things.

Elizabeth's mother had the greenest thumb I've ever seen in my life. It's possible that some of my success in gardening rubbed off from her. I always watched her work and there were flowers everywhere — inside and outside the house.

I think this background laid the solid foundation for our life together.

There's always talk, including in the Party, about how our position on equality for women affects the home life of Communists, especially leading Communists. In most cases, I'm sure it is better than the average American family. But to say it is fully applied in the home would not be true.

It is not true in my case. I cook when I have time or feel like it; Elizabeth does it whether there is time or not. I wash dishes when I'm not too busy or too tired; Elizabeth washes dishes whether she's tired or not.

Women who work still carry the load of two jobs — even sometimes in Communist households. Men should be carrying on a constant struggle with themselves to work toward sharing that load. Without such a self-struggle the gap between our political position and our personal lives will remain.

Max and Marian

MAX AND MARIAN WERE TWO BEAUTIFUL PEOPLE. THEY WERE both — and still are, because they are still living while I am writing this — charter members of our Party.

Max was an auto worker in Toledo in his youth, and for years and years a steelworker in Cleveland. As a matter of fact, Max and Elizabeth Hall together gave leadership to the Republic Steel local in Cleveland for a long time. Marian, besides taking care of the house and raising two wonderful daughters, worked in a number of trades and industries.

When I returned from Leavenworth, the Party was still in an internal factional struggle. As a matter of fact, many had left the Party because of this. They lost confidence in the leadership of the Party and so dropped from membership.

Marian and Max were different. They made a special bus trip from California (because that was cheapest) to see what was what in the national office in New York. After talking to other leading comrades they asked to see me. They had their questions all clearly formulated, obviously together. I answered one question after another to the best of my ability.

When it was all over, Max, in a very matter of fact way, turned to Marian and said, "So, are you satisfied?" Marian's answer was just as simple and direct; it was a few word, "Yes, I'm satisfied." With that, Max turned over an envelope to me. We shook hands and they departed. In the envelope was, I think, $3,000 for the Party. This was their demonstration that while they had lost confidence in some leaders of the Party, they had not lost confidence in the Party or the working class.

Therefore, the factional struggle was a momentary thing and the Party and the working class go on forever.

Years later Max and Marian made another trip to New York (again on a bus, because that was the cheapest way to travel). They had drawn up a will some time before so that the Party would get everything they had. They came because "they had talked it over and decided that the Party needed the money now." They turned over their total life savings. The sum was rather large. Saving was a way of life for Max and Marian. But the saving was for a purpose. They saved as much as they could because it was saving money for the Communist Party.

That is a dedicated lifestyle if I've ever seen one. They lived as if in poverty. For instance, Max always put two pairs of soles on their shoes so a pair of shoes would last ten years or more. When out of town, they would never eat in a restaurant: "It costs too much." They bought some bologna, bread and a bottle of milk. "What we've saved is Party money, and we don't want to waste it."

Max and Marian are beautiful examples of workingclass dedication and true commitment to the Communist Party. While making these contributions they have been active daily in mass work and Party work their whole adult life. They have, for instance, been showing films about socialism in the Soviet Union to small and large gatherings for almost 50 years.

Conversations with William Z. Foster

BILL FOSTER WAS A VERY UNIQUE AND MOST INTERESTING PERSON-ality. He was ill with heart ailments for a long period of time, so he was restricted to his home for long periods. Foster lived to old age due to the personal care of a great human being and top-notch doctor, Comrade Doctor Harry Epstein. Comrade

Epstein was Foster's doctor for most of his life, and in a sense, kept him going.

Such periods of isolation create their own problems, including political ones. But Foster kept up with developments and wrote most of his books and many articles during those long periods when he was restricted to his bedroom. There was a constant stream of visitors at his apartment and he was able to keep abreast of events in this way.

I had the good fortune of being assigned by the Political Bureau of our Party to be the live link between Foster and the rest of the leadership. I spent hours each week with Foster. We talked, joked, argued and discussed many things. My estimation of Foster grew during this process. We became very close friends.

Foster was unique because he came into the Party with the greatest accumulation of class struggle experience of anyone in U.S. history. He had the greatest experience in organizing workers into unions, in strike struggles, etc. From these experiences he developed the deepest understanding of the particular features and characteristics of the U.S. working class. He had a keen sense about how they would react to developments. He knew their strengths and weaknesses.

Foster also had no illusions about the U.S. ruling class. He had experienced first hand its brutality. Many of his earlier years were spent in the syndicalist movement. And I would say that not all Foster's experiences in the syndicalist movement were negative ones.

The class struggle and the working class was the pivot, the mooring, around which all of Foster's thoughts revolved. The working class was his point of reference. He would say things like, "You're as stubborn as the U.S. working class." Or he would say, "The working class has the necessary potential political muscle needed to overthrow U.S. capitalism." Or he would say nonchalantly, "Now that's a workingclass approach."

Foster's theoretical contributions and his depth were greatly underestimated by the Party. For a long period Earl Browder, who was then the general secretary, was considered

the theoretician, while Foster was seen as the practical tacti-
cian.

There were three errors in these assessments. One was that
when the theories had to meet the test of time, Browder turned
into the "practical" one, without the benefit of Marxist-Leninist
theory, and Foster proved to be the Marxist-Leninist who did
not waver and was able to pursue a correct course in tactics and
strategy as well. That was a test of one's theoretical understanding.

The second error was in thinking that a correct course in
strategy and tactics is not based on a deep understanding of
theory, even if one does not write articles of a theoretical nature.

The third error reflected an anti-workingclass influence that
Foster, the worker, could not make contributions in theoretical
developments because that is the work of intellectuals. I think
these three errors showed themselves in the concept of Foster's
theoretical understanding.

Once we were discussing Browder's revisionism. Foster
with great emphasis said, "Gus, if our Party and its leadership
sticks with the class struggle and the workingclass approach,
we will still most likely make mistakes and errors, but the important thing is that we will not make the big mistakes that
Browder, Kautsky, Trotsky and others made. Therefore, the
important thing is to stick to the workingclass emphasis, working class approach and the class struggle."

Foster gave me some advice the very day I was elected to
the Political Bureau. He said with a twinkle in his eye, "This is a
body of people with definite opinions and they express them
very vigorously. Therefore you have to push yourself into the
discussion. Don't wait until you have fully formulated your
thoughts. Put your name in right from the start of a discussion.
Otherwise, you will be sidetracked in the work of this important body of the Party." I think I have followed Foster's advice.

As a rule the discussions between Foster and me at his
home were rather calm and quiet and considered. At times
they were loud and sharp. But they never affected our comradely relationship. Esther, Foster's wife, used to call out when

we got loud, "Bill, you have to consider Gus's heart and not argue so vigorously!"

On a few occasions, because Foster was isolated for so long, he began to express some doubts about the position of the Political Bureau and questioned whether I had correctly or fully stated the facts. After a few such occasions I decided to confront the problem. I said: "Bill, if you and I are going to continue having a Communist-like relationship I will have to honestly accept, even if I disagree with some of your ideas, that you are fully stating your position and you will have to do the same with me." Foster was shocked at my sharp statement. He sat back in silence for a few minutes and then said, "Gus, you're right, and I appreciate your frankness. That's a workingclass approach." In fact, our relationship struck deeper roots.

However, that political isolation cannot be completely put on Bill's shoulders. There were weaknesses in the collective in not making the necessary effort to keep Bill in touch with the discussions and debates in the Political Bureau and Central Committee of the Party. I'm sure that would also have helped Foster make more contributions to the Party in that period.

On one of my visits to Bill, Ben Davis, who was then the National Secretary of our Party, came with me. Ben had been the New York State Chairman and was elevated to National Secretary.

As soon as we got into Bill's room, Bill said to Ben: "You made a mistake; you let Gus take you away from your base in New York" I said, "Bill, that's a trade union concept, not a Party concept. You know in the Party the base for all of us is the Party itself." He laughed and said, "Of course you're right. But it doesn't hurt to be closer to some districts than others." As a matter of fact, he pointed a finger at me and said, "You stay close to the industrial districts, especially to Ohio." I had to agree with that because I do.

As a rule I opened up on questions, unless Bill had written an article and he wanted to read it to me or to a few of us. I said I wanted to discuss with him the weaknesses of our Party in the struggle against racism and the influences of white chauvinism in the Party. I told him I thought this was a very important and basic question for us.

Bill said this was a very serious and somewhat difficult question. I said I wasn't interested in us making a record, or the formal side of the struggle. But how to fight racism and white chauvinism in a way that would be effective, that would burn it out as far as the Party is concerned and influence people, especially workers, against racism. I said, "Too often we consider only the formal aspects; too many of our white comrades are not convinced that we can make real headway on the important front of the struggle against racism. Too often the discussion goes into surface problems, like whether we should say we are a Black and white party or a white and Black party."

Bill interjected: "You know, you're right. I wrote an article for *Political Affairs* on that. Why not say it's both — Black and white and white and Black. We are a workingclass Party, but we are more than that. We are a Party of socialism. And more than that also. But let's get back to fighting racism in a way that gets concrete results, not just the formal aspect, so we can say we have rejected it.

"First we must be convinced that we can convince others. If we are not convinced, we cannot do this. And we must be confident that others can be convinced. Second, we must relate it to the self-interests of others, and most important, to the class interests of workers. That is a very important starting point in the struggle against racism. Third, we must be convinced that the struggle against racism is the most vital element of our movement and struggle."

He continued: "If we lay that as a basis we can make more headway than we have so far." I added that it is a struggle that must be a part of every day's activities. Like all struggle it must be constructive. Bill said, "It is easier to drive out all members in the Party who are affected by chauvinism than to correct them and win them over."

It's too bad such a conversation wasn't taped because I can't recall many parts of it. Comrade Foster talked about the many sides of the struggle for national liberation and the role of nationalism in that struggle. I recall his emphasis was on seeing and working with the positive aspects of nationalism, but he said Communists must never adopt it as the basis for their concepts and outlook.

He stated that there are both tendencies in the Party — not to see the progressive, positive role and therefore an outright rejection, and also a tendency to adopt nationalism as one's own. I recall raising the question of always seeing that the main arena of struggle must be against racism and white chauvinism. Bill agreed and added, "If the priorities are not right we would become apologists for racism."

It was a stimulating and interesting discussion, like so many I had with Bill. I am a better and wiser Communist because of Bill Foster.

Where Do Today's Lonely Men of the Woods Go?

AS A YOUNG MAN, AS A MATTER OF FACT A TEENAGER, I WORKED in the woods. Not in the close roadside lumber operations but in what was then called the deep woods. They were lumber camps that were mostly isolated from the rest of the world for at least six months of the deep winter. The men who gravitated toward these camps for work had many similar characteristics.

I believe this is true of many industries. The nature of the industry and the jobs tend to attract people who have similar ways of looking at life and the world around them. More than anything else the deep-woods worker was a lonely man; quiet and very considerate. There were very few youngsters like myself. As if to make up for the lack of help they got when they were young, the older workers went out of their way to be helpful and friendly to the newcomers who were young. For us that was very fortunate.

The old-time lumberjack tended to think about the world more in philosophical terms than practical or immediate terms. But when it came to tall tales, like Paul Bunyan stories, their imaginations ran wild. I was always surprised at their great interest in culture. As a matter of fact, it seems the great majority of the world's poets and songwriters were in these lumber camps!

There are many newspapers and books that do contain poetry by the lumberjacks. I read more poetry there that was never published, than all the poetry I've read since. I recall only one book of poems by a lumberjack. He was a very pleasant man, a lifetime friend of our family. The title of the book always struck me; it simply was "From the World of the Forgotten."

Lumberjacks have a deep love of nature, for the woods. They worked all week in the woods. But come Sunday, after dinner they would take long walks in the deep woods. Most of the lumberjacks had wild animal pets — chipmunks, a bird called the "lumberjack" (which hung around lumber camps), a bear or deer who they helped find food in the snow and cold. Looking back, it's interesting that while there was so much wildlife I don't recall ever seeing a deer or even a rabbit killed by a lumberjack.

I'm sure the lumber corporations knew some of the characteristics of the lumberjack and took advantage of his loneliness. They knew they were in a sense stuck there in the woods, either by their own choice or something in their lives. The wages were $30 per month.

Now these old type lumber camps of the deep woods are gone, pushed out of existence by new technology. I sometimes wonder where the beautiful, lonely, thoughtful poets who used to inhabit these camps go today.

Fern Dobbs

COMRADE FERN DOBBS WAS TRULY A MAN OF THE WOODS. ALL HIS life he lived and worked away from the cities and in the northern areas of Wisconsin and Michigan. He was a very kind and sociable individual. He enjoyed visitors and would drive his jeep 100 miles just to "drop in" on some old friend.

Fern heard rumors about my love for the woods and that each year I provided the deer for an annual venison dinner to raise funds for the Party in Cleveland. As a matter of fact these dinners became the most successful fundraising affair of each year. So when Fern heard these rumors he sent me an invitation to come to his cabin and hunt in upper Wisconsin. The cabin — as he called it — turned out to be a beautiful doll-like house, like a handcarved piece of sculpture that he had worked on for years. And there it stood, all alone in the deep woods. Inside the cabin was spotless, everything neatly in its place.

Fern was a man of the woods, living in isolation most of the time. But he was a Communist, a firm Marxist-Leninist all the way. He continued to read and study the workingclass science and was very anxious to discuss what he had learned.

Fern had an unusual way of doing "mass" work. Twice a year — every spring and fall — he would go to "the cities," as he would say, to the Marxist bookstores and buy literature. He would literally load up his jeep to the roof. Then he would go on his way — each trip would take about a month to a month and a half. Because he had been doing this for no one knows how many years, he had "regular customers" who waited for his biannual visit. His "customers" were farmers, workers, small-business owners — people working at gas stations and on the farms. He concentrated in the agricultural and small town areas. Sometimes he would trade Marxist books for some gas for his jeep. Even the McCarthy hysteria period did not stop Fern. He told me a million stories from his biannual trips. He was very proud of the fact that with each trip he found new customers and the sales kept on increasing. He originally started 20 to 30 years ago with only a few customers.

Fern was unusual in many ways. One November morning, I woke up in his cabin — I always slept on the top tier of the bunk he had built in the cabin. This was about 6:00 a.m. and the temperature outside was 40 degrees below or colder. Fern was not sleeping and I began to wonder whether he had slipped out to hunt. But through the window I saw an odd sight. There in the 40 below zero weather was old Fern standing in the nude, rubbing himself with a large towel. When he came in, I inquired about what the hell he was up to. He said he was taking his usual fresh-air bath and had been doing it for years, winter and summer.

Also, Fern would eat only poached eggs; fried and boiled weren't good for the health. Instead of corn flakes or wheatina, Fern would eat corn and wheat.

I didn't see Fern for a couple of years. Then one evening in Chicago, I was going upstairs to speak at a mass meeting. Before I reached the door, there was Fern, big smile on his face. He handed me an envelope and went on his way. When I opened the envelope, I found a few thousand dollars and a note which explained that in view of the fact that he had sold his "doll house" cabin and that he and I had had so many enjoyable discussions and laughs there, he thought the Party should get half the sale money.

When I last saw Fern he was in his late seventies. I have hesitated to write about him in the past tense because it may just be that with his fresh-air baths in below-freezing temperatures, Comrade Fern Dobbs is still very much alive. So, dear Fern, if you read these words, I'm sure you will overlook my seeming lack of confidence in your unusual approach to a long life.

The Quaker Who Made a Profession of Robbing Banks

I NEVER KNEW HIS FULL NAME, ONLY JOHN. HE WAS AN UNUSUAL person — as a Quaker and as a bank robber. He was born into a Pennsylvania Quaker family, went to Quaker schools. But somewhere he shifted gears. I met him in Leavenworth.

He almost created a riot over bird's-nests in the prisons. He could not stand seeing the prison guards destroying the nests the birds had built, where they were laying eggs and hatching them high over the prison walls. He won the fight and so I nicknamed him, "John the Baptist." That nickname stuck with him for the rest of his career.

John finished that prison term and was released before we were. He went to the national Party office and offered his services. But no one would believe his story, so his offer was rejected. Then there was a story in the press that John went to the Federal Prison Bureau in Washington and told them he had no moral right to be out of prison and free when people like Potash and Hall, whom he met and respected and who had done nothing wrong, remained in prison. Of course the prison officials didn't agree with him.

When I got out, Elizabeth and I visited John and his family in California. It seemed he had gone straight by then. But about a year later, when I was still on parole in Cleveland, I began to get notes from John. Each note referred to the church requirement — a tithing of ten percent — and each letter enclosed a clipping about a bank robbery.

One letter had two clippings from a local paper in Cleveland. It was a a story of a bank robber who had written a letter to the paper protesting an article which called him "cruel and cold hearted." In the letter he told the editor, "You go to (such and such) bank and you will see that the clerk is pregnant. I was going to rob that bank yesterday but when I saw the condition of the clerk I walked out. So you have no right to call me coldhearted. . . . " I guess that was the Quaker in John coming out. But the letters kept coming, each with a clipping about a new bank robbery. And I was as sure as I could be that it was John who was doing it all — robbing the banks, clipping the articles and sending the notes.

While the letters were coming to Cleveland, it was publicly announced that I would speak in Chicago at a mass meeting. The day before the meeting John was picked up near Chicago for bank robbery. He sent me a letter from the Cook County jail saying he was sorry he had not been able to get to the mass meeting. He also said that he wasn't going to be tried — he was going to use the trial to put the system on trial! He said, "It is the system that's no goddamned good." He had concluded that in fact it was the system that was all wrong.

In these past years I always know when John the Baptist is out of prison. When he's out, he sends me a New Year's card or sometimes a telegram.

Going back a moment, when I was in prison and John the Baptist was out, he sent Elizabeth ten roses, but sent them in my name. That was also the Quaker coming out in John.

In the Business of Trade Unionism

THERE WERE A LOT OF UNDERWORLD BIGGIES IN LEAVENWORTH. A small incident took place that showed how they saw the trade unions, and how little they knew about us. It also showed what had become of many of the trade unions, especially some trade union locals.

These underworld personalities knew we worked with trade unions. So they asked for a conference in the prison yard with Irving Potash and myself. Without hesitation they put the proposition on the table. They wanted to buy from us one or two trade union locals, even three if possible. The sums they offered were huge. They said they would put the money in escrow in banks and that we would not have to release our hold on the unions until we were assured the money was in the bank.

To their astonishment, we tried to explain that we do not buy or sell trade union locals and this was not our relationship to trade unions, and that we were interested only in building the trade unions for the sake of the trade unions themselves. They would not believe us.

Next day they asked for another conference and doubled the price; in fact they upped the price twice. When we would not agree, they decided that we would not sell because the price was not high enough and they weren't in a position to make it bigger. We were never able to convince them about our trade union policy. They saw trade unions as a business. And in business you buy and sell.

The Bank Robber
Who Changed his Mind

WHEN IRVING POTASH AND I ARRIVED AT LEAVENWORTH IN LEG-irons and handcuffs, we were put into a 30-day isolation block — isolated from the other prisoners. But because of the unbelievable effectiveness of the prison grapevine the prisoners knew days in advance that two Communist leaders were coming in as prisoners.

In prisons there are generally undeclared but accepted social structures. When we entered Leavenworth, within hours we heard that the influential people in this structure sent word that we were welcome and if we had any problems or needed anything we should send word to them and they would take care of it. Against all rules and taking the risk of being sent to "the hole," an elderly Black prisoner found ways of sending us cigarettes and razor blades almost as soon as we arrived. We have remained fast friends to this day.

One young bank robber had obviously not gotten the word about our acceptance. He told us the story later on. He was generally anti-Communist because he was raised as a Catholic. So he had made up his mind to start a fight and beat us up — at least one of us. He even told us later how he planned to start the fight. He was going to ask one of us a provocative question: "What about individual initiatives under socialism?"

Here he was, his own initiatives were limited to the prison cell and he was worried about the individual initiatives permitted under socialism. Later he admitted that it was all quite ridiculous.

Whether through design by the warden's office or by coin-

cidence this anti-Communist was put into the cell next to Irving
Potash. Of course, Irving knew nothing about the plans of this
anti-Communist. The 140-pound Irving would have been no
match for six-foot two-inch, 250-pound young bank robber
who, by the way, was the best weightlifter in the prison. But
the young bank robber met a different kind of match and lost —
or maybe one could say won, in the long run.

As the bank robber related the story months later, when the
cell gates were opened he confronted Irving with his challenge:
"What about individual initiatives under socialism?" Irving,
who was the most pleasant, kindest, considerate human being
on this earth, smiled, put out his hand in friendship and said,
"Well, it's an interesting subject. Let's you and me talk about
it." Later, the bank robber said, "How can you hit someone
who reacts like that?" But that's not the end of the story.

Irving, in his quiet way, kept explaining about socialism. A
few days later, I met the bank robber and we became good
friends. About a year or so later someone made some nasty
remarks about Communists and communism in the prison
yard. The young bank robber, who earlier was going to beat up
Communists, beat up the anti-Communist to the point where
he landed in the prison hospital.

Years went by. When the bank robber got out of prison, he
came to New York to proudly introduce us and the Party office
to his new family. He hasn't robbed banks since. But every so
often he drops by and leaves a small donation for "our good
cause."

May Day Flashbacks

FOR SOME NINETY YEARS WORKERS THROUGHOUT THE WORLD
have been celebrating, demonstrating and marching on May 1.
On this special day workers hold their heads higher and walk
with a jaunty spring to their step. This is their day. In many

small ways they reflect a deep pride and unwavering confidence in their class. Some consciously and others instinctively feel that our class has the task of clearing the path, providing the main force, in the struggle for social progress. On May 1 hundreds of millions of workers bask in the sunlit grandeur of the achievements, the victories and the historic role of our class. It is the day when class consciousness is on display. The mass demonstrations are public expressions of the meaning of May Day to workers. But the depths of May Day's roots can be more clearly noticed in the actions of individual workers who were not or are not in a position to take part in mass actions. The class roots of May Day have a special meaning for me and can be best illustrated in these flashbacks.

FOR FORTY OR MAYBE FIFTY YEARS, ANDY WAS A BARBER IN HIS one-man shop in the heart of a workingclass neighborhood. His shop was open six days a week. Andy's barbershop was also a center for workingclass education. On the first of May every one of those 40 to 50 years, Andy did his special, unique May Day thing, and it was done with dignity and "class." Andy, who ordinarily never wore a tie, would come to work wearing a bright red one. Not even the McCarthy cold war hysteria stopped Andy from observing May Day. He would open his shop and put up the old sign: "May Day — No Work Today."

Of course, all his workingclass customers knew that while Andy was not cutting hair on this day, the shop was open, including the door to his backroom apartment. It was open for coffee and donuts and interesting and lively conversation. The *Daily Worker* and Communist literature were always present in Andy's shop.

Besides being a good barber, Andy was an excellent teacher, propagandist and fighter. He used to say, "When a worker leaves my shop he has much less hair, but much more understanding and class consciousness." All one had to do was sit in his shop and observe in order to be convinced that what he said was true. Andy's customers were politically advanced. They were his students.

During the McCarthy hysteria days, the FBI tried to harass Andy and his customers. For instance, a few would come and sit in his shop. But when they returned the second or third time Andy decided to do something about it. He took out his razor strap and hung it on the wall next to the two agents. Then with very deliberate, calm strokes he began to sharpen his long razor. Years later, with a twinkle in his eye, he would relate how quickly the agents left his shop. Of course everyone who knew Andy also knew that he would not harm a fly; the FBI agents were not so convinced.

MATT, THE IRON MINER AND LUMBERJACK, NEVER WORKED ON May Day. He lost jobs because of this. But for Matt it was a matter of workingclass principle.

Instead of going to work, Matt would get a clean shave and put on his one good shirt without any fuss or planning because in a sense May Day was a special family day. Susan, his wife, who was fully conscious of the political meaning of the day, would add an extra egg for breakfast and a few extra pieces of meat to the stew for dinner. But more than anything else, it was a day when the family conversation invariably drifted to political matters. It was a day when, more than at other times, Matt would talk about his experiences in strikes and other mass actions of the workers.

As he related his experiences it seemed that the workers had lost most of the struggles. But Matt never referred to them as defeats. He would mention with obvious pride how he had been arrested for his strike activities and with a mixture of anger and sorrow he told of the time when the National Guard broke into the home of strikers and bayoneted them to death in their beds. They had been friends of Matt's. After 25 years he still refused to have anything to do with those who had scabbed during that strike.

May Day was the day when socialism and the first working-class state, the Soviet Union, were the centerpiece of family conversation. Racism was also a subject that was discussed on this day more than others — racism and its effects on the nearby Indian Reservation.

In this household there was a May Day atmosphere and a May Day family closeness. This was Matt and Susan's way of instilling in their family workingclass history and traditions, and pride in the working class. These warm memories of past May Days are reflections of my family's May Day roots.

JOHN HUDAK'S FAVORITE MAY DAY STORY ACTUALLY HAD NO-thing to do with May Day except that the events took place on May 1.

John was a Pennsylvania coal miner. One of his favorite workers did what many miners have done for generations. He did not trust the banks because "they were for the mining company." So the few dollars he saved he put into an old salt sack and hid it in a dark corner of the mine.

One morning when the miner went to check on his life's savings he found the salt sack had disappeared. He was beside himself with anger and frustration. But his friend, John, would not let him give up so easily. The next day John put a piece of cheese into an old Bull Durham bag and tied a long string to it. The following morning, just as he expected, the bag was gone. They followed the string for hundreds of yards. At the end of the line was a rat's nest and part of it was the salt sack with the money in it.

That would have been the end of it except that it was May Day and John was a Communist. He was not about to let such an opportunity pass. Each year after that he would repeat that story and the little speech he gave to his fellow miners on that day: "That same thing happens to us miners every day. The mining-company rats steal from us every day we work. If we were to put a string on the values we produce it would lead us to the bank. And there in the corporate vaults we would find the loot in the world's biggest salt sacks."

MAY DAY'S ROOTS ARE IN THE CLASS CONSCIOUSNESS OF WORKERS — in the history, the experiences, the memories handed down through generations, the treasured traditions and pride in their historic role.

May Day is and will always remain a day of tribute to the Andys, Matts, Susans and Johns — to the working class of our country who have sunk these roots. The roots of May Day belong to every worker. They are forever a part of the past, present and future of the working class.

Reference notes

Chapter 1: The Rise of Industrial Trade Unionism

1. William Z. Foster (1881-1961) was born in Taunton, Massachusetts. Leader of the Great Steel Strike of 1919; later founded the Trade Union Educational League (TUEL) and the Trade Union Unity League (TUUL). Elected national secretary of the Communist Party, USA in 1930 and later elected national chairman.

2. *The Great Steel Strike and Its Lessons,* William Z. Foster, B.W. Huebsch, NY, 1920.

3. Elbert H. Gary (1846-1927) was an Illinois corporate lawyer; chairman of United States Steel Corporation beginning 1901. He fought every attempt to organize the steelworkers. Gary provided the inspiration for the famous statement: "He never saw a blast furnace until his death."

4. In 1935 President Franklin Roosevelt established the Works Progress Administration. By 1936 over 3 million people were at work in WPA programs, which included construction of public buildings, schools, roads, parks, as well employment programs in the arts, theatre and literature. The Civilian Works Administration was another New Deal job-creating program.

5. The Committee (later Congress) of Industrial Organizations (CIO) was formed in 1935 by a number of American Federation of Labor and independent unions opposed to the AFL policy of organizing workers only on a craft basis. Organizing on an industrial basis, the CIO soon grew to become a major rival to the AFL until the two federations merged in December, 1955 and became known as the AFL-CIO.

6. The founding convention of the National Negro Congress was held in Chicago in February of 1936. The convention was called to address the overwhelming economic and social problems faced by Black Americans. Eight hundred delegates attended, from 585 organizations including churches, trade unions, farm and educational societies, business organizations and political parties — representing over one million people.

7. Refers to policies of Earl Browder (1891-1973) was General Secretary of the Communist Party, USA from 1930-1944; see glossary under "Browderism."

8. John Foster Dulles (1888-1959) was a corporation lawyer who was notorious for his corporate links with German industry prior to World War II, and his role in the pro-fascist "America First" organization. As Secretary of State under President Eisenhower, Dulles became notorious for his anti-Sovietism, his theory of "brinkmanship," and policies of "massive retaliation" against socialism and the "roll-back" policy towards Eastern Europe.

9. In 1948, twelve top leaders of the Communist Party, USA, including Gus Hall, were indicted under the Smith Act, charged with conspiring *at some future date* to advocate the violent overthrow of the U.S. government; since they had never advocated this they had to be charged with the "crime" of supposedly thinking about doing so in the future. They were convicted in 1949 in a trial which the author has characterized as an "out and out frame-up." In 1951, after the Supreme Court turned down their appeal, a nationwide wave of Smith Act arrests took place, and Party leaders were tried in many states. A number served prison terms. The major provisions of the Smith Act were later declared unconstitutional.

10. Anti-labor acts bearing the names of their chief authors, and passed by Congress after the end of World War II. Taft-Hartley (passed in 1947) greatly limited the rights of unions, and made it illegal for a Communist to hold any official position in a trade union. Landrum-Griffin (1959) compelled unions to hold elections under government supervision with provisions to punish unions disobeying the law with huge fines. The McCarran Act (1950), characterized the Communist Party as foreign-controlled, and required the registration of "Communist action," "Communist front," and "Communist infiltrated" organizations as agents of a foreign power. It also provided for concentration camps to be set up in the event of an "invasion" or "insurrection." The McCarran Act, along with the Smith Act, was a major weapon used to attack the Left and the Communist Party, and to weaken the trade union and peace movements. Their anti-Communist provisions were later thrown out by the courts.

11. Harry Bridges (1900-), born in Australia, was a top leader of the 1934 general strike in San Francisco set off by the longshoremen's strike and became president of the International Longshoremen's and Warehousemen's Union (ILWU). Efforts to frame him up and deport him failed, and in 1945 he became a U.S. citizen.

12. The National Industrial Recovery Act of 1933 guaranteed workers a minimum wage, reasonable hours, collective bargaining

and the right to join unions. In 1935 the Supreme Court declared the law unconstitutional. The Federal government then enacted the National Labor Relations Act (also called the Wagner Act after Senator Robert F. Wagner, who led the fight for the bill). The Wagner Act protected labor's right to organize and it also established the National Labor Relations Board to enforce the new law. Gradually, the NLRA and NLRB have been turned into tools used by employers against workers, particularly under the Reagan Administration. The Fair Labor Standards Act was passed in 1938 by Congress. It established a minimum wage for selected industries, the forty-hour week, overtime pay and the prohibition of child labor.

13. With Henry Wallace nominated as its leader, the Progressive Party was launched in Philadelphia in 1948. The party was heavily redbaited, and it was only able to get ballot status in 30 states. Nevertheless, in the 1948 elections, the Progressive Party received a million and a half votes.

14. The House Un-American Activities Committee (HUAC) (officially named the House Committee on Un-American Activities) was established in 1938, and was a thought-control force which wreaked havoc on the civil liberties of countless Americans in the decades that followed. On the charge that all progressive and liberal organizations, unions and mass movements for peace were under the control of the Communist Party, this Committee set out to destroy all dissent in the country.

15. Three-week strike by 70,000 members of the International Union of Electrical workers (IUE) against General Electric in 1960. Disunity between the different unions representing GE was a major reason for the defeat.

16. 1957 tugboat strike in New York harbor, by members of National Maritime Union Local 333, United Marine Division. Four thousand workers went out on strike, with 300 tugboats tied up. The strike lasted for 36 days.

Chapter 2: Fighting for Class Struggle Trade Unionism

1. Transport Workers Union (TWU), headed by Mike Quill, struck the New York City Transit Authority on January 1, 1966, demanding a four-day, 32-hour work week. The militant strike ended unsuccessfully on January 13. Quill was jailed. While in prison he collapsed and died, on January 28.

2. George Meany, see note 3. Walter Reuther (1907-1970), president of the United Auto Workers union (UAW) from 1946-1970; CIO president from 1952 until its merger with the AFL in 1955.

3. While George Meany (1894-1980) was president of the AFL-CIO he used his influence to put Jay Lovestone (1898-) — who had been exposed as working for the CIA and FBI for many years — in charge of the federation's Department of International Affairs, where he actively cooperated with the CIA in anti-Communist activities in the world labor movement.

4. David Dubinsky (1892-1982) became president of the International Ladies Garment Workers Union in 1932. The ILGWU became part of the CIO in 1935, but Dubinsky broke with the CIO in 1938. At his retirement in 1966 he boasted that he had saved the ILGWU from "communism."

5. I.W. Abel (1908-), president of the United Steel Workers (USWA) union from 1965-1977.

6. V.I. Lenin, *What Is To Be Done*, in *Collected Works*, Vol. 5, Progress Publishers, Moscow, 1961, p. 421.

7. John L. Lewis (1880-1969) was the son of a Welsh immigrant miner and a miner himself. He became president of the United Mine Workers union (UMWA) in 1920 and led the split with the AFL that resulted in the formation of the CIO in 1935. His understanding of the importance of working with Communists in building the CIO helped guarantee the success of the drive to organize the mass production industries.

8. During the Vietnam War it was revealed that the Nixon administration had secretly ordered the bombing of Kampuchea, (then Cambodia). In 1970, when Nixon admitted he had sent U.S. troops into Kampuchea, it set off a wave of protests.

9. Premiers Ky and Thieu led the U.S.-backed South Vietnamese government.

10. Dienbienphu was the last stronghold of the French colonialist army in Vietnam. It fell to Vietnamese liberation forces in 1954.

Chapter 3: The Class Struggle Today

1. The Mahoning River rises in Eastern Ohio and flows near cities of Alliance, Warren and Youngstown and into Pennsylvania. Until the recent shutdowns was a major steel-making center.

2. Lloyd McBride (1916-1983) succeeded I.W. Abel as president of the Steelworkers union in 1977.

3. Works Progress Administration, as described in note 4 for Chapter 1. Public Works Administration (PWA) was an early New Deal program with government financing of public projects through private employers.

4. The Lykes Corporation was later acquired by LTV corporation,

as were Jones and Laughlin and Republic steel. Reference to "corporate vultures" proved prophetic — when LTV took away pension rights of thousands of its retirees in 1986, workers came to refer to LTV as: "Liars, Thieves, Vultures."

5. Part of the U.S. Trade Act passed by Congress in 1974. It linked granting of U.S. trade credits to Soviet willingness to allow more emigration.

6. Russell B. Long was a U.S. senator from Louisiana from 1948 until his retirement. His positions and votes consistently supported the interests of his state's oil companies.

7. Edward Sadlowski was director of the United Steelworkers district covering the Chicago/Gary area. He was a contender for president of the USWA in the 1977 union elections to replace retiring president I.W. Abel, winning support from important sections of the rank and file. He lost to Lloyd McBride, who died in 1983 and was replaced by Lynn Williams, the current president.

8. The taconite strike in Minnesota (August to November, 1977) was the first major steel strike since 1959, and the longest up to that time. It involved 17 United Steelworkers union locals representing workers in Minnesota and Northern Michigan.

9. Allan Bakke was a white engineer who claimed that the University of California's minority admission plan resulted in making him a victim of "reverse discrimination." The U.S. Supreme Court's 5-4 decision on June 28, 1978 to require the University to admit Bakke was widely condemned as an attack on affirmative action and the struggle for Afro-American equality.

10. The Nuclear Freeze movement, which began in 1980, became a major peace organization in the U.S. attracting millions of Americans concerned about the danger of nuclear war, with extensive trade union participation.

11. During his 1984 attempt for the Democratic Party nomination for president, Gary Hart, senator from Colorado, campaigned on the idea that labor is a "special interest group" and attacked those receiving labor support.

12. In August, 1985, the International Typographical Union (ITU) struck the Chicago Tribune over hiring practices, job classification and transfer policies. The strikers had massive labor solidarity from other unions.

13. Chapter 11 refers to a reorganization of three sections of the old bankruptcy law into a new "Chapter 11." Under certain circumstances it allows companies to file their own reorganization plans, which often include demands for concessions from workers — it has been used as a major union-busting tool.

14. William Winpisinger (1924-) became president of the International Association of Machinists in 1977.

15. Albert Shanker, head of American Federation of Teachers; Lane Kirkland, president of the AFL-CIO. Both anti-Communist, they are identified with the Right-wing of the trade union movement.

16. Irving Brown was a leader of the AFL-CIO's International Affairs Department together with Jay Lovestone; like Lovestone, he has been accused of working with the CIA.

17. In May, 1886, workers demonstrating in Haymarket Square in Chicago for the eight-hour day were set upon by police when a bomb exploded. Eight leaders were arrested, not for throwing the bomb, but for "influencing by their teachings" the bomb-thrower who was never caught. Four were executed. The trial was so clearly a frame-up that the others were pardoned by Governor Atgeld of Illinois. In 1889, May Day (May 1) was designated by U.S. workers to commemorate the heroes of 1886. It has become an international workers' holiday.

18. At the 27th Congress of the Communist Party of the Soviet Union the Soviet Communist Party launched the policy of restructuring and upgrading the economy. The congress was held in February, 1986.

19. In 1902 an investigation of skilled labor among Afro-Americans was done by Atlanta University under the direction of Dr. W.E.B. DuBois. The results led to the publication of *The Negro Artisan,* Atlanta University Publications, No. 7, Atlanta. DuBois (1868-1963) was a major leader in the movement for Afro-American equality in the U.S. Born in Massachusetts, he became the first Black person to receive a Ph.D. from Harvard University. He wrote a number of studies on the struggle for Afro-American equality which are considered classics. He joined the Communist Party, USA in 1961.

Chapter 4: The Science of the Working Class

1. As of 1985 there are 115.5 million persons in the civilian labor force.

2. Barry Goldwater, Republican senator from Arizona, ran for president in 1964 and was defeated in a landslide by Lyndon Johnson.

3. As of 1985 the farm population had fallen to 5.3 million, and has declined steadily since.

4. V.I. Lenin, *Collected Works,* Vol. 15, Progress Publishers, Moscow, 1963, p. 18

5. "Mike Gold About John Reed," in *Mike Gold: A Literary Anthology,* International Publishers, New York, 1972. For John Reed, see note 1 for Chapter 5.

Chapter 5: The Party of the Working Class

1. Reference to John Reed's eyewitness account of the Russian Revolution, *Ten Days That Shook The World* (1919), which is considered a classic. Reed (1887-1920) was an American journalist who became one of the founders of the Communist Party in America.

2. Joe Curran was president of the National Maritime Workers Union (NMU). Louis Budenz was editor of the *Daily Worker.* They, along with Browder (see note 7, Chapter 1), became anti-Communist after being in or close to the Communist Party. Budenz testified against Communists during the McCarthy period. Curran moved to expel Communists from the NMU.

3. John Williamson (1903-1974) was born in Scotland and became a Communist leader in the U.S. He was deported during the McCarthy period to Scotland. He wrote a book about his experiences called *Dangerous Scott: The Life and Work of an American "Undesirable,"* New York, International Publishers, 1969.

4. The bitterly-fought strike by 1,400 meatpackers in Austin, Minnesota, against Geo. A. Hormel and Co. from August 1985 to September, 1986. "Picketing the bank" refers to the failed tactic by the local union leadership of picketing a local bank that was financially tied to Hormel.

5. Founded in 1924, the *Daily Worker* and then the biweekly *Worker* were published until 1968 when the *Daily World* was founded; in May, 1986, the *Daily World* merged with the West Coast *People's World* (1938) to found the *People's Daily World.* It is the only national workingclass daily newspaper in the U.S.

Chapter 6: Workingclass Unity

1. There are some 30 million Afro-Americans as of 1987.

2. Laws known as "Jim Crow" laws systematically discriminated against Afro-Americans. Ordinances were enacted requiring job and housing segregation, and restricting Afro-Americans to separate public facilities (drinking fountains, restaurants, theaters, parks and libraries). The civil rights movement fought these laws, resulting in Supreme Court decisions declaring the laws illegal. Laws prohibiting discrimination in public facilities were embodied in the Civil Rights Act of 1964.

3. The Knights of Labor was an important early labor organization

founded in 1869 by Uriah S. Stephens and other Philadelphia tailors. It was the first attempt to organize workers into a single union rather than separate unions, and welcomed Afro-Americans and women into its ranks. It led a number of strikes, particularly in the railroads. It reached its peak in 1889 under Terence V. Powderly but by 1900 had ceased to function.

4. Letter to the workingmen of Manchester, January 19, 1863, *Senate documents*, 3rd Session, 37th Congress, 1862-1863.

5. *Cheerful Yesterday*, 1898, pp. 115-117; quoted by Herman Schluter, *Lincoln, Labor and Slavery*, New York, 1913, p. 38. Thomas W. Higginson (1823-1911) was a U.S. abolitionist and clergyman.

6. *Lincoln, Labor and Slavery*, pp. 40, 43

7. Ibid. p. 100

8. As of 1985 women constitute 45 percent of the civilian workforce.

9. The Tennessee Valley Authority (TVA) was a successful New Deal project in 1933, the idea of which was to build a series of dams and provide cheap electricity to the depressed farmers in the area. The Reagan administration is trying to sell it to private industry, but it has been pointed to as an example of how government initiative can outclass private capitalist initiative.

10. My Lai was a village in Vietnam that was destroyed by U.S. troops in 1970. Lieutenant William Calley ordered the killing of 347 old men, women and children. Later, on trial for the massacre, Calley pleaded that he didn't know he wasn't supposed to kill them, as long as they were Communists. Though found guilty, Calley never served any prison time.

Chapter 7: The Working Class in Our Era

1. V.I. Lenin, *Collected Works*, Vol. 22, Progress Publishers, Moscow, 1964, pp. 355-56

2. V.I. Lenin, *Collected Works*, Vol. 30, Progress Publishers, Moscow, 1965, p. 293

3. Official government statistics do not take into account of discouraged or involuntarily part-time workers. Labor economists estimate actual unemployment to be at least twice the official figures.

4. Members of the United Steelworkers union were locked out by USX Corporation on August 1, 1986. The union proposed to extend the old contract while negotiations continued, but the company refused. The union then charged that the work stoppage

was not a strike but a lockout, which involved 22,100 steelworkers at 16 USX plants in nine states.

Chapter 8: Socialism and the Working Class

1. Lenin's Letter to American Workers, written on August 20, 1918, was brought to America by special messenger and was widely circulated in socialist ranks. See V.I. Lenin, *Collected Works*, Vol. 28, Progress Publishers, Moscow, 1965.
2. There was mass opposition to intervention by the U.S. into Soviet Russia, in the U.S. as in other countries throughout the world. The U.S. sent a detachment of some 5,000 troops to Siberia to help the counterrevolutionaries there in 1920. After defeats and disillusionment the soldiers had to be recalled.
3. The resolution was approved by the Congress and published on March 15, 1918 in *Pravda*, No. 49. *Draft Resolution on Wilson's Message, Collected works*, Vol. 27, Progress Publishers, Moscow, 1965, p. 171.
4. Douglas A. Fraser (1916-) was born in Scotland and served as president of the United Auto Workers union from 1977-1983. He became a member of the board of directors of Chrysler Corporation in 1980. The letter he wrote to the *New York Times* about a supposed strike by Soviet autoworkers was based on a report that turned out to be a fraud.
5. In December, 1979 Congress approved a massive bailout of Chrysler Corporation, which President Carter signed the following January. It was the largest federal bailout of a private corporation, and provided the company with a $1.5 billion federal loan guarantee if the company could raise $2 billion from workers, dealers and other creditors. Part of the deal required Chrysler workers to forego $462.5 million in raises for the next three years.
6. "The Reindustrialization of America," *Business Week*, June 30, 1980.
7. "Soviets" — Russian word for "councils." First formed during the 1905 Russian revolution, the soviets became a central means for exercising workers' political power.
8. A law passed in New York State in 1967 which prevents public employees from exercising their right to strike. Later law amended to include stiff fines for individual strikers.
9. Refers to the federal bailout of Chrysler (see note 5, this chapter) and the $250 million bailout of the Lockheed Corporation in 1971.

Glossary

All-people's front: policy of organizing people of all classes, including business, on a common program of struggle. Recently the term is used to refer to the "all-people's front against Reaganism," a tactic first advanced by the Communist Party, USA.

Anti-monopoly coalition: policy of the Communist Party of seeking to unite the great mass of people around a program of fighting the monopolies: workers, Afro-Americans and other oppressed groups, women, farmers, small-business people, students and intellectuals, even sections of business.

Browderism: refers to political line developed by Earl Browder, General Secretary of the CPUSA from 1930 to 1944. Browder championed the idea that after World War II, U.S. imperialism would voluntarily cooperate with the socialist world; this carried with it the notion that imperialism could change its nature and that the class struggle could be eliminated or channeled into cooperation with capital. Under Browder the Communist Party was dissolved from 1944 to 1945 and replaced with the Communist Political Association. The Party was restored and Browderism rejected at an emergency convention of the Party in 1945. Browder was expelled in 1946.

Bourgeoisie: originating from the French, in the days of the Paris Commune. Means the capitalist class, the individuals and corporations who own the means of production under capitalism — the factories, mines, mills, etc. "Society as a whole is more and more splitting up into two great classes directly facing each other: bourgeoisie and proletariat." (Marx and Engels, *Communist Manifesto*.)

Center forces: in the trade union movement, those that stand between the Left and the Right; such forces usually move toward unity with the Left as struggles intensify.

Class collaboration: trade union policies of non-struggle class "partnership," accommodating the wishes of the boss rather than the needs of the workers.

Class consciousness: awareness on the part of workers that they and they only produce the wealth of society, that they constitute a class and in their unity is their strength. Abraham Lincoln had this to say on the subject: "Labor is prior to, and independent of, capital. Capital is only the fruit of labor, and could never have existed if labor had not first existed. Labor is the superior of capital, and deserves much the higher consideration." (Message to Congress, 1861.)

Class struggle: Marx and Engels observed in the *Communist Manifesto* that "the history of all hitherto existing society is the history of class struggles. Freeman and slave, patrician and plebian, lord and serf, guild-master and journeyman, in a word, oppressor and oppressed, stood in constant opposition to one another, carried on an uninterrupted, now hidden, now open fight. . . ."

Communism: a socioeconomic system that will be a society of abundance where each works according to their ability and receives according to need, where all people will be freed from want to pursue their creative potential. Communism as a movement refers to Communist parties which work to build the workingclass movement in their own countries to replace capitalism, and then to build socialism toward the stage of communism.

Cyclical crisis: see "three-layered crisis."

Dialectics: Marxist-Leninist philosophical method, described by Engels as "the science of universal interconnection" and "the general laws of *all* motion." An example of dialectics is seen in the *Communist Manifesto*: "Does it require deep intuition to comprehend that man's ideas, views and conceptions, in one word, man's consciousness, changes with every change in the conditions of its material existence, and its social relations and in its social life?"

Dictatorship of the proletariat: term developed by Marx and Engels to refer to the state of workingclass rule in which the government protects the interests of working people against the efforts of the former capitalists to restore the old system; the term was used in contrast to the "dictatorship of the bourgeoisie" that characterizes government under capitalism. This phrase has been used out of context by enemies of the working class to slander the Communist movement.

Dual unionism: the Industrial Workers of the World (IWW) and other syndicalists in the early part of the century believed that it was impossible to work inside the "bosses' union," the AFL, and that workers should organize their own union — a dual union. Lenin denounced this idea, and William Z. Foster, who belonged to the IWW before joining the Communist Party, broke with this concept and championed the idea of all militant workers joining the unions in existence and working to strengthen them and improve their policies.

Economism: term used in Lenin's day, referring to a tendency in the socialist movement among some to reduce all trade union questions to their strictly "economic" form, separating out politics.

Exploitation: extracting from workers as much value/profit as possible. The optimum rate of exploitation aimed at by capitalists is to leave the worker with just enough to keep working and able to reproduce, with only enough education as needed to do the work that the level of technology requires.

Fascism: the open, terroristic rule of monopoly-finance capital. Characterized by a police state, complete repression of labor and all progressive forces, and violent anti-Communism.

General crisis of capitalism: see "three-layered crisis."

Imperialism: the stage of capitalism characterized by the growth of monopoly corporations, whose greed for superprofits drives them to increase exploitation at home and expand operations around the world in search of cheap raw materials and low wages; along with economic penetration in foreign countries comes political domination. The classic work on the subject is Lenin's *Imperialism, The highest Stage of Capitalism.*

Industrial concentration: Communist Party policy of concentrating efforts on building the organizations of industrial workers and increasing their role in the broader movements for social progress, and in the process seeking to raise their revolutionary and class consciousness, and thereby build the Communist Party as well.

Industrial unionism: unions of all the workers in a shop or industry, regardless of their particular skill or craft. It formed the basis of the CIO, which broke off from the AFL because it rejected this form of organization.

Left forces: in the trade union movement, organized groups of class conscious workers, including Communists, who see the interests of workers and bosses as irreconcilable. Left-wing positions in the labor movement include fighting against concessions, for affirmative action and workingclass unity, organizing the unorganized, nationalization of basic industries, for international trade union cooperation, including with the socialist countries, opposition to policies of U.S. imperialism, etc.

Marxism-Leninism: the term given to the science pioneered by Karl Marx and Frederick Engels, and further developed by V.I. Lenin. It is the science of the working class that sees human history moving in the direction of socialism and finally to communism.

McCarthyism: the period in the 1950s when U.S. monopoly capitalism launched a massive campaign promoting anti-Communist hysteria. It takes its name from Senator Joseph McCarthy who conducted witchhunts throughout the country. Americans finally rejected McCarthyism and demands were made for McCarthy's impeachment.

Monopoly capitalism: the stage of capitalism (reached in the USA about 1900) when the main industries have been consolidated under a single capitalist or a handful of corporations. The monopolies can then exercise almost complete control over production, distribution, prices, etc., as well as tremendous leverage over government policy.

Nationalization: when an industry is taken over by the government and run for the benefit of the people. The Communist Party calls for basic industries in the U.S. to be nationalized and run democratically by representatives of labor and community.

Open shop: refers to non-union mass production industries, particularly in the period before the massive organizing sweep of the CIO in the 1930s; "open shop" employers were viciously anti-union.

Opportunism: characteristic of unprincipled people who sacrifice long-term principles for immediate, often personal, advantage.

Petty bourgeois: refers to owners of small businesses, professionals, etc. In an anti-monopoly coalition this group enters into an alliance with the working class and others whose interests are opposed to the monopolies.

Proletariat: the industrial section of the working class.

Proletarian internationalism: identification with the world working class; seeing that the workers of the world have their basic interests in common.

Redbaiting: the labor journal *Labor Today* defines redbaiting as "a common form of political name-calling. It is supposed to make people worry about whether there are 'Communists' or 'subversives' in their midst — instead of worrying about what we need in the next contract, or speedup, or whether grievances are being handled right."

Right forces: in the trade union movement, those who cling to policies of class collaboration and anti-Communism, and resist policies of class struggle trade unionism.

Sectarianism: working in such a way that excludes others and prevents unity; policies that lead to isolation and an "inner" orientation.

Social democrats: those who profess a belief in socialism but reject scientific socialism, i.e. Marxism-Leninism. There are two main tendencies of social democracy in the U.S. trade union movement today: right-wing, as represented by the Social Democrats, USA, which tries to impose policies in the interests of U.S. imperialism into the labor movement; and that which is represented by the Democratic Socialists of America, which takes positions that can be characterized as Center and Center-Left.

State monopoly capitalism: the merging of the power of financial and corporate interests of monopoly capitalism with the power of government.

Structural crisis: see "three-layered crisis."

Surplus value: what is *not* paid to the worker for his or her work out of what is produced, above and beyond the use of the worker's labor power, i.e. wages. Wages under capitalism fall far short of the value the worker adds to a commodity by his or her labor; the surplus value is appropriated by the capitalist. (See "exploitation.")

Three-layered crisis: refers to the intertangling of the cyclical, structural and general crises of capitalism. The cyclical crisis is the periodic "booms and busts" of the economy resulting from capitalists' greed — producing more while reducing workers' ability to buy what they produce (by cutting real wages.) The structural crisis refers to the systematic destruction of the U.S. industrial base by Big Business in search of low-wage, non-union havens, including overseas, and the refusal to reinvest their superprofits in modernizing the industries at home. The general crisis refers to the fact that imperialism is steadily losing ground in the worldwide struggle between capitalism and socialism.

Trotskyism: originated with Leon Trotsky, a participant in the Russian Revolution who held a theory of "permanent revolution" and rejected the idea that socialism can be built in one country. Trotsky became a major figure in worldwide anti-Sovietism. His followers opposed the policy of the united front against fascism; in the U.S. they opposed building the CIO. There are different varieties of Trotskyite "phony-Left" groups — all disruptive of mass people's organizations, reflecting a lack of confidence in the working class. Their appeal is to petty-bourgeois intellectuals.

United front: strategy of organizing the working class and people around a common program of struggle — such as against fascism, against monopoly, against the nuclear war danger, etc. Building the united front against Hitler fascism became a key initiative of Communist parties following George Dimitrov's famous speech to the 7th Congress of the Communist International in 1935.

Index